Corpora in Language Teaching and Learning

english corpus linguistics

Thomas Kohnen · Joybrato Mukherjee (eds.)

Volume **13**

PETER LANG
Frankfurt am Main · Berlin · Bern · Bruxelles · New York · Oxford · Wien

Yvonne Alexandra Breyer

Corpora in Language Teaching and Learning

Potential, Evaluation, Challenges

PETER LANG
Internationaler Verlag der Wissenschaften

Bibliographic Information published by the Deutsche Nationalbibliothek
The Deutsche Nationalbibliothek lists this publication in the Deutsche Nationalbibliografie; detailed bibliographic data is available in the internet at http://dnb.d-nb.de.

Cover Design:
Olaf Gloeckler, Atelier Platen, Friedberg

ISSN 1610-868X
ISBN 978-3-631-63041-9

www.peterlang.de

To my husband Justin for his unwavering support and unconditional love and to our beautiful children, Connor and Charlie, who are just that – beautiful.

Table of contents

List of abbreviations and acronyms

ALA	Association of Language Awareness
ASCII	American Standard Code for Information Interchange
CALL	Computer-Assisted Language Learning
CCED	Collins COBUILD English Language Dictionary
CEFR	Common European Framework of Reference
CGEL	Comprehensive Grammar of the English Language
CLOC	ColLOCation
COBUILD	Collins Birmingham University International Language Database
COCOA	word COunt and COncordance generation on the Atlas computer
DDL	Data-Driven Learning
EAGLES	Expert Advisory Group on Language Engineering Standards
EFL	English as a Foreign Language
ELT	English Language Teaching
ESL	English as a Second Language
ESP	English for Specific Purposes
GSL	General Service List of English
GUI	Graphical User Interface
HTML	Hyper Text Mark-up Language
IBM	International Business Machines Corporation
ICAME	International Computer Archive of Modern & Medieval English
IT	Information Technologies
KWIC	KeyWord-In-Context
LDOCE	Longman Dictionary of Contemporary English Online
LGSWE	Longman Grammar of Spoken and Written English
LTE	Language Teacher Education
MI	Mutual Information score
NATO	North Atlantic Treaty Organization
OCP	Oxford Concordance Program
PDF	Portable Document Format
POS	Part-Of-Speech
SGML	Standard Generalized Mark-up Language
SLA	Second Language Acquisition
TALC	Teaching And Language Corpora (Conference)
TEFL	Teaching English as a Foreign Language
TEI	Text Encoding Initiative
TESOL	Teaching English to Speakers of Other Languages
XML	eXtensible Mark-up Language

List of abbreviations and acronyms: corpora

ACE	Australian Corpus of English
ANC	American National Corpus
BE06	British English 2006 Corpus
BNC	British National Corpus
BoE	Bank of English
Brown	Brown University Standard Corpus of Present-Day American English
CANCODE	Cambridge and Nottingham Corpus of Discourse in English
CIC	Cambridge International Corpus
CLC	Cambridge Learner Corpus
COCA	Corpus of Contemporary American English
COLT	Bergen Corpus of London Teenage Language
ELISA	English Language Interview Corpus as a Second-Language Acquisition
FLOB	Freiburg-LOB Corpus of British English
FROWN	Freiburg-Brown Corpus of American English
ICE	International Corpus of English
ICLE	International Corpus of Learner English
LeaP	Learning Prosody in a Foreign Language
LINDSEI	Louvain INternational Database of Spoken English Interlanguage
L-LC	London-Lund Corpus
LLC	Longman Learners' Corpus
LOB	Lancaster-Oslo/Bergen
LONGDALE	LONGitudinal Database of Learner English
LSWE	Longman Corpus of Spoken And Written English
MICASE	Michigan Corpus of Academic Spoken English
Padova MEC	Padova Multimedia English Corpus
T2K-SWAL	TOEFL 2000 Spoken and Written Academic Language
TeMa	Corpus of Textbook Materials

Figures

Tables

1 Introduction

The advent of computers has brought about major changes to the study of language. In fact, linguistic research methods and, as a result, language descriptions have changed significantly since modern computer technology has become readily available to the research community. The ability to electronically store large amounts of language data and to access and retrieve this data through a software interface has paved the way for the emergence of corpus linguistics. The main focus of this type of linguistic inquiry is language data stored in digital format, referred to as corpora. Leech (1992: 106) highlights the impact of computer technology on linguistics as follows:

> [T]he computer's ability to search, retrieve, sort, and calculate the contents of vast corpora of text, and to do all these things at an immense speed, gives us the ability to *comprehend*, and to *account for*, the contents of such corpora in a way which was not dreamed of in the pre-computational era of corpus linguistics. (Leech 1992: 106)

For the first time, aided by computer technology, researchers were able to observe and analyse large amounts of naturally occurring language data. This added a quantitative dimension to language study by providing statistics on the frequency and patterns of occurrence of linguistic items. The visual output and functionality of corpus analysis software, most frequently referred to under the umbrella-term 'concordancer', has enabled researchers to discover patterns in language usage that had previously remained hidden from view. However, the computer only acts as a facilitator; the processing and interpretation of the data depend on "the observational and generalizing skills of the investigator" (Leech 1992: 114). A rapidly expanding number of publications and of corpus research centres around the globe are evidence of the impact the analysis of machine-readable corpora has had on the study of language.

At an early stage of the development of corpus linguistics, a strong and continuing bond to language learning and teaching was formed. The process of 'discovering facts about language' was quickly recognised as highly relevant for language learning. Even before the release of the worldwide first, entirely corpus-based dictionary, the *Collins COBUILD English Language Dictionary* (*CCED*) (Sinclair 1987a), publications began to appear which discussed the potential of corpora and concordances for language learners and teachers (e.g. Ahmad, Corbett & Rogers 1985; Johns 1986; Skehan 1981).

Johns (1986) was among the first to suggest putting corpus tools and resources into the hands of language learners. He named this approach 'data-driven learning' (DDL) and defined it as "the use in the classroom of computer-generated concordances to get students to explore regularities of patterning in the target language" (Johns & King 1991: iii). Johns (1988: 15), widely recognised as the most influential advocate of this approach, has claimed that "the concordancer is [...] one of the most powerful tools that we can offer the language learner".

This development took place in a period in which the role of computers in the classroom was mostly seen in the computer-as-tutor function. However, as a tutor, computers have failed to convince because, despite great advancements in technology, computers cannot match the capacity of humans to comprehensively understand, interpret, and correct natural language. The unreliable nature of spell-checkers (even today) serves as a vivid reminder of this. In contrast, Johns (1991a: 2) proposed to make the computer an informant and, instead of making the system intelligent, "we simply provide the evidence needed to answer the learner's questions, and rely on the learner's intelligence to find answers". Thus, Johns essentially views the learner's role in this task similarly to the one expressed by Leech (1992) above; in other words, the learner becomes the language investigator.

Claims about the potential of the approach of using corpus data with learners in the language classroom – frequently referred to under the umbrella-term DDL – have been made in relation to several aspects: learners are exposed to naturally occurring language data from the respective corpus and engage in authentic research tasks to solve 'real' language problems (e.g. learner-initiated questions such as "What is the difference between convince and persuade?", Johns 1991a: 4). This approach arguably allows for authenticity of script, purpose, and activity (see Johns 1988: 10). Furthermore, by developing strategies for solving such language problems, learners take a more active role in the learning process and may become increasingly autonomous (see Johns 1988: 14). Finally, investigations of language items as proposed by Johns should ultimately lead to an increase in language awareness which "should have direct pay-off in terms of use of the language and ability to communicate in it" (Johns 1988: 14).

Over the past three decades, direct corpus applications in language learning have featured heavily in publications in this growing area of research. In the early phase, many publications presented ideas on how to use corpora in the classroom (e.g. Honeyfield 1989; Johns & King 1991; McEnery & Wilson 1993; Tribble & Jones 1997), some dealt with the technical aspects of the approach (e.g. Johns 1986, 1997; Levy 1990), and some presented evaluations of the effectiveness of concordancing for language learning (e.g. Stevens 1991b; Cobb 1997, 1999). The field has since expanded rapidly, and the use of corpus data has been showcased in a great variety of learning scenarios for a broad range of purposes; for example, vocabulary acquisition (e.g. Allan 2006; Lee & Liou 2003; Yeh, Liou & Li 2007), in-depth study of selected grammatical aspects (e.g. Daud & Abusa' 1999; Davies 2004; Estling Vannestål & Lindquist 2007), development of writing skills (e.g. Chambers & O'Sullivan 2004; Cresswell 2007; Gilmore 2009; Papp 2007), the analysis of literary texts (e.g. Bednarek 2008; Daud & Husin 2004), and error analysis and self-correction by learners (e.g. Gaskell & Cobb 2004; Gabel 2001). A large majority of publications on corpora in language education are concerned with English as a Foreign Language (EFL) for general or special purposes as well as specific fields like English for Academic Purposes (EAP). The present study also focuses predominantly on EFL as this is the subject which the teacher trainees at the centre of the case study presented here are studying. However, research in this field is by no means restricted to English, as is evidenced by the growing number of publications on the learning of other languages. These include, among others, Chinese (e.g. Lixun 2001; Smith, Chen & Kilgariff 2008; Szakos 2000), French (e.g. Chalmel 1998; Chambers & O'Sullivan 2004; Cobb, Greaves & Horst 2001; Whistle 1999), German (e.g. Belz 2004; Belz & Vyatkina 2005, 2008; Möllering 2001, 2004), Italian (e.g. Kennedy & Miceli 2001, 2002, 2010; Zorzi 2001), and Portuguese (e.g. Berber Sardinha 1999; Santos Pereira 2004).

The combining of corpus linguistics and language teaching research was also reflected by the first *Teaching and Language Corpora* (*TALC*) conference in 1994. This conference was the result of a growing number of scholars interested in the educational aspects of corpus use who had previously been presenting their research at the *International Computer Archive of Modern and Medieval English* (*ICAME*) conference, perhaps the most important conference for corpus linguists at that time. The *TALC* conference has since been held biannually with continuing success. In addition, conferences that had previously focused purely on either corpus linguistics (e.g. the biannual *Corpus Linguistics* conference) or on language education (e.g. the annual *EUROCALL* conference) added corpora and language learning to their list of topics for presentations.

In sum, over the past three decades, the direct use of corpora in language teaching has been heavily promoted by an international research community. Yet, in recent years, the question has been raised as to what degree corpora have actually made a difference to the theory and practice of language teaching and learning. In particular, there is growing concern over a persisting gap between research efforts and actual application in teaching practice. Despite the fact that a multitude of publications report on studies using corpora in the classroom, the impact on mainstream teaching has remained extremely limited. Tribble (2000: 31) notes that "not many teachers seem to be *using* corpora in their classroom". In the following year, he concludes from a survey he conducted in the United Kingdom that "IT (let alone corpus analysis) remains mysterious to most of [his] professional colleagues" (Tribble 2001: 7). At Vienna University in Austria, Seidlhofer (2002: 216) discovers that "there is very little awareness amongst teachers and students [...] of the enormous impact of corpus linguistics on both language description and on the preparation of the very language teaching materials and reference tools they all use". In reference to the German context, Mukherjee (2004: 239) remarks that "in reality, the influence of applied corpus-linguistic research on the actual practice of English language teaching is still relatively limited". Similarly, Kaltenböck and Mehlmauer-Larcher (2005: 66) observe that, while there is more progress in tertiary education, "in secondary education and general ELT (English Language Teaching) classes, however, computer corpora are still conspicuously absent". Braun (2005: 48) concludes that "corpora, while being the 'buzzword' in language research departments, are still far from being part of mainstream teaching practice, if not *terra incognita* altogether".

Given the considerable research output, as evidenced above, there is no readily apparent reason as to why corpora have not been more widely accepted into mainstream teaching. Furthermore, the claims about the advantages of using corpus data in the classroom appear to make it a desirable addition to every teacher's repertoire. Publications addressing the question of how to advance the use of corpora in mainstream language learning and teaching have since begun to emerge (e.g. Boulton 2007a; Chambers 2005; Mukherjee 2004).

The purpose of this book is to make a contribution to the ongoing efforts of promoting corpus use in language education and to move the discussion forward in order narrow the gap between research and practice. This contribution is presented in the form of a two-staged critical analysis to identify key factors in advancing the use of corpora, a survey as well as expert interviews of teacher educators, a case study with teacher trainees on learning *and* teaching with corpora, and finally, a proposal for tailor-made concordancing software for classroom use. The main hypotheses underlying this study are:

(i) The use of corpus data in language learning and teaching has significant potential; however, in spite of this, corpora do not appear to play a significant role in mainstream teaching.
(ii) The transfer of a research approach into an educational environment is problematic and requires careful adjustments and considerations which should be informed by language pedagogy.
(iii) Teachers play a pivotal role in the popularisation of corpus use in language education but their perspectives on teaching with corpora have remained largely unexplored.
(iv) Only adequate training enables teachers to use corpora for teaching purposes. This training is ideally placed in pre-service language teacher education.

Consequently, the present book is structured as follows: Chapter 2 reviews the development of corpus linguistics, the impact of corpora on language description, as well as corpus tools and resources. Even though a comprehensive treatment of each individual aspect is not within the scope of this study, this discussion is an integral part of the study as it introduces concepts, tools, and resources that are discussed in the remainder of this research project.

Chapter 3 demonstrates the impact and potential of corpora in language education in the form of indirect and direct applications. This chapter concludes with a close examination of direct corpus applications for learners in relation to their relevance to the following concepts central to contemporary language education: authenticity, learner autonomy, and language awareness. This discussion establishes the relevance of the corpus approach to these desirable goals in current language pedagogy.

Chapter 4 focuses on the gap between productive research endeavours on the one hand and the apparent lack of application in language classrooms on the other. The discussion in this chapter takes place in the form of two analyses: firstly, evaluative studies on the effectiveness of using corpora for learning, studies on learner strategies, and on learner and teacher responses to the use of corpus data in the classroom are critically reviewed; secondly, an in-depth analysis is presented which examines the three core elements involved in the corpus investigation process – corpus, software, user. This analysis is conducted with particular focus on potential issues that arise due to the transfer from research context to classroom environment. Key factors in advancing the use of corpora for language learning purposes are identified as a result of these analyses.

Teachers play a crucial role as they represent the main conduit from research to classroom application. Therefore, they are possibly the most significant factor in advancing the use of corpora in language education. This view is in line with Mukherjee (2002, 2004, 2009) who has previously stated that "it is the teachers to whom particular attention should be paid in this process of popularization" (Mukherjee 2004: 244; see also Conrad 2000; Mauranen 2004a). Yet, the teacher's role and the teacher's perspective on teaching with corpora are two areas which have remained largely unexplored. Thus, gaining insight into the challenges and the potential of corpora as perceived by language teachers who are not 'corpus experts' is vital in order to move the discussion of advancing the use of corpora in language classrooms forward.

It is further argued here that, in order to be motivated and skilled enough to use corpora in the classroom, it is of particular importance that teachers receive adequate training. This training ideally takes place in pre-service language teacher education (LTE). A variety of learning opportunities with corpora have already been shown to have great benefits for many aspects of teacher training (e.g. Allan 1999, 2002; Amador Moreno, Chambers & O'Riordan 2006; Farr 2008, 2010a; Tsui 2004). Within this context, trainees can discover the potential of corpora for learning which may motivate them to use corpora later on as part of their teaching repertoire. LTE also provides opportunities for trainees to learn how to teach with corpora which will prepare them to use corpora confidently in their future classrooms.

Chapter 5 presents a survey of teacher educators at universities in Germany in two areas of pre-service LTE: language practice and language teaching methodology. The purpose of this survey is to gauge the extent to which corpora play a role in these areas as they represent those parts of teacher education that provide opportunities for teacher trainees to either learn language with corpora (language practice) or learn how to teach language with corpora (teaching methodology). The discussion of the survey is complemented by outcomes from expert interviews with five survey participants in order to expand and elaborate on the issues at hand.

Chapter 6 presents a case study with teacher trainees of EFL. This study is situated within the context of a course for teacher trainees at a university in Germany on learning *and* teaching with corpora. The purpose of this case study is to observe teachers' responses to teaching with corpora and to examine their perspective of using corpora as learners *and* as teachers. The results highlight a number of challenges teachers experience when teaching with corpora. In addition, the case study shows the great potential of corpora in LTE for raising language awareness as well as teaching awareness in teacher trainees.

Chapter 7 demonstrates the design of a tailor-made concordancer for classroom use. The proposal for this software design represents an example of corpus technology informed by the needs of language pedagogy in line with the hypothesis that this approach is a key factor in successfully transferring a research tool into the classroom context.

Chapter 8 presents a final discussion that brings together the results from the previous chapters and presents an outlook on future research on corpora in language education.

2 Corpus linguistics

Driven by the advent of computers in the 1960s, a new approach to investigating language has emerged: corpus linguistics. The analysis of electronic language corpora with powerful retrieval and analysis software has since provided insights into naturally occurring language data that were previously not attainable. The present chapter introduces the core methods, key principles, and tools of the corpus approach.

2.1 The development of corpus linguistics

> It is my belief that a new understanding of the nature and structure of language will shortly be available as a result of the examination by computer of large collections of texts. This kind of study, which has been in progress for thirty years but is just becoming fashionable, is called 'corpus linguistics'.
>
> (Sinclair 1991b: 489)

Corpus linguistics is most closely associated with the empirical analysis of electronically stored naturally occurring language data. Such a collection is referred to as a 'corpus' which can be defined as an electronic "collection of texts assumed to be representative of a given language, dialect, or other subset of a language, to be used for linguistic analysis" (Francis 1982: 7). Corpus research aims to produce descriptions of language based on the observation of language in use. In this it differs radically from the theoretical approach to linguistics which has been mainly associated with models put forward by Noam Chomsky. His views of what constitutes language study have dominated the field of linguistics during the latter half of the twentieth century. Early advocates of (pre-electronic) 'corpus-based' linguistics[1] (e.g. Harris and Hill, from the era of American structuralism in the 1950s) had regarded the actual language evidence as the primary object of linguistic study (see Harris 1951). In line with positivist and behaviourist theories, these post-Bloomfieldian linguists considered the value of introspection as only secondary. Underlying this belief was the assumption that language is finite, and that, if sufficiently large, a corpus can contain the totality of a language.

---

1 The term 'corpus linguistics' was not used until much later and is reportedly linked to the publication *Corpus linguistics: Recent developments in the use of computer corpora in English language research* by Aarts and Meijs (1984; see Leech 1992: 105).

By the early 1960s, the value of observable data had come under sharp attack by Chomsky. Reminiscent of Saussure's (1983 [1916]) distinction between *langue* and *parole*, Chomsky had introduced the dichotomy between 'competence' and 'performance'. However, there are some significant differences between the two concepts. Whereas Saussure had developed his theory as an approach to the analysis of actually occurring language use, Chomsky (1965) explicitly states that

> linguistic theory is concerned primarily with an ideal speaker-listener, in a completely homogenous speech-community, who knows its language perfectly and is unaffected by such grammatically irrelevant conditions as memory limitations, distractions, shifts of attention and interest, and errors (random or characteristic) in applying his knowledge of the language in actual performance. (Chomsky 1965: 3)

In regard to what should be the object of linguistic study, Chomsky (1965) further believes that

> linguistic theory is mentalistic, since it is concerned with discovering a mental reality underlying actual behaviour. Observed use of language [...] may provide evidence as to the nature of this mental reality, but surely cannot constitute the actual subject matter of linguistics, if this is to be a serious discipline. (Chomsky 1965: 4)

Chomsky (1965: 4) views linguistics as the study of competence which he describes as "a system of generative processes", the theory of which must be able to describe every possible grammatical sentence and the underlying generative rules. In his view, the study of linguistics has to focus on building models that explain a language speaker's competence to generate an infinite amount of unpredictable sentences. Thus, competence is described as a speaker's internalised knowledge of language, while performance is the actual use of language. Based on this distinction between competence and performance, Chomsky emphasises that a corpus of actual language use is an inadequate basis for linguistic analysis because a corpus consists merely of externalised utterances, in other words performance data, which can only be seen as a poor reflection of the speaker's language competence:

> Any natural corpus will be skewed. Some sentences won't occur because they are obvious, others because they are false, still others because they are impolite. The corpus, if natural, will be so wildly skewed that the description would be no more than a mere list. (Chomsky 1962: 159)

Consequently, his focus is on the study of introspectively produced samples of language. Chomsky (1965) further argues that native speaker intuition plays the most significant part in judging what is and what is not grammatical in a language. In order to demonstrate the importance of native speaker intuition, Chomsky (1957: 15) had once presented the (in-) famous example sentence "Colorless green ideas sleep furiously" which, although nonsensical, is intuitively deemed perfectly grammatical. Particularly, in the United States, Chomsky's criticism and his influential theories played a significant role in the development away from linguistics based on empirical studies in favour of a more rationalist framework for the study of language.

Another crucial argument, that further weakened the case for corpus research prior to the development of computers, was brought forward by Abercrombie (1965) in the early 1960s. He criticised the 'pseudo-procedures' of the corpus approach, which in his view although not "literally impossible; [...] would be so arduous and time-consuming as a way of conducting an investigation that no one in their senses would ever set out to use it" (Abercrombie 1965: 114-115). Without the processing power of modern computers, it can easily be seen how the manual work with large text collections would be enormously time-consuming, expensive, and error-prone.

Despite these very strong arguments against it, the corpus approach was never entirely abandoned during the time in which Chomsky's theories dominated the field of linguistics. In 1959, Quirk had commenced his work on the influential *Survey of English Usage* (see Quirk 1968) in Britain, and, in the United States, Francis and Kučera completed the *Brown University Standard Corpus of Present-Day American English* (hereafter: *Brown Corpus*) in 1964. Francis (1982) describes the scepticism he encountered from his colleague Robert Lees, later described by Aarts (2000: 5) as a "staunch Chomskyite", in this famous anecdote:

> In 1962, when I was in the early stages of collecting the Brown Standard Corpus of American English, I met Professor Robert Lees at a linguistic conference. In response to his query about my current interests, I said that I had a grant from the U.S. office of education to compile a million-word corpus of present-day American English for computer use. He looked at me in amazement and asked, 'Why in the world are you doing that?' I said something about finding out the true facts about English grammar. I have never forgotten his reply: 'That is a complete waste of your time and the government's money. You are a native speaker of English; in ten minutes you can produce more illustrations of any point in English grammar than you will find in many millions of words of random text'. (Francis 1982: 7-8)

Despite all criticism and the considerable influence of Chomsky's theories on the linguistic discipline in the United States, the development of the *Brown Corpus*, the first machine-readable language corpus, went ahead. Combined with the advent of modern computer technology, it helped to promote the emergence of corpus linguistics. The use of computer technology thus enabled linguists to gain a whole new perspective on language and is a central aspect of corpus linguistics:

> Computers make it possible to identify and analyze complex patterns of language use, allowing the storage and analysis of a larger database of natural language than could be dealt with by hand. (Biber, Conrad & Reppen 1998: 4)

The efficiency, reliability, and accuracy displayed by the power of computer processing were simply not feasible through manual labour alone. This development added a new dimension to empirical research in language studies. Criticisms of using 'pseudo-procedures' could now be refuted, and there has been an increasing use of quantitative data from linguistic corpora ever since. As a consequence, the value of naturally occurring data was re-examined. Due to unprecedented possibilities of storage, access, retrieval, and analysis of naturally occurring language data, its many advantages became available to the research community. In contrast to language samples retrieved through native-speaker introspection, which could be considered artificial and unreliable, language data stored in electronic corpora was observable and verifiable. Sinclair (1991a), who is probably one of the strongest proponents of corpus linguistics, discusses the limitations of introspection for the study of language as follows:

> The problem about all kinds of introspection is that it does not give evidence about usage. The informant will not be able to distinguish among various kinds of language patterning – psychological associations, semantic groupings, and so on. Actual usage plays a very minor role in one's consciousness of language and one would be recording largely ideas about language rather than facts of it. (Sinclair 1991a: 39)

However, as much as it may appear that these two approaches to linguistic study are mutually exclusive, it is important to note that this is in fact not the case. In a well-known and widely quoted anecdote, Fillmore (1992), a theoretical linguist himself, draws up the caricature of an 'armchair' (theoretical) linguist and a corpus linguist. He writes:

> These two don't speak to each other very often, but when they do, the corpus linguist says to the armchair linguist, 'Why should I think that what you tell me is true?', and the armchair linguist says to the corpus linguist, 'Why should I think that what you tell me is interesting?' (Fillmore 1992: 35)

It appears, then, that modern linguistics is divided into two opposing viewpoints concerning the object of linguistic inquiry. However, recognising the two approaches, so that each can benefit from the other, seems the most productive approach to the study of language. As Fillmore (1992) states:

> I don't think there can be any corpora, however large, that contain information about all of the areas of English lexicon and grammar that I want to explore; all that I have seen are inadequate. The second observation is that every corpus that I've had a chance to examine, however small, has taught me facts that I couldn't imagine finding out about in any other way. (Fillmore 1992: 35)

Since the 1980s, a change of paradigm has become noticeable, and the status of corpora for the descriptive analysis of English has grown significantly. As Halliday (1982: 11) observed, linguistic research had moved from making "rules for generating ideal sentences" to "studying what people actually say and write".

The contribution of the development of computer technology in this process is significant as Sinclair (1992: 379) predicted early on: "The advent of computers has improved the quality of many scientific disciplines in recent years, but in none of them is the effect so profound as it will be in the study of language". The next section examines some of the changes brought about by corpus research in the creation of dictionaries and grammars, and in our overall understanding of how language works.

2.2 Corpora for language descriptions

> [L]anguage looks rather different when you look at a lot of it at once.
> (Sinclair 1991a: 100)

This current section takes a closer look at the impact of corpus studies on reference works and at language patterns that have emerged through the study of large language corpora.

2.2.1 Dictionaries and grammars

The corpus approach has had a profound impact on many areas of linguistic research. Most significantly, it has revolutionised the writing of dictionaries and grammars. Lexicographers have used language data long before the emergence of modern corpus linguistics. However, prior to the advent of computers, the process of describing language usage for dictionary creation was a long, arduous process and usually involved a great number of people. One of the last comprehensive English dictionaries produced entirely without computers was *Webster's Third New International Dictionary of the English Language* (Gove 1961). The definitions and different meanings of each dictionary entry were derived from the manual analysis of nearly ten million paper citation slips of recorded language usage (see Gove 1961: 4a).[2] As a consequence, computers were initially "thought of as having principally a clerical role in lexicography – reducing the labour of sorting and filing and examining very large amounts of English in a short period of time" (Sinclair 1991a: 2). In the mid- to late 1970s, John Sinclair became one of the founders of the *Collins Birmingham University International Language Database* (*COBUILD*) project which set out to compile a corpus of contemporary English for lexicographical research purposes. The corpus consisted of 20 million words of mainly written contemporary English. Sinclair reported that, while the team had initially not expected any revolutionary findings, it soon became apparent that the traditional approaches to dictionary writing were no longer acceptable (Sinclair 1987b). They discovered that collocation, semantics, and pragmatics had to be taken into account as language patterns, and a new perspective on language emerged in the process (Sinclair 1991a). Frequency of occurrence, collocation, phraseology, the connection between lexis and grammar, and, as a whole, the importance of investigating naturally occurring language data, have since become central to dictionary writing. After all, "[o]ne does not study all of botany by making artificial flowers" (Sinclair 1991a: 6). During lexicographic research conducted with the *COBUILD Corpus*, Sinclair (1991a) encountered many examples which proved intuition is not a reliable guide to inform language description:

> The commonest meanings of the commonest words are not the meanings supplied by introspection; for example, the meaning of *back* as 'the posterior part of the human body, extending from the neck to the pelvis' (*Collins English Dictionary* (CED) 2nd edition 1986 sense 1) is not a very common meaning. Not until sense 47, the second adverbial sense, do we come to 'in, to or towards the original starting point,

[2] As Francis (1992: 22) notes, "[i]t is an interesting coincidence that the year of its publication, 1961, was the year chosen to be the year of publication from which the samples in the Brown Corpus were selected".

> place or condition', which is closer to the commonest usage in our evidence. (Sinclair 1991a: 112)

The *CCED* (Sinclair 1987a) was the first dictionary based entirely on the analysis of a corpus, in this case the *COBUILD Corpus*, which later became the *Bank of English* (*BoE*). At the time, the *CCED* was unique in that it provided information about the usage of words that was previously not supplied in traditional dictionaries. Information about the frequency with which a word occurred was now provided and complemented with example sentences taken from the corpus for each definition (See Figure 2-1 for an example of the entry for *back* in the 5th edition of the *Collins COBUILD Advanced Learner's English Dictionary* (*CCAED*) (Sinclair 2006)). The example of the *CCAED* reflects aspects from Sinclair's statement above and demonstrates the details provided by corpus-based reference materials. While at first glance this dictionary entry may appear similar to traditional references, the corpus approach provides information about the usage of the headword not commonly found in traditional dictionaries. Each entry is supplemented with an 'Extra Column' which provides additional information derived from corpus analysis. This column contains information about frequency (the three diamond symbols indicate that the headword is a high-frequency item), grammar and patterns, pragmatics, as well as synonyms and antonyms. Furthermore, the individual definitions include examples taken from the corpus; in other words, they are naturally occurring language examples. The examples themselves are chosen to reflect the most typical collocates of each word. In addition, information on style, usage, and pragmatics is provided. Below is the example of *back* as a noun (part of the body) and its meaning listed under 2 (7):

> You can use **back** in expressions such as round the back and out the back to refer generally to the area behind a house or other building. [BRIT, SPOKEN]

The information in brackets informs the reader that the expression round the back or out the back is used in spoken British English. This type of information has great potential for language learners as it introduces them not only to the meaning of a word but also how to use it. Lexis and lexical patterns are clearly the focus of the *CCAED* and signify the contributions of corpus research to language description; for example, by highlighting the strong links between lexis and grammar.

back

① ADVERB USES
② OPPOSITE OF FRONT; NOUN AND ADJECTIVE USES
③ VERB USES

87

back ◆◆◆

① **back** /bæk/

In addition to the uses shown below, **back** is also used in phrasal verbs such as 'date back' and 'fall back on'.

→ Please look at category 17 to see if the expression you are looking for is shown under another headword.

1 If you move **back**, you move in the opposite direction to the one in which you are facing or in which you were moving before. □ *The photographers drew back to let us view the body... She stepped back from the door expectantly... He pushed her awary and she fell back on the wooden bench.* — ADV: ADV after v, oft ADV prep

2 If you go **back** somewhere, you return to where you were before. □ *I went back to bed ... I'm due back in London by late afternoon... Smith changed his mind and moved back home... I'll be back as soon as I can... He made a round-trip to the terminal and back.* — ADV: ADV after v, be ADV oft ADV prep/adv

3 If someone or something is **back** in a particular state, they were in that state before and are now in it again. □ *The rail company said it expected services to get slowly back to normal... Denise hopes to be back at work by the time her daughter is one.* — ADV: ADV after v, be ADV, oft ADV prep

4 If you give or put something **back**, you return it to the person who had it or to the place where it was before you took it. If you get or take something **back**, you then have it again after not having it for a while. □ *She handed the knife back... Put it back in the freezer... You'll get your money back.* — ADV: ADV after v oft ADV prep

5 If you put a clock or a watch **back**, you change the time shown on it so that it shows an earlier time, for example when the time changes to winter time or standard time. — ADV: ADV after v

6 If you write or call **back**, you write to or telephone someone after they have written to or telephoned you. If you look **back** at someone, you look at them after they have started looking at you. □ *They wrote back to me and they told me that I didn't have to do it... If the phone rings say you'll call back after dinner... Lee looked at Theodora. She stared back.* — ADV: ADV after v, oft ADV prep

7 You can say that you go or come **back to** a particular point in a conversation to show that you are mentioning or discussing it again. □ *Can I come back to the question of policing once again? .. Going back to the school, how many staff are there?* — ADV: ADV after v, ADV *to* n

8 If something is or comes **back**, it is fashionable again after it has been unfashionable for some time. □ *Short skirts are back... Consensus politics could easily come back into fashion.* — ADV: ADV after v, be ADV, oft ADV prep

9 If someone or something is kept or situated **back from** a place, they are at a distance away from it. □ *Keep back from the edge of the platform... I'm a few miles back from the border... He started for Dot's bedroom and Myrtle held him back.* — ADV: ADV after v, be ADV, oft ADV *from* n

10 If something is held or tied **back**, it is held or tied so that it does not hang loosely over something. □ *The curtains were held back by tassels.* — ADV: ADV after v

11 If you lie or sit **back**, you move your body backwards into a relaxed sloping or flat position, with your head and body resting on something. □ *She lay back and stared at the ceiling... She leaned back in her chair and smiled.* — ADV: ADV after v ≠ *forward*

12 If you look or shout **back** at someone or something, you turn to look or shout at them when they are behind you. □ *Nick looked back over his shoulder and then stopped, frowning... He called back to her.* — ADV: ADV after v, oft ADV prep

13 You use **back** in expressions like **back in London** or **back at the house** when you are giving an account, to show that you are going to start talking about what happened or was happening in the place you mention. □ *Meanwhile, back in London, Palace Pictures was collapsing... Later, back at home, the telephone rang.* — ADV: ADV with v, ADV prep

14 If you talk about something that happened **back** in the past or several years **back**, you are emphasizing that it happened quite a long time ago. □ *The story starts back in 1950, when I was five... He contributed £50m to the project a few years back.* — ADV: ADV with v, ADV prep, n ADV [emphasis]

15 If you think **back to** something that happened in the past, you remember it or try to remember it. □ *I thought back to the time in 1975 when my son was desperately ill.* — ADV: ADV after v, ADV *to* n

16 If someone moves **back and forth**, they repeatedly move in one direction and then in the opposite direction. □ *He paced back and forth.* — PHRASE: PHR after v

17 to **cast** your **mind back** → see **mind**.

② **back** /bæk/ (**backs**) ◆◆◆

→ Please look at category 17 to see if the expression you are looking for is shown under another headword.

1 A person's or animal's **back** is the part of their body between their head and their legs that is on the opposite side to their chest and stomach. □ *She turned her back to the audience... Three of the victims were shot in the back.* — N-COUNT: Oft poss N

2 The **back of** something is the side or part of it that is towards the rear or farthest from the front. The back of something is normally not used or seen as much as the front. □ *... a room or the back of the shop... She raised her hands to the back of her neck... Smooth the mixture with the back of a soup spoon.* — N-COUNT: usu sing, oft *the* N *of* n ≠ *front*

3 **Back** is used to refer to the side or part of something that is towards the rear or farthest from the front. □ *He opened the back door... Ann could remember sitting in the back seat of their car. ...the path leading to the back garden.* — ADJ: ADJ n ≠ *front*

4 The **back** of a chair or sofa is the part that you lean against when you sit on it. □ *There was a neatly folded pink sweater on the back of the chair.* — N-COUNT: usu sing with supp

5 The **back** of something such as a piece of paper or an envelope is the side which is less important. □ *Send your answers on the back of a postcard.* — N-COUNT: *the* N, usu sing ≠ *front*

6 The **back** of a book is the part nearest the end, where you can find the index or the notes, for example. □ *...the index at the back of the book.* — N-COUNT: *the* N, usu sing ≠ *front*

7 You can use **back** in expressions such as **round the back** and **out the back** to refer generally to the area behind a house or other building. [BRIT, SPOKEN] □ *He had chickens and things round the back.* — N-SING: prep *the* N

8 You use **back** in expressions such as **out back** to refer to the area behind a house or other building. [AM] □ *Don informed her that he would be out back on the patio.* — N-UNCOUNT: prep N oft N *of* n

9 In team games such as football and hockey, a **back** is a player who is concerned mainly with preventing the other team from scoring goals, rather than scoring goals for their own team. — N-COUNT = defender ≠ forward

10 In American football, a **back** is a player who stands behind the front line, runs with the ball and attacks rather than defends. — N-COUNT

PHRASES

11 If you say that something was done **behind** someone's **back**, you disapprove of it because it was done without them knowing about it, in an unfair or dishonest way. □ *You eat her food, enjoy her hospitality and then criticize her behind her back.* — PHRASE: PHR after v [disapproval]

12 If you **break the back** of a task or problem, you do the most difficult part of what is necessary to complete the task or solve the prob-lem. □ *It seems at least that we've broken the back of inflation in this country.* — PHRASE: V inflects, PHR n

13 If two or more things are done **back to back**, one follows immediately after the other without any interruption. □ *... two half-hour shows, which will be screened back to back.* — PHRASE

14 If you are wearing something **back to front**, you are wearing it with the back of it at the front of your body. If you do something **back to front**, you do it the wrong way around, starting with the part that should come last. [mainly BRIT] □ *He wears his baseball cap back to front... The picture was printed back to front.* — PHRASE: PHR after v = *backwards*

Figure 2-1: Entry for *back* in *CCAED* (Sinclair 2006, pp. 86-87)

Today, many major publishing houses base language reference works for English on large-scale corpus analysis. Publishers hold commercial corpora with millions of words which are used to create dictionaries, grammars, and teaching materials. Cambridge University Press, for example, is host of the *Cambridge International Corpus* (*CIC*) which at the time of writing contains over one billion words and is made up of several sub-corpora, including both written and spoken corpora of British and American English. The *CIC* also includes a learner corpus of English.

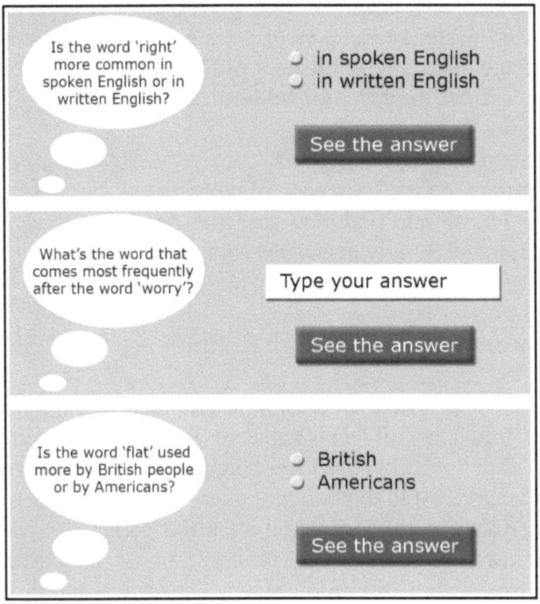

Figure 2-2: Observation vs. Intuition

Basing language descriptions on corpora has seemingly become a seal of quality. The Cambridge University Press website advertises the value of their corpus with the slogan 'Real English Guarantee'.[3]

Furthermore, their web site also entices the reader to consider the advantages of language analysis based on observation versus intuition (see Figure 2-2).

---

3 See '*Cambridge International Corpus*' website. Available at http://www.cambridge.org/us/esl/catalog/subject/item2701617/cambridge-international-corpus/.

With three short questions the reader is invited to test his/her intuition, and a click on 'See the answer' will reveal the answer based on corpus research. The idea, of course, is to demonstrate to the reader that only observation of language data can accurately reflect language use and that introspection, even by native speakers, cannot provide all the answers and is inevitably fallible.[4]

In addition to dictionaries, corpus-based grammars have been developed such as the *Comprehensive Grammar of the English Language* (*CGEL*) (Quirk, Greenbaum, Leech & Svartvik 1985) and the *Longman Grammar of Spoken and Written English* (*LGSWE*) (Biber, Johansson, Leech, Conrad & Finegan 1999), whereby only the latter is entirely corpus-based.[5] Similarly to lexicography, the role of corpora in grammar research is to provide language evidence in order to conduct quantitative analyses and retrieve examples of grammatical phenomena from naturally occurring language data. The publishers of the *LGSWE* describe the features that set this grammar apart from traditional ones as follows:

- Entirely corpus-based grammar of English
- Over 350 tables and graphs showing the frequency of constructions across different registers, from conversation to fiction to academic prose
- 6,000 authentic examples from the *Longman Corpus Network*
- British English and American English grammar compared
- New and challenging findings
- Reveals the differences between spoken and written English

Thus, the corpus-based approach adds a new dimension to grammar research in that it takes into account the frequency of occurrence in order to determine whether a feature is commonly or typically used. Although it is important to note that frequency data itself is not used to explain grammar, "the usefulness of frequency data (and corpus analysis generally) is that it identifies patterns of use that otherwise often go unnoticed by researchers" (Biber, Conrad & Cortes 2004: 376). Native-speaker introspection can guide judgement on grammatical accuracy. It is, however, much less reliable in detecting grammatical patterns in language use and their frequency of occurrence, specifically across variations of English or registers (e.g. spoken vs. written English). Most significantly, corpus analysis has contributed to a new view of grammar that is less concerned with the traditional dichotomy between grammatical or ungrammatical and more focused on what is likely and what is unlikely to occur. Chomsky (1957) put forth his conviction regarding the grammar of a language as follows:

---

[4] This activity is located on the '*Cambridge International Corpus*' website (Footnote 3).

[5] For a detailed comparison of the *CGEL* and the *LGSWE*, see Mukherjee (2006a).

> The fundamental aim in the linguistic analysis of a language L is to separate the *grammatical* sequences which are the sentences of L from the *ungrammatical* sequences which are not sentences of L [...]. One way to test the adequacy of a grammar proposed for L is to determine whether or not the sequences that it generates are actually grammatical [...]. (Chomsky 1957: 13)

In contrast, Stubbs (2009: 118) has observed that corpus investigations often lead the researcher to discover that "absolutely fixed patterns are extremely rare, and a frequent conclusion is that a given pattern is 'typical' or 'canonical', but that it has variants". Corpus investigations of such patterns have also shown that the associations between grammar and vocabulary are much stronger than previously assumed. *That*-clauses as described in the *LGSWE* illustrate the lexico-grammatical phenomenon well. The analysis of the *Longman Corpus of Spoken and Written English* (*LSWE*)[6] showed that all verbs that commonly occur in post-predicate position with *that*-complement clauses come from just three semantic domains: mental verbs (e.g. *think*, *know*); speech act verbs (e.g. *say*, *tell*), and other communication verbs (e.g. *show*, *prove*, *suggest*) (Biber, *et al.* 1999: 661). Another example is the passive and active voice. The authors conclude that "lexical factors strongly influence the choice between active and passive: whereas some verbs normally take the passive voice, other verbs very rarely do so" (Biber *et al.* 1999: 479). Register also plays a role in variation, as the example of verbs in the passive voice in NEWS shows:

> In news, a different set of verbs commonly occurs in the passive. Many of these report negative events that happened to someone, omitting mention of the person who performed the activity:
> *He* ***was accused*** *of using threatening or insulting behaviour.* (NEWS)
> *He* ***was jailed*** *for three months.* (NEWS)
> (Biber *et al.* 1999: 480)

The model of pattern grammar (Hunston & Francis 1998, 2000) draws heavily on these discoveries. Hunston (2002b: 169) defines pattern grammar as "an approach to the grammar of English which prioritises the behaviour of individual lexical items", and it is her belief that "awareness of pattern is important to language teaching because it can facilitate the development of both accuracy and fluency" (2002b: 167).

---

6 The *LSWE* is made up of 40 million words of written and spoken American and British English from four different registers: conversation, fiction, news, academic prose.

To summarise, the production of language reference works has undergone enormous changes since the advent of computers and the introduction of electronic language corpora. Quantitative and qualitative methods, taking both frequency and probability into account, have uncovered patterns in language that have previously gone unnoticed and have furthermore led to necessary revisions of existing beliefs about language. Sinclair (1985) formulates the implications of corpus research early on as follows:

> On the one hand, there is now ample evidence of the existence of significant language patterns which have gone largely unrecorded in centuries of study; on the other hand there is a dearth of support for some phenomena which are regularly put forward as normal patterns of English. (Sinclair 1985: 251)

The next section provides an overview of some of the patterns that have emerged from research undertaken with corpora.

2.2.2 Emerging patterns

The 'vertical' reading of concordance lines can make language patterns observable which have remained hidden from view in traditional horizontal reading of texts. The electronic analysis of large text collections has enabled researchers to closely investigate the environment of words in order to determine what effect this has on the meaning of the word. As a result, language patterns have been discovered which have had a lasting impact on how we understand language today.

Collocations

Firth (1957a: 11) once famously said that "you shall know a word by the company it keeps". The idea of studying meaning and context is a key notion in his approach to linguistics. According to Firth, the meaning of a word is not solely found in the word itself but is created by the associations of words which he named 'collocations' (Firth 1957b: 194). The analysis of language data in electronic corpora has greatly enhanced the possibilities of studying such extended units of meaning. Collocational patterns are often subtle and difficult to explain even for native speakers. For example, it is not readily apparent why it seems natural to refer to *a strong argument* and *a powerful argument*, when *tea* can be *strong* but not *powerful* (see Halliday 1966). Grammatically, all of these combinations are correct but there are clearly restrictions on a lexical level that dictate the use of these words. Native speaker intuition can provide some guidance as to whether two words occurring together 'sound right'. However, such intuitive judgements are limited and the tendency of two words to co-occur can most reliably be tested based on statistical analyses conducted on large language corpora. While the concept of collocations was not new, the unique retrieval capacities of concordancing software have since enabled researchers to conduct quantitative studies that can show the strength of association between particular words.

Learning collocations is an important step towards speaking idiomatically correct language. As Lewis (2002: 26) points out: "Collocations provide learners with a powerful organisation principle of language". Corpus studies of collocations have resulted in valuable reference works on collocations (e.g. *The Oxford Collocations Dictionary: For Students of English*, McIntosh, Francis & Poole 2009) and language learning materials (e.g. *Phrasal Verbs and Collocations (American English)*, Barlow & Burdine 2006). Shin and Nation (2008: 340) believe that "collocations help learners' language use, both with the development of fluency and native-like selection" and propose a list of collocations based on the analysis of a 10 million word spoken component of the *British National Corpus* (*BNC*).

A recent development in collocational research, which may also be of benefit for language learners, is the study of lexical repulsion. This phenomenon, proposed by Renouf and Banerjee (2007: 419), describes the "intuitively observed tendency in conventional language use for certain pairs of words not to occur together", specifically when there is "no explanation other than convention". The authors give some examples: "it is conventional in English to say *sheer guts*, but not *utter guts*; and *utter peace* but not *sheer peace*" (2007: 419). The research on lexical repulsion is very much in its infancy. However, as Renouf and Banerjee (2007: 439) point out, it may lead to the generation of "lists of words which cannot normally combine naturally with a given headword, for the benefit of language learners and non-native-speakers wishing to optimise the quality of their textual composition".

Semantic prosody

The analysis of large corpora has further unveiled semantic prosodies (a term introduced by Louw 1993) which are created through the typical use of a lexical item in a certain cotext. Hunston (1995a: 137) summarises this collocational phenomenon as follows: "[A] word may be said to have a particular prosody if it can be shown to co-occur with other words that belong to a particular semantic set". Sinclair (1991a), who is credited with the identification of semantic prosodies, delivers a corpus-driven[7] description of the phrasal verb *set in* and notices that "[t]he most striking feature of this phrasal verb is the nature of the subjects. In general, they refer to unpleasant states of affairs" (Sinclair 1991a: 74). Some examples of the vocabulary he finds are: "*rot*, *decay*, *malaise*, *despair*, *ill-will*, *decadence* [...]" (1991a: 75). It is important to note that at the core of this concept lies the idea that meaning is created beyond the boundaries of the single word; that a 'unit of meaning' is found in the co-occurrences of this lexical item. These patterns can only be discerned through the observation of large amounts of language data.

Semantic prosody can mostly be described as positive or negative; however, negative ones appear to be much more frequent (Louw 2000). Another such example is the verb *cause* which, as Stubbs (1995: 26) discovers, most frequently collocates with negative collocates concerning "problems, trouble and damage, death, pain and disease". Hunston (2007: 253) later refines this definition in her analysis of *cause* and adds that "[i]t seems reasonable to conclude that CAUSE implies something undesirable only when human beings, or at least animate beings, are clearly involved" (reprinted in Hunston 2009: 89).

Units of meaning

In his seminal publication *Corpus, Concordance, Collocation*, Sinclair (1991a: 109) describes the traditional view of language as "a way of seeing language text as the result of a very large number of complex choices. At each point where a unit is completed [...], a large range of choice opens up and the only restraint is grammaticalness". However, according to Sinclair, this model of the 'open-choice principle' cannot sufficiently explain real language use and meaning creation. Sinclair (1991a: 110) proposes the 'idiom principle' which basically says that "a language user has available to him or her a large number of semi-preconstructed phrases that constitute single choices, even though they might appear to be analysable into segments". This principle, which Sinclair regards as "at least as important as grammar in the explanation of how meaning arises in text" (1991a: 112), allows for different degrees of lexical and syntactical variation. Some words or phrases heavily attract others (i.e., strong collocations), some tend to occur with a particular grammatical structure, and some seem to occur most frequently in a specific semantic environment (i.e., semantic prosodies). These insights into language behaviour are all derived from the empirical analysis of naturally occurring language data in corpora. At the core of this corpus-based research is the belief that form and meaning in language use are

---

7 See Tognini-Bonelli (2001) for her proposed distinction between corpus-*based* and corpus-*driven*.

inseparable. Furthermore, the unit of meaning in language cannot be carried by a single item but can only be derived from the cotext of that word.

Based on machine-readable corpora and corpus analysis software, the field of corpus linguistics allows the study of language under a variety of different aspects. As a consequence, the development of corpus methodologies, tools, and resources has enabled a wealth of new research which was unimaginable prior to the development of sophisticated computer technology. Leech (1992: 106) puts forth his view of (computer) corpus linguistics as "a new research enterprise, and in fact a new philosophical approach to the subject. The computer, as a uniquely powerful technological tool, has made this new kind of linguistics possible". Corpora have, for example, made a significant contribution to the fields of forensic linguistics, translation studies, corpus stylistics, sociolinguistics, and discourse analysis.[8]

Another area upon which corpus research has greatly impacted and which is the focus of this study is language education. The impact of corpora and their direct and indirect applications in language learning and teaching will be examined in Chapter 3.

2.3 Corpus tools and resources

The quality of corpus linguistic analysis depends to a large degree on the quality of the tools and resources employed. The key components are corpora and corpus access software. Thus, the first part of this section begins with an overview of corpus design and typology. The second part presents the basic functions of concordancing software and takes a closer look at the most common concordancers. The third part discusses corpus annotation and mark-up languages.

2.3.1 Corpora: design and typology

> Thirty years ago when research started it was considered impossible to process texts of several million words in length. Twenty years ago it was considered marginally possible but lunatic. Ten years ago it was considered quite possible but still lunatic. Today it is very popular.
>
> (Sinclair 1991a: 1)

Innovations in computer technology have played a central role in corpus development. Text input or conversion techniques, storage capacity, and processing

---

[8] Hunston (2002a: 97ff) provides an informed overview of these areas.

power were key factors in corpus compilation and processing. In the early days, text materials existed in hardcopy only and had to be converted into electronic format. This happened either through keyboarding (i.e., keying in the texts manually) or through optical scanners, which were notoriously unreliable at the time. Renouf (2007) reports on the work undertaken to create the *Birmingham Corpus* (approx. 20 million words) in the 1980s:

> We had two operators working simultaneously non-stop for many months, and to keep up production I had to acquire special dispensation to have women students as well as male working overnight on campus; I processed many books myself. (Renouf 2007: 31)

Optical character recognition has come a long way since; however, depending on the quality of the source material, it is still a time- and labour- intensive process that requires manual checking for errors. In contrast, Baker (2009), who has compiled a corpus of written British English published around 2006 (*BE06 Corpus*) modelled after the *Lancaster-Oslo/Bergen Corpus* (*LOB Corpus*), reports that it took approximately twelve working days to build the one million word corpus. This is of course largely due to the fact that Baker (2009: 312) exclusively used texts that "had been originally published in paper form, then placed on the internet".

Tognini-Bonelli and Sinclair (2006) provide a helpful historical outline to sketch the development of corpora over the years:

a The first 20 years, c. 1960-1980; learning how to build and maintain corpora of up to a million words; no material is available in electronic form, so everything has to be transliterated on a keyboard.
b The second 20 years, 1980-2000; divisible into two decades:
  i. The 1980s, the decade of the scanner, where with even the early scanners a target of 20 million words becomes realistic.
  ii. The 1990s, the First Serendipity, when text becomes available as the by-product of computer typesetting, allowing another order of magnitude to the target size of corpora.
c The new millennium, and the Second Serendipity, when text that never had existence as hard copy becomes available in unlimited quantities from the Internet.

(Tognini-Bonelli & Sinclair 2006: 208)

Although technological advances have played a key role in the development of corpora, it is important to distinguish between a mere collection of machine-readable texts and a corpus that was constructed according to linguistic principles. Compiling a corpus is a complex task and requires much careful consideration.

In order to derive valid statements from a corpus, it has to either cover the target language exhaustively or be representative of the respective subject of inquiry. With the exception of specialised corpora of finite subsets of language for a specific research purpose (e.g. a corpus of all the research articles from a selected journal in order to research the language used in that journal), corpora generally cannot contain all instances of a language or a subset thereof. In particular, the totality of general language cannot be known and as a consequence cannot be captured in its entirety. As Hunston (2002a: 28) concedes, "[t]he problem is that 'being representative' inevitably involves knowing what the character of the 'whole' is. Where the proportions of that character are unknowable, attempts to be representative tend to rest on little more than guess-work". In his seminal article, 'Representativeness in corpus design', Biber (1993) presents a detailed discussion on the topic of representativeness. He argues that a selection of samples of the target language should be taken according to a clear definition of the limits of the analysed language. This definition is called the 'sampling frame'. The more precisely the purpose of the corpus is formulated, the easier it is to establish criteria of representativeness. The method of sampling has been devised in an attempt to approximate maximum representativeness. McEnery, Xiao and Tono (2006: 19) define samples as "scaled-down versions of a larger population". Before samples can be selected, the sampling frame has to be defined which largely depends on the research purpose. Studies on formal, non-fictional written British English should, for example, include newspaper texts and governmental documents but exclude novels and private email correspondence. This approach is called "*stratified random sampling*, which first divides the whole population into relatively homogeneous groups (so-called *strata*) and samples each stratum at random" (McEnery *et al.* 2006: 20). This process requires listing the different categories and then sampling from each of them.

The *Brown Corpus* is a good example to illustrate this point. It consists of one million words and is made up of 500 sample texts, each comprising approximately 2,000 words. As this corpus had been created to serve as a strategic sample of written American English published in 1961, the chosen categories were to cover all relevant written sources of American English. Table 2-1 lists the categories chosen for informative and imaginative prose of the *Brown Corpus*:

Table 2-1: Text categories (*Brown Corpus*, Francis & Kučera 1979)

	I. Informative Prose (374 samples)	
A	*Press: Reportage*	*44*
B	*Press: Editorial*	*27*
C	*Press: Reviews*	*17*
D	*Religion*	*17*
E	*Skills and Hobbies*	*36*
F	*Popular Lore*	*48*
G	*Belles Lettres, Biography, Memoirs, etc.*	*75*
H	*Miscellaneous*	*30*
J	*Learned*	*80*
	II. Imaginative Prose (126 samples)	
K	*General Fiction*	*29*
L	*Mystery and Detective Fiction*	*24*
M	*Science Fiction*	*6*
N	*Adventure and Western Fiction*	*29*
P	*Romance and Love Story*	*29*
R	*Humor*	*9*
	Grand Total:	*500*

The precise documentation of the *Brown Corpus* is described in the corpus manual (Francis & Kučera 1979), and it has become a matter of good practice to provide a corpus manual that informs about the sampling techniques and other vital details about the design of the corpus like corpus annotation and mark-up which is discussed in Section 2.3.3 below. This allows researchers today to replicate the composition of a given corpus in order to build diachronic corpora of materials published at different times for studies of language change. In the case of the *Brown* and *LOB* corpora, comparable corpora of materials published 30 years later were created for American English (*Freiburg-Brown Corpus of American English, FROWN Corpus*) and for British English (*Freiburg-LOB Corpus of British English, FLOB Corpus*). Baker (2009) also reports that further versions of the British corpus are in progress with materials from 1931 and 1901 respectively. Baker (2009) himself recently compiled the *BE06 Corpus* which contains materials produced 15 years after the *FLOB Corpus*. As Lee (2010) points out, however,

> [t]his multiple copying of the original Brown/LOB design is not because the sampling criteria and genre proportions therein are considered ideal (indeed, they are not). It is rather because the

> compilers wanted maximal comparability for regional and diachronic research. (Lee 2010: 109)

Therefore, one needs to be aware that whenever research is based on sampling, there is always a risk of leaving something out and, consequently, of working with samples that represent the entire body disproportionally.

The ideal size of a corpus is dependent on the research purpose for which the corpus is intended. Francis (1982: 13) remarks that "[w]hen the purpose of the corpus is lexical, all thought of complete coverage must be abandoned. So large is the lexicon of a language and so almost infinitely numerous the possibilities of collocation that we cannot imagine a corpus, however large, that can contain it all". This is reflected, for example, in the great size of commercial corpora employed by publishing houses for the purpose of lexicographical research. However, it must be noted that obtaining large volumes of language data can be a difficult, expensive and laborious process. Consequently, as Atkins, Clear and Ostler (1992: 3) rightly observe, "the need for large volumes of data may lead one to adopt a more opportunistic approach to the collection of text". Copyright restrictions imposed by publishers and limited funds available through research grants can be influential factors to drive corpus compilation.

However, the more particular the research question and the more limited the context, the smaller a corpus can be while still maintaining a degree of representativeness. The *IBM Manuals Corpus* at Lancaster University is an example of such a case. The corpus contains one million words and is made up of manuals for IBM products. McEnery and Wilson (1996: 147ff.) discovered during a case study on 'sublanguages' (language from restricted domains) that the *IBM Manuals Corpus* reaches closure on a lexical basis at approximately 110,000 tokens (i.e., the number of individual words in the corpus). After this, it exhibits no significant growth in lexical types at all; in other words, it has reached the zero-growth point. A further increase in size therefore means no increase in lexical types. It is worthwhile mentioning though that McEnery and Wilson treat this subject with great caution. They come to the conclusion that the IBM manuals seem to represent a very restricted register of language with a high degree of closure and that the sublanguage hypotheses may indeed be valid. Yet, there are many issues they could not explore, and therefore they do not draw any definite conclusions (McEnery & Wilson 1996: 165-166).

There is still much debate among linguists on what constitutes the 'ideal' corpus in terms of representativeness, structure, the balance and size of samples, and the size of the entire corpus, yet the answer is ultimately a matter of the intended purpose it is designed for. Despite ever refined methods and theories on corpus design, the creation of a perfectly balanced and representative corpus remains "an act of faith" (Kennedy 1998: 21). Stubbs (2004) proposes that

> [a] realistic aim is a corpus which samples widely, is not biased toward data which are easy to collect (e.g. mass media texts), does not under-represent data which are difficult to collect (e.g. casual conversation), and is not unbalanced by text-types which have over-specialized lexis and grammar (e.g. academic research articles). (Stubbs 2004: 112)

Types of corpora

Corpora have proved to be especially useful for refining current descriptions of language features and contextualising language use. There are many different types of corpora and applications of these corpora can be found in many different research areas. In the following, some of the most common types of corpora are introduced and possible applications for them reviewed. The following corpus types will be discussed:

(i) Sample (or reference) corpus,
(ii) Monitor corpus,
(iii) Parallel and comparable corpus,
(iv) Specialised corpus,
(v) Spoken corpus, and
(vi) Learner corpus.

(i) Sample (or reference) corpus

This type of corpus is designed to contain a broad selection of all the registers and genres of a given language. The *Brown Corpus* and the *LOB Corpus* are considered to be the first reference corpora for American and British English respectively, although by current standards they are much too small and neither of them contains any spoken material. Contemporary reference corpora, like the *BNC*, consist of at least 100 million words or more and are often split into subcorpora that are available for smaller-scale or more specialised research. The *BNC*, for example, also includes transcripts of spoken language. As opposed to monitor corpora, which will be discussed below, their size is finite, in other words, their content is static. An important characteristic is that the material they contain is broadly heterogeneous. Thus, sample or reference corpora should reflect the general usage of language without specialised language from one particular genre creating an imbalance.[9] Classic examples of sample corpora are the *Brown* and *LOB* corpora, as well as their regional counterparts (e.g. the *Australian Corpus of English, ACE*). The *International Corpus of English* (*ICE*) project has produced a range of comparable sample corpora of worldwide English varieties. These corpora are similar in design to the *Brown* and *LOB* corpora; however, they also include transcripts of spoken language. Another ongoing project is the *American National Corpus* (*ANC*). This project is divided into several stages. One aim is to create an American counterpart to the *BNC* which will be designed to be comparable to the British version. In addition, "an 'opportunistic' component of potentially several hundreds of millions of words, chosen to provide both the broadest and largest selection of texts (and, where available, annotations) possible" (*ANC* website)[10] is in preparation. The latter is more akin to a monitor corpus which is described below.

(ii) Monitor corpus

Sinclair (1982: 4) defines a monitor corpus through "its capacity to hold a 'state of language' for research purposes". As the name suggests, this type of corpus is dynamic, it 'monitors' language. New data is added continuously while outdated materials are extracted according to a scheme that is intended to ensure that the language data remains contemporary. Monitor corpora are generally very large and grow continuously; most of them are opportunistic while some are compiled after a more rigid plan. One frequently quoted example for a monitor corpus is the BoE.[11] According to the *Collins* website, the *BoE* currently contains approximately 650 million words.[12] This large collection of text was designed to reflect current usage of English and contains written and spoken materials, the latter in the form of transcribed speech. Due to its massive size and the large variety of genres it covers, the *BoE* is an excellent source for a wide range of research and is of special interest to the production of reference materials. The *BoE* is part of the *Collins Corpus*, which according to the publisher's website contains 2.5 billion words of "written material from websites, newspapers, magazines and

---

9 Sinclair (1991a: 24) also notes that a sample corpus "does not purport to be a valid sample of each genre. […] If a million words is hazarded as a reasonable sample of one state of a language, then the sub-categories necessary to balance the sample are not in themselves reasonable samples because they are too brief".

10 '*American National Corpus*', website. Available at http://www.americannationalcorpus.org.

11 Although more recently, Davies (2010) has stressed the apparent unbalance of genre in the *BoE* which make diachronic studies based on this corpus problematic.

12 'About the *Collins Corpus* and the *Bank of English*', website. Available at http://www.mycobuild.com/about-collins-corpus.aspx.

books published around the world, and spoken material from radio, TV and everyday conversations". New data is continuously added in order to keep the language in the corpus 'up-to-date'.

A recent example of a monitor corpus of American English is the *Corpus of Contemporary American English* (*COCA*). According to the developer of the corpus, the *COCA* is arguably the "first balanced monitor corpus of any language" as it is "divided almost equally between spoken, fiction, popular magazines, newspapers, and academic journals" (Davies 2010: 453). Through an online interface, registered users can search the corpus by "substring, lemma, part of speech, collocates, synonyms, and limit and compare by sections of the corpus" (2010: 462).

(iii) Parallel and comparable corpus

A parallel corpus (sometimes also referred to as a translation corpus) actually consists of at least two corpora, one including texts in the original language and the other the translation of the first, generally aligned by sentence or at least by paragraph. Parallel corpora are often made up of official proceedings from multilingual organisations such as the EU or NATO and bilingual countries such as Canada (e.g. the *HANSARD Corpus*) but may include any other text type as well. The *INTERSECT Corpus*, for example, is made up of texts from a variety of genres; these include, fiction, news, business, government, and science. This type of corpus has become appealing to different areas of research although they are of primary interest to the field of translation. More recently, they have also become popular for the use in the language classroom (e.g. Barlow 2000; Frankenberg-Garcia 2004, 2005), particularly of course for training translators (e.g. Beeby, Rodriguez Inés & Sánchez-Gijón 2009; Laviosa 2002; Zanettin, Bernardini & Stewart 2003).

A comparable corpus consists of texts from two or more languages that are similar in subject matter and text type. The ICE collection is an example of comparable corpora. Such corpora are a valuable tool in translator education as they can aid in the process of developing more natural sounding translations while parallel corpora can provide examples of professional translation strategies. As Philip (2009: 59-60) highlights, "rather than studying previous translation choices (in a translation corpus), comparable corpora reveal how the word, phrase or term is actually rendered by native-speakers of the TL [target language], allowing the translator to produce text which passes as native-like".

(iv) Speech corpus

Speech corpora are usually multimodal. They contain the actual audio recordings as well as the respective orthographic transcripts. The *Bergen Corpus of London Teenage Language* (*COLT*) consists of approximately 500,000 words of spontaneous conversations between 13- to 17-year old boys and girls from socially different school districts. The compilation and annotation of spoken corpora is still a very time-consuming and expensive enterprise despite advances in computer technology. As a consequence, speech corpora are generally not freely available. A notable exception is, for example, the *Michigan Corpus of Academic Spoken English* (*MICASE*). This corpus is freely available through the *MICASE* website.[13] Users can access the corpus either through an online interface, browse the transcripts or listen to the recorded sound files.

Speech corpora are also used within the fields of speech science and speech technology in order to create acoustic models for speech recognition engines. Applications are, for example, automatic directory assistance and similar telephone-based automatic speech recognition systems. Some corpora are created for use outside of natural language research and frequently contain scripted and read-out-loud speech and are highly specialised (e.g. the *Alphadigit Corpus* which is a collection of 78,044 recordings from 3,025 speakers who say six digit strings of letters and digits over the phone).

(v) Specialised corpus

Specialised corpora are generally much smaller than monitor or reference corpora. They contain language material from one particular and usually restricted domain; for example, business letters, legal texts, geography lecture notes etc. Thus, while the statements derived from such a corpus cannot be projected onto general language use, they can, however, be compared with large general corpora in order to identify differences and similarities. The category of specialised corpora is quite broad and can be applied to other types of corpora; for example, the above mentioned *MICASE* is a specialised corpus as it consists only of spoken English in an academic setting. Specialised corpora can be used in any given language research context. In the context of language learning, specialised corpora are frequently used in teaching (e.g. English for Specific Purposes, ESP), "where such small, easy-to-collect specialized language samples were in many senses considered precisely what was needed" (Gavioli 2005: 55).

---

[13] '*MICASE*', website. Available at http://micase.elicorpora.info.

(vi) Learner corpus

Learner corpora are made up of texts and materials produced by language learners from different language backgrounds. This type of corpus is used as a resource for more insight into the interlanguage of the foreign language learner. Error analysis has brought many insights, such as over- and underuse of certain features, and has identified many learner needs that had previously gone undetected. The most famous project of this kind is the *International Corpus of Learner English* (*ICLE*), initiated in 1990 by Sylviane Granger (see Granger 1993, 1994). The *ICLE* contains learner language material from 12 language backgrounds. Fan, Greaves and Warren (1999) discuss the benefits of learner corpora. A more detailed discussion of the role of corpora in the study of learner language follows in Section 3.1.2 below.

(vii) Web as Corpus

The ready availability of text through the internet has led to suggestions of using the internet as a source of texts for corpus creation or to search the Web directly as a dynamic corpus. As a source of linguistic information, the internet offers unprecedented access to tremendous amounts of text from all kinds of genres. In particular, the internet provides instant access to language data that can give insight to rare items, and neologisms. In addition, new text types (e.g. emails, blogs, and chat room logs) can be searched. In this capacity, the Web-as-corpus has great advantages over traditional reference corpora which are quite laborious, expensive, and slow to compile. The concept of the Web-as-corpus, however, is also highly controversial and the "theoretical objections to using the Web as a corpus come thick and fast" (Renouf 2007: 42). These objections include the inability to control or know the language data which leads to the necessary abandonment of a number of the most central principles of corpus linguistics: the notion of representativeness has to be ignored, searches cannot be replicated by other researchers because the data changes constantly, exhaustive study is impossible, and "the significance and interpretability are thrown into question" (Renouf 2007: 42).

These are just some of the most commonly used corpora. Thus far, an official corpus typology has not been established. The *Expert Advisory Group on Language Engineering Standards* (*EAGLES*), an initiative of the European Commission, has published a first draft of such a typology which is available online.[14] However, this document does not appear to have been updated since 1996. Sinclair believes that rather than producing 'official standards', "it is safer

---

[14] '*EAGLES*', website. Available at http://www.ilc.cnr.it/EAGLES/corpustyp/corpustyp.html.

in such a fast-developing field to rely on groups of scholars sharing the procedures that they find useful" (personal correspondence, 22 July 2003).

2.3.2 Corpus analysis software

Hunston (2002a: 3) rightly remarks that "[a] corpus does not contain new information about language, but the software offers us a new perspective on the familiar". Thus, computer programs play a central role in the process of analysing corpora. The software employed by linguists in order to analyse corpora is often referred to as a concordancer although such programs almost always include other functions such as frequency count and collocation search. For ease of understanding, the term 'concordancer' will be used from here on in order to refer to corpus analysis software. These programs, essentially very advanced search engines, access electronic language data stored in a corpus. The two core functions of concordancers are the production of frequency lists and of electronic concordances which Sinclair (1991a: 32) defines as "a collection of the occurrence of a word-form, each in its own textual environment". Such concordances are produced in the form of KeyWord-In-Context (KWIC) lists which present every retrieved instance of the search string, also known as the node word, in a centred column with the context displayed on the left and on the right side of that column. Examination of such concordance lines can show patterns that exist in language use but that would be impossible to detect based on introspection alone. These patterns are an essential feature of language and a concordance "makes visible recurrent patterns, and allows us to count them" (Stubbs 2009: 117).

Types of concordancer

Tribble and Jones (1997: 9-10) distinguish between streaming concordancers, text-indexers and in-memory concordancers. The latter was developed when computing capacity was extremely limited. The entire text was loaded into the memory of the computer for very fast access but the permissible size of the respective text was extremely limited. The us of text-indexers is usually limited to large-scale corpus work. The most typical program used today is the streaming concordancer such as, for example, *AntConc, MonoConc Pro* and *Wordsmith Tools*. These programs are stand-alone concordancers, in other words, they require external corpora and can be run on an offline systems. For some time, an increasing number of corpus research centres have also made corpora or parts of corpora freely available through so-called online concordancers.

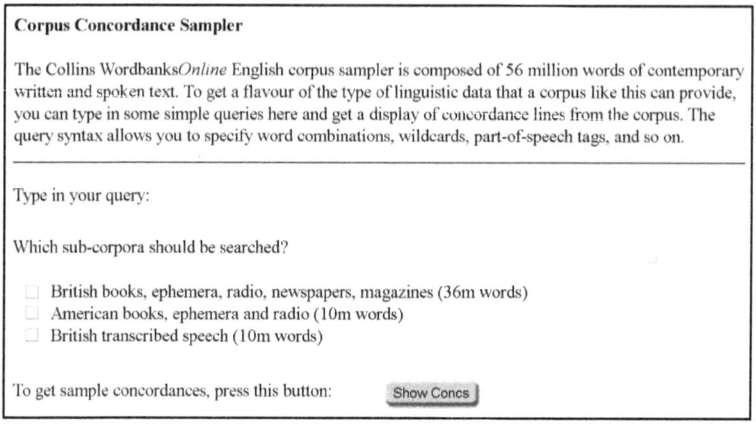

Figure 2-3: *Collins WordbanksOnline English Corpus Sampler*

One example is the *Collins WordbanksOnline English Corpus Sampler* (hereafter: *Collins Corpus Sampler*).[15] While the output of both the concordance and the collocation sampler is limited, this online platform provides access to a fairly large general corpus and is a great starting point for basic concordancing activities.

Concordancers offer a unique perspective on language that can aid in identifying multiple contexts of a search string, a list of all the words that occur in a particular corpus, as well as the frequency of their occurrence, and the collocations of that search string. Barlow (2004: 207) observes that "the most radical transformation of a text used in linguistics analyses is to, in effect, rip it apart to produce a wordlist". The output generated by concordancers reflects the quantitative dimension of the corpus approach and demonstrates the true potential of computer technology in this type of linguistic analysis. Producing a full concordance of the one-million-word *Brown Corpus*, for example, would have taken many researchers months if not years to complete manually and, even then, accuracy could not have been guaranteed. In the early days of computing technology, "Henry Kučera reported that the concordancing of the one-million-word *Brown Corpus* took the total mainframe capacity of Brown University Computer Unit for a day" (Renouf 2007: 31). In contrast, the corpus software *Concordance 3.3* (Watt 2009), run on a current standard desktop computer by the author of this present study, finished analysing the entire *Brown Corpus* in 33.36 seconds (with alphabetical sorting). The remainder of this

[15] Please note that the *Collins Corpus Sampler* has recently been updated on the Collins webpage to the subscription-based service *Wordbanks Online*. Available at http://www.collins language.com/wordbanks/default.aspx.

section will take a closer look at the various functions of concordancers. A review of concordancing software is provided in Section 7.1.

Word search

The word search option locates all occurrences of a particular search string. The result is generally displayed in the KWIC format which aligns the samples in such a way that the keyword is centred in the middle as shown in Figure 2-4:

Nr	Comment	Left context	KWIC	Right context
31		These are war-games. You're	important	because you're sitting on Cassidy's files; but for the ...
32		... a conservative selection). Drusilla Modjeska's	important	book Exiles at Home (Angus and Robertson,...
33		...-related diseases had elapsed. Thirdly, and most	important	, both Drew's estimates of tobacco-induced deaths ...
34		... which is based on eights, there is an immensely	important	boy called "The Ninth Man In The Monarch." I have ...
35		... southern Africa question. He was a member of the	important	Brandt Commission which studied questions ...
36		... of the area, especially the Fishermen Islands, are	important	breeding grounds for nine species of sea birds and ...
37		... is sad that society pigeonholes motherhood as an	important	but low-status job because the going rate for ...
38		... or by bringing more land into production. Also	important	(but perhaps more painful) has been the exit of ...
39		... of manufacturing in Queen+sland and the lack of an	important	capital city there has never really been the ...
40		... rarely in practice. In 1951 Enderby studied the more	important	case of a dilute suspension of weakly-charged ...
41		... for restraint. He also served notice on industry that	important	changes had to be made. The Government ought to ...
42		<h>3.1 INTRODUCTION </h> Eight	important	coal rich areas are discussed in this report. They are ...
43		... operating in India. <h> ZINCALUME </h> The most	important	coating development in three decades was inspired ...
44		... in the walled garden. Where no doubt a lot more	important	concerns had begun. Mr Gladstone walking the paths.
45		... of the physics of how molecules interact, with	important	consequences for the chemistry of molecular ...
46		... While an appropriate balance of State members is an	important	consideration in the selection of assess+ment panels,...
47		... the party who received it before marriage, that is an	important	consideration. (f) The strength of a contribution ...
48		... Carol leaves Lindsay. The film also looks at other	important	contempo+rary relationship issues: managing as a ...
49		... competition faced by local manufacturers, two	important	determinants of the extent to which an industry is ...
50		... and a streamlining of practices and organisation. An	important	development in 1985-86 has been a restructuring of ...

Figure 2-4: KWIC display (*My Concordancer*; Corpus: *ACE*)

This format provides a clear display of the keyword in its context. There are a number of very important characteristics that make the KWIC format so essential to successful research. First of all, the most obvious feature is that the query word is listed in the centre and can therefore be seen directly in its various contexts. The second feature, which combined with the first makes it very easy to discover patterns, is the option to sort the context of the keyword. In the above example, the first word to the right of the query was sorted alphabetically. A more advanced sorting is available in most current concordancers. If the concordance lines are sorted according to the original occurrence of the query in the corpus, this can be very helpful for identifying the change of use of a word throughout a text (e.g. in literary texts). Here is an illustration of the advanced sorting option that the corpus investigation software *MonoConc Pro 2.2* (Barlow 2002) provides:

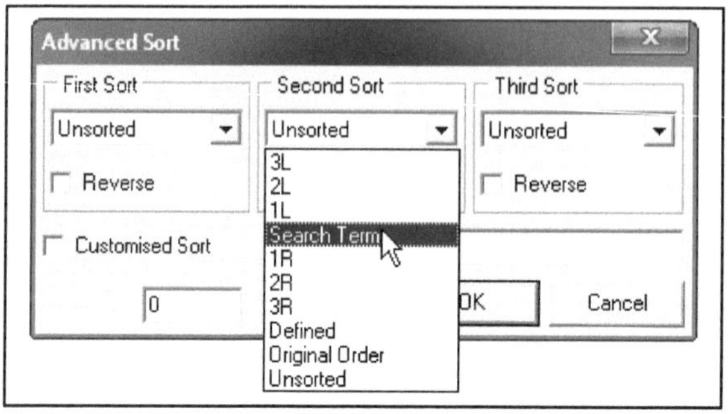

Figure 2-5: *MonoConc Pro*, advanced sorting options

The concordance output can be customised as well. The number of characters displayed to the right and to the left can be adjusted, and many programs can show the results in the KWIC format as well as in complete sentences or paragraphs. The instant retrieval of words and their original context through the concordancer is one of the most powerful features of the corpus approach.

Query syntax

The query syntax of concordancers can help to identify these patterns more easily and help to conduct more complex searches. A search query can be modified in a number of different ways. In particular, wildcards are a valuable tool to make a search more flexible or more precise. Here are some of the standard wildcard characters (although these may differ in different programs):

* = 0 or more characters
% = 0 or 1 character
? = exactly 1 character
@ = covers the range of words (customisable)

A search for 'encourag*' finds any occurrences of *encourag-e*, *encourag-ed*, *encourag-ement(s)*, *encourag-er(s)*, *encourag-es*, *encourag-(e)ing* as well as *encourag-ingly*. A search for 'thr?w' displays all occurrences of *throw* as well as its past tense form *threw*. The @ wildcard is a further interesting option. It searches for word *x* followed by word *y* within a customisable range of words: the search string 'has @ been' displays all results of *has been* constructions; for example: *has also been*, *has always been*, *has not ever been*. Unfortunately, the query syntax of concordancing software often varies but is normally well-documented in a help file.

Frequency and word lists

Frequency lists, either in alphabetical or in frequency order, are lists of all the words that occur in a corpus complemented by the number of occurrence of each individual item. These lists can be a useful initial approach to a corpus or a particular subset of the corpus. Frequency lists are also used to compare one corpus to another, although this is only meaningful if the corpora are of the same size. Frequency lists have, for example, demonstrated that functional words are much more frequent than lexical words. It is important to note though that the frequency of an item is not always a reliable guide to its usage. Consider the example of *like* which appears 1,017 times in the *ACE*. This information alone does not allow one to draw any conclusions, however, because *like* could occur as a verb, a preposition, or an adverb. Raw frequency data is only a first indication, and further manual analysis is needed. As will be seen in Section 2.3.3 below, annotated corpora provide better means for frequency searches as they allow, for example, to automatically count the frequency of *like* as a verb only.

Collocations

The study of collocations has been greatly enhanced by the use of electronic concordancers. A KWIC list shows the word or phrase in question in its natural co-text. Standard tools such as *MonoConc Pro 2.2* (Barlow 2002) calculate the frequency of neighbouring collocates while more sophisticated tools such as the 'KeyWords' function in *Wordsmith Tools 5* (Scott 2008) help in the study of words that are semantically related and which co-occur in the same text and contribute to its cohesion. Another function, 'Wordlist', can also calculate the Mutual Information (MI) score which relates one word to the next. The formula to calculate the MI score not only takes into consideration how often a word co-occurs with the search string but also how often the word occurs well away from it (a typical example would be *the*) which would then result in a low MI score.

Pitfalls of concordancing

A concordancer is a unique tool to access language data in a way that was not possible without computers. Yet, there are some important issues that need to be considered when working with concordancers. A concordancer only ever displays results according to what it was asked to show. Such a program has no understanding of the concept 'word' but simply reads the input as a string of characters. Therefore, the search string 'seperate' will most likely end with no results as the word is spelled incorrectly. A search for 'be' will not produce results of all the forms of *be* (*am, is*, *are*, *been*, *being*, *was*, *were*). On the other hand, a search for 'like' will not only display the verb *like* but also, for example, *like* as preposition or adverb, which in turn will result in a huge number of (likely unwanted) results.

Concordances can be misleading as one often only notices the results and not the things that are absent. The missing of negative evidence does not necessarily justify the formulation of a rule, as results are entirely dependent on the quality of the corpus. A concordancer cannot find *nothing*. Some questions are concordance-ready, others are not. As will be shown in the next section on corpus annotation, a search for all adjectives in a corpus is possible (keeping the unreliability of automatic taggers in mind); concordancing for all adjectives with derogatory meaning is not. There is generally a danger of over-generalisation; where a "possible tendency" can be mistaken for a "definite tendency" which in turn easily turns into a "definite rule" (Johns 1988: 25).[16]

2.3.3 Annotation and mark-up

Successful corpus-based research, facilitated through the functionality of corpus analysis software, is primarily dependent on the corpus itself. While concordancers are sophisticated search tools, they are not linguistic experts and cannot, for example, identify the grammatical functions of words. In fact, as mentioned above, concordancing software can only process the search word or phrase as the actual string of characters entered. The concordance therefore reflects exactly that string which may produce unwanted results. The case of homographs and polysemes in English offers a good illustration of this problem. Here, a string of letters stands for more than one lexeme, and the concordancer cannot distinguish between one or the other. A search for the string 'minute', for example, which may stand for the noun (a small unit of time) or the adjective (very tiny), will result in a concordance listing both meanings. As a result, such a concordance requires manual analysis in order to distinguish the samples of *minute* as a noun and as an adjective.

Frequency lists are also affected by this phenomenon. In particular in the case of English, a language with many homographs, frequency lists drawn from raw text corpora need to be analysed with caution. Another problem would be to

[16] Corpus literacy for learners and learner strategies in using corpus data will be discussed in Chapter 4.

search for the different morphological variants of a lemma (or dictionary headword). For example, the verb *be* has eight different forms (*be*, *am*, *is*, *are*, *was*, *were*, *been*, *being*), it also can appear in abbreviated forms (e.g. *there's*), and as such cannot be automatically distinguished from other instances (e.g. abbreviations of *has*, or possessive *'s*). This makes an accurate search for all forms of *be* rather complex and requires a lot of manual analysis on behalf of the researcher.[17] This often results in concordances with unwanted results which more often than not "are difficult if not impossible to predict and therefore exclude" (Whistle 1999: 449). One way of tackling these shortcomings of concordancers is with the help of corpus enhancements in the form of annotation schemes or mark-up language.

To begin with, a corpus exists in its raw state of plain text. It is, however, possible to 'enhance' this with additional linguistic information in the form of annotation or mark-up. There are various types of annotation that can be applied to a corpus. The most common level is grammatical word-class tagging or the so-called part-of-speech (POS) tagging, followed by syntactic annotation. Nowadays, both of them can be applied at least semi-automatically. More complex types of annotation include semantic, discoursal, prosodic, pragmatic, and stylistic annotations which are mostly applied by the use of mark-up languages. POS annotation as well as mark-up languages will be briefly reviewed in the following section. A discussion of the advantages and disadvantages of annotated corpora concludes the section.

Part-of-speech tagging

Grammatical tagging or POS tagging means that each word in a corpus is associated with a tag or descriptor to indicate its grammatical class; for example, 'noun', 'verb', and 'adjective'. Prior to the tagging process a scheme has to be devised that lists the abbreviations used for each word class. The tags are then added to the words, usually separated from them with a predetermined character such as '_' or '/'. Below is an example of a sentence taken from the tagged version of the *LOB Corpus* (annotated version):

> Ordinary_NN Williams_NP said_VBD he_PPS ,_, too_RB ,_, was_BEDZ subjected_VBN to_IN anonymous_JJ calls_NNS soon_RB after_CS he_PPS scheduled_VBD the_AT election_NN.

---

17 It is worth mentioning here that concordancing languages other than English is potentially even more complicated due to accents, changing verb stems, and inflected forms.

The list of tags described in the manual of the *Brown Corpus* provides the key to encode the tags used in the example above:

Table 2-2: Part-of-speech tags (*Brown Corpus*, Francis & Kučera 1979)[18]

Tag	Description
AT	article
BEDZ	D=past tense Z=3rd person singular (of the verb be)
CS	subordinating conjunction
IN	preposition
JJ	adjective
NN	singular or mass noun
NNS	plural noun
NP	proper noun or part of name phrase
PPS	3rd. singular nominative pronoun
RB	adverb
VBD	verb, past tense
VBN	verb, past participle

As the example of *minute* has shown, annotation can prove very useful in concordancing. If one was interested in the uses of *minute* only as a noun, the query to a tagged corpus – for example, the *Collins WordbanksOnline English Corpus* – looks like this: 'minute/NOUN'. This would result in a concordance that only contains occurrences of *minute* as a noun. POS tagging can therefore greatly enhance the efficiency of corpus searches by excluding unwanted returns from the beginning. Furthermore, this feature also permits searches for a word class at a particular position. For example, if one was interested in adjectives preceding the noun *impact*, the search string could be formulated with a wild-card: '* impact'. This search, performed on the *Corpus of Contemporary American English* (*COCA*), returns results of *an impact*, *the impact*, *its impact* as the three most frequent uses. POS tagging permits the user to conduct a more precise search with the string: '[j*] impact' which lists all only adjective/noun combinations for *impact*. Table 2-3 shows a list of the ten most frequent combinations:

18 The complete list of tags is available in the manual of the *Brown Corpus* (Francis & Kučera 1979) at http://khnt.hit.uib.no/icame/manuals/brown/INDEX.HTM#bc6.

Table 2-3: Adjective/noun combinations of *impact* (in *COCA*)

	ADV + NOUN	**Total**
1	*environmental impact*	*822*
2	*negative impact*	*699*
3	*significant impact*	*653*
4	*economic impact*	*647*
5	*positive impact*	*555*
6	*major impact*	*377*
7	*potential impact*	*367*
8	*big impact*	*345*
9	*profound impact*	*287*
10	*greater impact*	*266*

POS tagging is also highly useful when looking at high-frequency words like *can*. A tagged corpus would allow the user to exclude any results of *can* as a noun if the verb is the desired keyword. The grammatical tagging of the *Brown Corpus* was a laborious process and done manually over the course of many years. The automatic tagger that was employed to process the *Brown Corpus* achieved only 77% accuracy (see Greene & Rubin 1971) at the time. Modern taggers achieve around 97% accuracy for languages like English. However, highly inflected languages such as Russian and Polish are much more difficult to tag and accuracy levels hover around 80-90% (see Brants 2006).

Mark-up languages

Mark-up languages like SGML (Standard General Mark-up Language) and XML (eXtensible Mark-up Language) are used to add information to the corpus that was lost during the process of transferring the text electronically to the corpus file. This information often relates to the formatting of the original document; for example, page numbers, headlines, and typeface (bold, italics). However, mark-up languages are very flexible and provide limitless options of annotation. In order to separate text from this added information, the so-called tags are set in diamond brackets. Below is an example from the *FLOB Corpus*:

<#FLOB:A01\><h_><p_>Labour pledges reversal of NHS hospital opt-outs<p/>
<p_>By Stephen Castle<p/>
<p_>Political Correspondent<p/><h/>

> <p_>ROBIN COOK, Labour's health spokesman, yesterday repeated party opposition to the internal market in the National Health Service and said there had been <quote_>"no secret pacts with health service <}_><-|>manager<+|>managers<}/>"<quote/> to maintain hospital trusts.<p/>

The information in the brackets restores some of the information from the original documents lost in the process of conversion into raw text and is decoded in the manual accompanying the *FLOB Corpus* (Hundt, Sand & Siemund 1999).

Table 2-4: List of SGML codes (*FLOB Corpus*, Hundt *et al.* 1999)[19]

<table>
<tr><th>Tag</th><th>Description</th></tr>
<tr><td><#FLOB:\></td><td>FLOB category (e.g. <#FLOB:C03\>)</td></tr>
<tr><td><p_></td><td>begin paragraph</td></tr>
<tr><td><p/></td><td>end paragraph</td></tr>
<tr><td><h_></td><td>begin headline</td></tr>
<tr><td><h/></td><td>end headline</td></tr>
<tr><td><h|></td><td>one word headline</td></tr>
<tr><td><quote_></td><td>begin quotation</td></tr>
<tr><td><quote/></td><td>end quotation</td></tr>
<tr><td><}_><-|><+|><}/></td><td>Misspelling</td></tr>
</table>

Plain text vs. annotated corpora

There is some debate between corpus linguists about whether annotation actually enhances a corpus or whether it contaminates it. Sinclair (1991a: 21) argues that "[t]he safest policy is to keep the text as it is, unprocessed and clean of any other codes". In the description of his "clean-text policy", Sinclair (1991a) advocates the use of raw text for the purpose of analysis for two reasons: firstly, he argues that research agendas differ and therefore annotation schemes may not be universally useful, and, secondly, due to a lack of linguistic standards, annotation bears the risk of obscuring or hiding patterns that would otherwise be detectable in raw text. Furthermore, even though some standards have been established (e.g. the *Text Encoding Initiative* (*TEI*) guidelines for SGML and XML mark-up), most annotation schemes differ widely because they are developed on a needs basis for individual projects. In response to this, Leech

19 A complete list of codes in the *FLOB Corpus* can be found in the online corpus manual at http://khnt.hit.uib.no/icame/manuals/flob/FLOBKOD.HTM.

(1993) has formulated seven maxims which should be considered when annotating corpora. To name a few, he demands that annotation should be removable, that the scheme of annotation be documented and that theory-neutral principles be applied for this scheme. One solution is to keep plain text copies of corpora in addition to the annotated version. Some concordancers have a function that will suppress tags when displaying search results. This way one can search tagged corpora without having to deal with the quite confusing-looking output. While the success rates of automatic tagging and parsing are fairly high these days, one has to be aware of possible mistakes of course and should take this into consideration when working with annotated corpora.

2.4 Corpus research: 'too serious to be left to the researchers'

This chapter has provided a brief review of the development of corpus linguistics, the impact on language description, as well as corpus tools and resources involved in this approach.[20] As will become evident in the following chapters, the development of corpus linguistics and the uses of corpora and corpus tools have also had very significant impact on language education. Johns, one of the earliest and possibly most influential proponents of giving learners access to corpora, once famously stated that "research is too serious to be left to the researchers" (1991a: 2). It is perhaps no coincidence that Johns developed the DDL approach while working at the University of Birmingham, where, at the same time, Sinclair headed up the *COBUILD* team and was in the process of developing the first corpus-based dictionary. The potential of corpora, corpus use, and results from corpus studies for language learning and teaching became soon apparent. In the following chapter, the present discussion expands to the use of corpora, indirectly and directly, within the context of language education. In addition to demonstrating the wide array of possible applications of corpora for language learning, the chapter further highlights the significance of this approach in light of central tenets of current language pedagogy.

[20] A number of informative introductions are available (see, e.g. Hunston 2002a; Mukherjee 2009). A comprehensive overview is provided in McCarthy and O'Keeffe (2010), and for further in-depth studies on corpus linguistics see, for example, Biber, Conrad & Reppen (1998), Meyer (2002), Sinclair (1991a), and Tognini-Bonelli (2001).

3 Corpora in language education

> While the use of computer text corpora in research is well established, they are now being used increasingly for teaching purposes. This includes the use of corpus data to inform and create teaching materials: it also includes the direct exploration of corpora by students, both in the study of linguistics and in the study of foreign languages.
>
> (Announcement of the first *TALC* conference, Gurney 1994: 102)

The impact of corpora on the study of language has been likened to a 'corpus revolution' (Rundell 2008; Rundell & Stock 1992). The impact on language education has been equally profound. The empirical analysis of machine-readable corpora has resulted in new descriptions of language which have contributed significantly to the creation of new learner dictionaries and reference grammars. These insights have also led to new developments in syllabus design. Furthermore, corpus studies have revealed that textbook language and language use, as attested in large authentic language corpora, differ considerably. These developments and their implications for language education are discussed in Section 3.1. Subsequently, a review of learner corpus research demonstrates the enormous potential of this rapidly expanding field for language education. While the analysis of learner corpus data has indirectly impacted on references and materials, it now also increasingly features directly in applications for the classroom. Thus, learner corpus data represents the connection between indirect and direct corpus use for language learning. Leech (1997: 5) has stated that the indirect contributions corpora have made to teaching are the "periphery" of corpus-aided language teaching. The core, as he defines it, is the direct use of corpus tools and methods in teaching which is reviewed in Section 3.2. Firstly, the early connections formed between corpus linguistic research and the language teaching profession will be explored. Secondly, this is followed by a detailed discussion of corpus applications by learners and teachers, mainly in the form of DDL. The chapter ends with an analysis of the significance of corpora for current paradigms in language pedagogy in Section 3.3.

3.1 Indirect applications of corpora in language education

As was shown in Section 2.2.1, observations derived from corpus research have impacted on language description as evidenced in dictionaries and reference grammars. Language patterns have been discovered that prior to computer corpus analysis had gone unnoticed or at least could not be fully explored such as collocations and semantic prosodies. As the current section will show, corpus studies have also impacted on pedagogical textbooks and syllabus design. The selection of language features, the order of which to teach them in, and how to teach them has been influenced by research based on large corpus collections.

3.1.1 Corpora for syllabus and textbook design

The idea of applying results of corpus-based analyses to language pedagogy is already reflected in vocabulary lists for learners created based on pre-electronic text collections. The best-known examples are Thorndike's *The Teacher's Word Book* (1921) and *General Service List of English Words* (*GSL*) by West (1953). However, these lists have since proved to be inadequate as they left the learner "seriously under-equipped to deal with authentic language" (Fox 1979, quoted in Nunan 1991: 118). In order to stress his point, Fox presented the following text where he substituted each word that is not on the *GSL* with made-up words:

> Many persons who 'talk' with their hands are blunk. They have doubts about what they are saying, so they try to dover up by drolling a false parn of excitement and urgency. These same people are usually very gruk and may be overtalkative and speak too loudly. Hurbish feelings are belave by the person who tries to keep all leeds to a monton; such a person is nep, porded, and lacking in self-ruck.[...] (Nunan 1991: 118)

The *GSL* was nevertheless widely used for the creation of ELT materials. However, the advent of machine-readable corpora has brought about many changes. The *COBUILD* project, as introduced in Section 2.2.1, resulted not only in the production of reference materials, such as grammars and dictionaries, but also aided in the development of teaching materials and syllabus design. An improved understanding of phrases, collocations, and lexico-grammatical patterns has helped to address known problem areas of language learners. Aston (2001b) has summarised the significance of such contextual patterns as follows:

> Concordancing corpora can help teachers and learners to identify recurrent patternings of these kinds. By so doing they may not only acquire the patterns, but also become aware of the extent to which these and other schemata – and not just single words and morphemes – constitute the building blocks of language use. (Aston 2001b: 16)

Syllabus design

New insights gained from computer-based corpus analysis have had significant impact on the discussion of what to teach and thus on syllabus design. Sinclair and Renouf (1988: 151) see the remarkable ability to reliably detect existing patterns of an item as one of the most significant achievements of corpus analysis: "The retrieval systems, unlike human beings, miss nothing if properly instructed – no usage can be overlooked because it is too ordinary or too familiar". The rationale for the 'lexical syllabus' they proposed based on these findings is that "[t]he common words [in English] are very common indeed, and mastery of them is rewarding in practice" (1988: 154), and thus they advocate a syllabus that is organised around lexis. Accordingly, Sinclair and Renouf (1988: 148) suggest that language learners should focus on:

a) the commonest word forms in the language;
b) their central patterns of usage; and
c) the combinations which they typically form.

Willis (1990) developed the concept of the lexical syllabus further and applied the results in the course book *Collins COBUILD English Course* (Willis & Willis 1988). The value of computer-based analysis is reflected in the findings derived from frequency analyses and other corpus investigations conducted as part of the *COBUILD* research project. These led Willis (1990: iv; 'Introduction') to conclude that "[w]hat emerges very strongly once one looks at natural language, is the way the commonest words in the language occur with the commonest patterns". The fact that 700 of the most frequent words in English make up approximately 70% of the English language is a powerful argument for the teaching of these words. Consequently, the lexical syllabus approach operates on the assumption that a syllabus should be designed based around the most frequent lexical meanings and uses as well as their patterns of occurrence. It appears that the lexical syllabus was never fully realised in mainstream textbooks; however, corpus studies quickly began to focus on the content of existing teaching materials.

Textbooks vs. authentic language

New discoveries about language use have also led to a number of comparative studies of authentic language data in corpora and language data found in textbooks for English as a foreign/second language:

> A corpus approach, because it is empirically based, allows us to test assumptions about language use against patterns found in naturally occurring discourse and then to review our pedagogical practices in light of this information. In fact, corpus-based research shows that the actual patterns of function and use in English often differ radically from prior expectations (Biber, Conrad & Reppen 1994: 171).

Many of these studies have concluded that considerable discrepancies exist. In an early study, Holmes (1988: 40) compared expressions of doubt and certainty in textbooks with frequencies of occurrence in both the *LOB* and the *Brown* corpus. She came to the conclusion that "[s]ome textbooks are positively misleading" and that "[s]ome books give little or no attention to the topic". In a comparative study of Teaching English as a Foreign Language (TEFL) textbooks used in Swedish schools and both in the *COBUILD* and the *London-Lund Corpus* (*L-LC*), Ljung (1990) found that the most frequent vocabulary items in those corpora differed significantly. Modal verbs, future time orientation, and conditional clauses were the focus of Mindt's (1996) comparative study of a textbook corpus and the *L-LC*. Mindt (1996: 246) concluded that "the order of these items in syllabuses very often does not correspond to what one might reasonably expect from corpus data of spoken and written English". In her study of *if*-clauses, Römer (2004b: 162) found that the "mismatches [...] make it clear that, at least with respect to if-clauses, the language of German EFL textbooks does not mirror authentic language use". A great number of studies have been conducted comparing language use in textbook with use found in large language corpora. Topics include, for example, present perfect tense (Schlüter 2002), future time expressions (Mindt 1986, 1987, 1997), linking adverbials (Conrad 2004), modal auxiliaries (Römer 2004a), and *would*-clauses without adjacent *if*-clauses (Frazier 2003).

Biber and Reppen (2002) investigated aspects of materials development for grammar instruction by comparing English as a Second Language (ESL) and EFL materials with results from empirical corpus studies. They come to the conclusion "that there are often sharp contrasts between the information found in grammar materials and what learners encounter in the real world of language use" (Biber & Reppen 2002: 199). They argue that a revision of grammar references based on corpus investigations of actual language use could help to improve the language learning process.

3.1.2 Learner language in corpora

As we have seen in the previous section, corpus-based research plays an important role in the design of syllabuses and has resulted in improved descriptions of language which have impacted on the production of language teaching materials. However, as Granger, who has played a pivotal role in the development of learner corpus studies, points out, research based on native speaker corpora will "always be of limited value and may even lead to ill-judged pedagogical decisions unless [it is] complemented with the equally rich and pedagogically more relevant type of data provided by learner corpora" (2002: 21-22).

Granger (2002) has proposed the following definition of learner corpora which she adapted from Sinclair's (1996) definition of machine-readable corpora:

> Computer learner corpora are electronic collections of authentic FL/SL textual data assembled according to explicit design criteria for a particular SLA/FLT purpose. They are encoded in a standardised and homogeneous way and documented as to their origin and provenance. (Granger 2002: 7)

Typical features of learner corpora are that they are monolingual, they contain non-specialist language, are mostly written, and they are generally synchronic in nature; that is, they do not track language development.

Since the 1990s, learner corpus research has contributed significantly to Second Language Acquisition (SLA) research (e.g. Aijmer 2002; Altenberg 2002; Belz 2004; Granger 1998, 2009; Housen 2002) and the field of learning and teaching of foreign or second languages (e.g. Allan 2002; Flowerdew 1998; Meunier 2002; Nesselhauf 2004a, 2004b). Non-native speaker corpora enable research studies with large amounts of learner output which was, prior to the development of computer corpora, not possible. Learner corpora are mainly used for contrastive interlanguage analysis – that is, comparative studies of native and non-native data, and for learner language error analysis. In particular, the latter plays an important role for the production of improved learning and teaching materials; an aspect which research based on native speaker corpora cannot deliver. As Granger (1994: 25) rightly points out, "[h]aving access to comprehensive frequency lists may well help course designers compile better lexical syllabuses, but it will not give them access to learners' actual lexical problems". Consequently, learner corpora have become a valuable instrument for learner needs analysis which in turn has great potential to inform tailor-made teaching materials. Research in this area has focused on a range of known problematic areas for language learners: for example, collocations (Chi, Wong & Wong 1994; Gilquin 2007; Nesselhauf 2003, 2005), use of tenses (Granger 1999; Virtanen 1997), and connectors (Granger & Tyson 1996; Milton & Tsang 1993).

Granger and Tribble (1998) have taken this concept one step further by suggesting the use of learner data to create form-focused DDL activities. They attest to great potential for these types of exercise as they "can help students become aware of a fossilised error in their interlanguage" (Granger & Tribble 1998: 203) and, in addition, they may also serve well to engage their interest because they deal with "not just with any old grammatical or lexical problem but their own attested difficulties" (1998: 203). Seidlhofer (2002: 213) called this approach of letting learners take on the role of researchers of their own language productions "working with learning-driven data". She also concluded that such an approach was highly motivating for the students, because they perceived the task as relevant. Her students "discovered that close scrutiny of the language of a text in which they had a personal investment can be a fascinating process rather than a pedantic, tedious affair" (2002: 230).

The high levels of activity in this research area have produced a great variety of learner corpora (for comprehensive overviews, see Pravec 2002; Nesselhauf 2004b). The majority of currently available learner corpora appear to be in learner English from various language backgrounds. The *Longman Learners' Corpus* (*LLC*) and the *Cambridge Learner Corpus* (*CLC*) are examples of very large commercial learner corpora maintained by big publishing houses. The *CLC* currently contains over 30 million words and is still growing. The corpus is made up of exam scripts written by students taking Cambridge TESOL English exams. This corpus currently holds more than 95,000 such scripts. Textbook authors, who work for Cambridge University Press, can access the corpus data to aid in the production of dictionaries and ELT textbooks. The *LLC* currently consists of 10 million words made up of student essays. Access to this corpus is also restricted to members of the Longman publishing house who use it for the production of dictionaries and course materials. The *International Corpus of Learner English* (*ICLE*) databank project was launched in 1990 (Granger 1993). It currently contains over three million words of non-native speaker written English in the form of essays produced by advanced EFL learners from 21 different language backgrounds. The *ICLE* webpage provides a detailed overview of all the available subcorpora.

As mentioned above, most learner corpora are synchronic, which means that they are not monitoring language development. However, more recently, projects that are longitudinal in character have been created. One example is a corpus of telecollaborative correspondence of German and English based on learner and expert speaker language monitored over a period of two years (Belz 2004; Belz & Vyatkina 2005, 2008). The analysis of this corpus is part of a larger project that explores the benefits of such learner corpus research for the development of L2 linguistic competence, particularly in relation to pre- and in-service teacher training (see Belz 2006).

The *Centre for English Corpus Linguistics* of the University of Louvain (Belgium), which also hosts the *ICLE* corpus, launched the *LONGitudinal DAtabase of Learner English* (*LONGDALE*) project in early 2008. As the title suggests, the aim of this project is to compile a longitudinal database of learner English. The first data collection will take place with the same group of learners over the course of three years. Spoken or speech corpora of learner language are also rare because their compilation remains difficult and cumbersome. There are two projects worth mentioning here: Firstly, the *Louvain INternational Database of Spoken English Interlanguage* (*LINDSEI*) which is made up of approximately 100,000 words of transcripts of interviews with French learners of English; and secondly, the *Learning Prosody in a Foreign Language* (*LeaP*) *Corpus* which was compiled for the teaching of phonology and pronunciation (Gut 2006).

Granger (2008: 349) rightly concludes that "[a]lthough learner corpora are still in their infancy, the buzzing activity in the field and the number of learner-corpus informed reference and teaching tools that have already been produced are a clear indication that they are here to stay". According to her, expanding research from English to other languages, increasing the range of learner populations, and applying the results in language teaching materials are primary research goals for the future.

3.2 Direct applications of corpora in the classroom

Halliday (1982: 15) once stated that "[m]ost linguistics is not classroom stuff; but it is there behind the lines, underlying our classroom practices, and our ideas about children, and about learning and reality". Corpus linguistics is in this sense quite unique. It has not only made indirect contributions to the field of language teaching but from an early stage language practitioners and applied linguists have recognised the potential of employing corpus resources and tools directly in the classroom. These direct applications of corpora will be explored and discussed in the following section.

3.2.1 Early encounters

The first series of publications on corpus-related activities for language learning appeared in the 1980s. This period was characterised by the transition from powerful and expensive mainframe computers to more affordable micro computers that provided researchers and teachers with ready access to computers for the first time. It was also a time in which the debate on the role of the computer in teaching emerged and caused considerable concern among practitioners (e.g. Last 1984: ix-xiii). Computer-assisted language learning (CALL) applications had been developed since the 1970s but were largely restricted to terminal-based tutoring packages, and a break away from this more traditional approach appeared desirable. Software was largely characterised by "teacher-created tests, drill-and-practice exercises and programmed learning" (Johns 1983: 89). Its popularity was credited to "the active feedback on success/failure that the machine can give, and, linked to that, the possibility of 'having another go'" (1983: 89).

The increasing availability of micro computers in the late 1970s meant that "either at school or at home some language-teachers [had] begun to experiment with ways in which they could be used in their teaching" (Johns 1983: 90). Furthermore, Higgins (1986: 147) postulated that "EFL teachers do not need to confine themselves to EFL software". Such experiments outside the traditional realm of CALL applications included forays into the newly found possibilities offered by corpus tools and resources. One of the earliest publications to be found is by Skehan (1981) who made a case for using the mainframe software package *CLOC* (Reed 1977) in order to create word lists for ESP teachers.[21] *CLOC* is an acronym derived from the word *'ColLOCation'*, and this suite of text analysis programs had facilities to create collocations, concordances, and word lists based on frequency counts. Skehan (1981) was one of the first to highlight the usefulness of this last feature for the systematic introduction of specialist vocabulary. He recommended the use of the *CLOC* package to the average teacher in order to produce these word lists and also pointed to the value of creating concordances and collocations. While Skehan recommended the use of concordances for teachers, he also recognised the benefits of using collocations with learners. This led him to conclude that "the potential is considerable" (1981: 118).

Despite the fact that they were still working on a mainframe computer, Ahmad *et al.* (1985) decided to give their students, advanced learners of English as L2, direct access to a corpus in order to explore specific language points (e.g. "the choice of semantic or grammatical agreement with certain nouns in English, e.g. *government*", Ahmad *et al.* 1985: 4). In particular, they stressed the usefulness of such activities to retrieve genuine examples from a corpus which allowed them to investigate various kinds of language features. They concluded that

> [w]hile CALL practitioners have naturally concentrated on providing material for beginners, CALL nevertheless offers exciting prospects for advanced learners. The area which lies on the border between

---

21 McEnery and Wilson (1997: 12) mention that Peter Roe had used LSP corpora with students in 1969 but there are no publications available on this; Leech (1997: 2) states that he has been using a prototype of the *LOB Corpus* with postgraduates since 1976. Antoinette Renouf has reportedly been working with concordances (*COBUILD Corpus*) with her language students in Birmingham since the early 1980s (see Johns 1986: 159).

language learning and linguistics appears to us to be particularly promising in this regard. (Ahmad *et al.* 1985: 6)

Although these early studies relied on working with mainframe computers, it was the increasing availability and affordability of micro computers to individuals that had a lasting impact on the use of corpora in language teaching. Early publications were characterised by detailed descriptions of self-made program routines and first explorations into the various types of applications for learners (e.g. Davison 1983). One of the most frequently cited articles from that time is Johns's (1986) seminal publication on his concordancing software *MicroConcord.*[22] He described in great detail the architecture, design, and functionality of the program. Indeed, the description of the software took up two-thirds of the article. Towards the end of his paper, Johns (1986: 158) identified three potential users of this software: the linguistic researcher, the teacher, and the language learner. Later on, Johns (1991a: 2) coined the term 'data-driven learning' or DDL to describe the approach of using this research software in the language classroom. DDL has since become an umbrella term for the direct use of corpora in the language classroom. The specific form of DDL as presented by Johns will be discussed in detail in the next section.

3.2.2 Data-driven learning

The *COBUILD* project, described in Section 2.2.1, can be seen as the first attempt to develop reference materials for English learners based on actual language usage. The *COBUILD Corpus* at the time also provided the data for the first concordance printouts Tim Johns used in his classroom. In 1986, Johns introduced *MicroConcord*, a concordance program which he had developed specifically for the language teacher and learner, accompanied by a number of small corpora (Johns 1986). However, in contrast to the approach *COBUILD* had taken – for example, providing reference materials, guides for syllabus design, and teaching materials based on corpus analysis – Johns (1991b: 30) wanted to "cut out the middleman" and give students direct access to authentic language data, in effect turning them into linguistic researchers or "language detectives" (Johns 1997: 101). One central aspect of this approach was Johns' s redefinition of the computer not as a "surrogate teacher or tutor" but as an "informant" (Johns 1991a: 1). The type of 'informant' Johns had in mind is not a machine of artificial intelligence that acts as an 'expert system' but rather an electronic resource of authentic language data. Within this model, the traditional 'flow of questions and answers' – teacher *initiation*, student *response*, teacher

[22] The software *MicroConcord* was later further developed and published by Scott and Johns (1993).

feedback – (Sinclair & Coulthard 1975) is reversed. The learner initiates the question, the informant (computer) provides language data, and then it is up to the learner to interpret the data. Thus, the computer is not made more intelligent but the learner. Johns (1991a) sees the role of the teacher changed to that of a research director and coordinator. The changing roles of learners and teachers within corpus-aided learning and teaching will be discussed in detail below in Section 4.3.3. Johns's Kibbitzer webpage is a prime example of this approach.[23] Created in 1996, this website served as an archive for the results of one-to-one discussions between Johns and his students on language points (lexical, syntactic, and discoursal). The students generally initiated the question; for example, 'What is the difference between *predict* and *forecast*?'. Guided by the teacher, the student then analysed the corresponding concordance lines in order to discover the subtle differences between the two words.

Thus, DDL is based on the notion "that the task of the learner is to 'discover' the foreign language, and that the task of the teacher is to provide a context in which the learner can develop strategies for discovery – strategies through which he or she can 'learn how to learn'" (Johns 1991a: 1). DDL task procedures generally entail inductive learning strategies, especially "strategies of perceiving similarities and differences and of hypothesis formation and testing" (Johns 1991b: 31). The special characteristics of concordancing software play a significant role in this process of DDL:

> Viewed as 'intake' for language learning (Corder 1967), a KWIC concordance occupies an intermediate position between the highly organized, graded, and idealized language of the typical coursebook, and the potentially confusing but far richer and more revealing 'full flood' of authentic communication. By concentrating and making it easy to compare the contexts within which a particular item occurs, it organizes data in a way that encourages and facilitates inference and generalization. (Johns 1986: 159)

The procedures of concordance analysis are either inductive or deductive. The inductive, or "bottom-up" (Murison-Bowie 1996: 193), approach presents the language data as evidence, and it is the learner's task to infer descriptive generalisations from it. Three steps guide this process (see Johns 1991a: 4):

---

[23] The original Kibbitzer website by Johns no longer exists. After Johns retired in 2001, the Birmingham English for International Students Unit took over the maintenance of the website; however, this also appears to be offline now. The *MICASE* website has recently established a Kibbitzer webpage at http://micase.elicorpora.info/micase-kibbitzers.

1) Observation/Identification;
2) Classification;
3) Generalisation.

The first step of observation involves the discovery of regularities: that is, of patterns found in the evidence. Thus, the functions of a concordancer play a crucial rule in this process by displaying the KWIC and by sorting the context either by left- or by right-sort or by even more advanced sorting combinations. The example of *brook* shows that the sorting of the context can immediately reveal some observable patterns:

1	... hing in that time."Nor will he	brook	any implied criticism of John ...
2	... who thought the party would not	brook	continued participation in the ...
3	... ttack, the Judges' Council will	brook	no criticism. Its memo proclaim ...
4	... of the Union. Ministers should	brook	no such thought: enlargement is ...
5	... the terrifying Hackman who will	brook	no vigilantes in his town and ...
6	... tolerant teachers, as they will	brook	no mispronunciation or mis-acce ...
7	... artistic freedom and who need	brook	no interference from moneymen. ...
8	... that society would not always	brook	such nonsense. They had only to ...
9	where she was going and she	brooked	no opposition. In an article in ...
10	... on a national holiday. He	brooked	no opposition, ordering the ...
11	... position, at least the winner	brooked	no argument. It was made by ...
12	rather embarassed him--Smith	brooked	no stuffy formality. Sweater ...
13	... ut clear, directed only to her,	brooked	no repudiation. She had been ...

Figure 3-1: Concordance of *brook* (*Collins Corpus Sampler*)

This concordance is sorted by search word (or KWIC) and then by the first word in the right context. The pattern in the right context is immediately visible: *brook* is frequently followed by the determiner *no*. An analysis of the left context for lines 1, 2 and 8 reveals that the remaining three samples also show *brook* in a negated sense. From this first observation it can be assumed that brook characteristically occurs with a negative. At the time this corpus query was run, these were the only instances of *brook* as a verb that were found in a 56 million word corpus (*Collins WordbanksOnline English Corpus*). Thus, a first tentative generalisation might be that *brook* rarely ever occurs in the positive sense.

The deductive approach to concordancing proceeds from the opposite direction. It starts out with a previously learned rule which learners have to apply to concordance lines for verification, which means that in effect they are required to 'test' previously acquired knowledge. The expected result is that their knowledge will be consolidated and even refined. Johns has proposed a numbers of such activities; for example, gap-filling and matching jumbled lines. One example is the *One item, multiple tasks* activity, which "deals with an area of language – preposition usage – that is on the 'collocational border' between syntax and lexis. It is on that border that DDL methods seem to be most effective" (Johns 2002: 109). Another benefit Johns sees in this type of exercise is that it is "gapping on the main meaning-carrying element in the collocation – here, the noun" (2002: 110):

One item, multiple contexts
Prepositions: Nouns in the right context of *on*

1.)	Paz (Baja) and all meals from lunch on	______	2 to dinner on day 8 are included;
	meals from lunch on day 2 to dinner on	______	8 are included; He just never stops
	He just never stops working. On the	______	I arrived-Wednesday-Bollettieri was
	and your own-minds at rest on the	______	, think carefully now about the kind
	You can travel out and return on any	______	of the week, choosing from 7 ferry
2.)	I complained to Rentokil on your	______	, it dropped its request for an
	pressure group which campaigns on	______	of refugees says Britain's prepared to
	itain's prepared to speak out on their	______	not anymore. Everton goalkeeper
	speak for themselves and not on	______	of outside interests. But Tory is do
	But Tory is donating 2,000 books on	______	of the APL project to hospitals
3.)	rise to ascendancy, poised on the	______	of the final mass extinction and of
	and of Ferguson has been on the	______	of becoming very famous for quite
	With one Balkan country on the	______	of civil war, trouble breaking out
	uncertainty as she stands on the	______	of a new relationship. 'You tried
	face of a 41-year-old man on the	______	of achieving his dreams. One ca

Nouns: *behalf, day, brink*

Figure 3-2: *One item, multiple tasks* (Johns 2002: 108-109).

Such an exercise is very suitable as a follow-up activity; for example, after the students have analysed the behaviour of the preposition *on* by means of concordancing a POS-tagged corpus. Inductive and deductive procedures in the context of DDL are thus not clearly separated. However, inductive strategies alone are often not sufficient in order to arrive at a valid generalisation. Moreover, results need to be tested deductively in order to confirm their validity. Murison-Bowie (1996: 185) notes that "much of what might be understood intuitively as rules are not supported by the evidence, and much of what can be observed is not commonly described by existing rules". This means that in order to arrive at an acceptable generalisation, the first rule derived from induction frequently has to be checked against more evidence, possibly revised, refined, restructured or altogether abandoned. This provides a very interesting background for authentic communication among learners including the negotiation of the validity of their results from concordance analyses. Whether or not these discussions take place in the target language depends on the level of language proficiency of the individual learner group. This form of communication is an important characteristic of DDL and makes it a valuable addition to classroom activities. The discussion on language awareness in Section 3.3.3 will discuss this feature of learners talking about language or 'languaging' in more detail. The processes of a data-driven exercise are thus comparable to what Prabhu (1987: 46) has coined a reasoning-gap activity, which "involves deriving some new information from given information through processes of inference, deduction, practical reasoning, or a perception of relationships of patterns".

DDL offers a great variety of activities in the language classroom. Honeyfield (1989: 47-50) offers a typology of exercises:

T1. Filling blanks in concordance material.
T2. Completing, or guessing the wider context of concordance material.
T3. Using concordance material as a reference tool for various exercises focusing on grammar, usage, vocabulary, etc.
T4. Discourse-oriented exercises involving the use of concordance material.
T5. Comparing the meanings or uses of given expressions in different types or samples of writing.
T6. Exploring emotional tone or style.
T7. Freely using a concordancing program to assist writing, correction or comprehension.

Figure 3-3: Typology of DDL exercises (Honeyfield 1989: 47-50)

Such tasks are generally teacher-controlled in the sense that they require a certain amount of premeditation and preparation on behalf of the teacher. However, Johns (1988: 21) proposes a further use of concordances that he calls "serendipity learning". His proposal is to give learners large amounts of sorted corpus output prepared by the teacher in the form of printouts. Together with the teacher, the learners are then encouraged to explore the concordance lines guided only by a number of questions provided by the teacher. Bernardini (2000,

2001, 2002) takes this one step further and proposes a corpus-browsing activity which gives learners direct access to very large corpora guided only by a common starting point (e.g. very unusual, highly connotated words like *vibe(s)* in the context of *watering hole*, Bernardini 2000: 229). As a framework she proposes a 'pedagogy of discovery' which she bases on Widdowson's (1990) conclusion that "language is learned as a contingent consequence of carrying out activities which engage the language with the learners' knowledge and experience of things" (Widdowson 1990: 121).

The use of concordances in the classroom has since gained great popularity and a wide range of applications have been developed. These applications and some attempts at evaluating them will be explored in the following section.

3.2.3 Further uses of corpus data

DDL activities yield great potential in the area of vocabulary and grammar teaching. The *MicroConcord* manual (Murison-Bowie 1993) contains a number of helpful suggestions for possible investigations with the concordancer. These investigations tackle difficult areas for learners such as polysemy, collocations, synonyms, confusables, and false friends. A number of publications introduce the possibilities afforded by DDL in classroom teaching and at the same time provide examples of potential learning activities (see, e.g. Flowerdew 1996; Fox 1998; Kettemann 1995; Mukherjee 2003; Tribble 2000; Tribble & Jones 1997). However, direct applications of corpora in the classroom are by no means restricted to the areas of lexis and grammar. The potential of using corpora and concordances for language learners has been explored in many other areas as will be discussed below.

In literary studies, the usefulness of working with electronic texts and concordances lies particularly in the ability of the concordancer to provide access to features of the given text that are much more difficult to detect otherwise. Rautenhaus (1997: 158) laments the fact that learners often fail to penetrate literary texts, in particular in the case of longer novels, as they perceive an in-depth analysis as painful and unnecessary in view of the volume of text to deal with. According to Rautenhaus (1997) the use of a concordance to analyse literary texts can increase the learners' motivation to engage more actively with such texts:

> Konkordanzprogramme können dazu beitragen, daß den SchülerInnen der Literaturunterricht mehr Spaß bereitet und sie ein Gefühl für die

> Vielschichtigkeit literarischer Texte entwickeln. (Rautenhaus 1997: 158)[24]

The characteristics of the KWIC display, the search functionality of the concordancer, and the ability to create frequency word lists, make it a powerful interpretative device for literary analysis and provide learners with a new type of access to the texts:

> Concordancing is a powerful tool for literary analysis because it makes text accessible to students and researchers in wholly new ways, by focussing attention on the contexts in which an individual lexical item [appears] at different points in the text, rather than on intensive or extensive reading of a text (Kowitz 1991: 148).

Such an approach can reveal facts about language as much as content. Kettemann (1995: 38-40) illustrates this with an example by looking at collocations of personal pronouns to investigate the changing characterisation of men and women throughout an emancipatory short story. Daud and Husin (2004) present an experimental case study in order to test whether a concordancer can help learners develop critical thinking skills based on the analysis of literary texts with the aid of the software. The results of the experiment show that "[t]he use of the concordancer was found to enhance students' ability to think critically" (Daud & Husin 2004: 485). In her study on introducing corpus stylistics into a literary course on three novels discussed from literary and linguistic perspectives, Bednarek (2008: 10) found that the "corpus stylistic methods were extremely successful in allowing the students to engage with their own research projects and to come up with innovative findings". Large collections of literary works available in the public domain provide ready access to thousands of texts in electronic format which makes them immediately available for classroom concordancing.[25]

The use of small, specialised corpora has produced considerable interest in using concordances with learners in the context of ESP and, in particular, in EAP. Such corpora provide an excellent basis for syllabus (Flowerdew 1993) and materials design (Collins 2000; Donley & Reppen 2001; Thurstun & Candlin 1997, 1998), in ESP and EAP contexts, and especially in increasingly specialised fields where textbooks are often unavailable (Rilling, Dahlmann, Dodson, Boyles & Pazvant 2005; Rilling & Pazvant 2002).

---

24 My translation: "Through using concordancing software students may experience literature as more fun and at the same time develop a feeling for the complexity of literary texts."

25 See especially the online archives *Project Gutenberg* (available at http://www.gutenberg.org) and the *Oxford Text Archive* (available at http://ota.ahds.ac.uk).

The field of academic writing has received considerable attention, and the use of corpora as a reference tool has been proposed for the acquisition of essay writing skills (Cresswell 2007; Garton 1996), to improve academic reading skills (Brodine 2001), for error analysis of learner productions (Gabel 2001; Gaskell & Cobb 2004; Seidlhofer 2000a, 2002), and for self-correction with concordances (Chambers & O'Sullivan 2004; Papp 2007; Todd 2001).

The areas of error analysis and self-correction of errors in learner writing appear particularly promising. A research project with French postgraduate students showed that "native language interference [was] reduced as a result of corpus consultation, and idiomatic phrases [were] adopted which the students would have had difficulty producing as a result of consulting a dictionary, grammar or course book" (Chambers & O'Sullivan 2004: 170; the second phase of the project is dealt with in O'Sullivan & Chambers 2006). Gabel (2001: 287) concluded from his study with postgraduate students that learners benefit from investigating their own interlanguage and comparing it with native speaker usage as it enables them to "bridge the gap between their own performance and that of native speakers". Furthermore, students showed great interest in the task of improving their own productions by means of concordancing native speaker corpora (Seidlhofer 2000a: 222). Depending on the level of language proficiency, however, careful guidance of learners appears important to ensure that the process of self-correction arrives at valid results (Todd 2001). In the context of general second language learning, Mukherjee (2002: 138ff.) suggested the use of concordances as a correction aid for teachers when marking student essays. In particular, he highlighted the potential for corpus use in providing teachers with the opportunity for in-depth corrections that are closer approximations to native speaker usage (see also Mukherjee 2009: 174-175).

Translation studies is another field that has readily welcomed the potential of corpora (for an overview, see Olohan 2004). Parallel and comparable corpora can provide important insights for translators-in-training and have become a valuable reference tool in this area. Bernardini (2004: 20) has pointed out that "[e]ducating learners to use comparable corpora as reference tools in their everyday activity may result in better-documented, more accurate as well as more fluent translations".

Similarly, the use of parallel corpora has also been suggested for second language learning purposes (Barlow 2000; Frankenberg-Garcia 2004, 2005; Groß 1998; Roussel 1991). Frankenberg-Garcia (2005) argued that parallel corpora provide learners with the opportunity to explore the target language with the help of their native language and aid them with language reception and correction. In contrast to results from monolingual corpora, "parallel concordances can help learners express in L2 what they already know how to say in L1" (Frankenberg-Garcia 2005: 194).

As can be seen from this overview of a selection of direct applications of corpora in the classroom, the range of possible applications is broad and holds much potential for language learning. There are now a great number of edited volumes available, often comprising papers delivered at conferences, that provide an excellent overview of direct applications of corpora in the classroom (e.g. Aijmer 2009; Aston 2001a; Aston, Bernardini & Stewart 2004; Braun, Kohn & Mukherjee 2006; Burnard & McEnery 2000; Hidalgo, Quereda & Santana 2007; Kettemann & Marko 2002; Sinclair 2004).

3.3 Corpora and language pedagogy

The approach of DDL, and the general idea of learners accessing corpus data to explore aspects of language use, is very similar to corpus analysis undertaken by researchers. However, in a research context, valid outcomes of the analysis (i.e., to arrive at accurate descriptions of language) take priority. In the classroom context, the focus is generally on the process of investigating concordance lines. It is the methodology itself which provides valuable opportunities for learner- and learning-centredness. Corpora and concordancers are transformed into pedagogical tools that have the potential to promote learner autonomy, to raise language awareness and to not only provide access to authentic materials but create task authenticity. These central tenets of current language teaching and learning – awareness, autonomy and authenticity – (van Lier 1996) are cornerstones of the communicative approach to language learning. They will be explored in relation to direct corpus applications in the classroom. What emerges is that these paradigms are not only closely interconnected as shown by van Lier (1996), but corpus classroom activities embody that very interconnectedness.

3.3.1 Authenticity of text, task, and purpose

Most corpora consist of electronic collections of naturally occurring language drawn from a variety of sources.[26] As such they present a valuable source of authentic materials for language learners. Furthermore, they provide learners with the opportunity, facilitated through the concordancer, to access large reservoirs of genuine target language data designed to be representative of a specific language or a subset thereof.[27] Learners can perform research tasks

---

[26] Unless this is explicitly stated otherwise in the corpus manual; as it would, for example, in the case of a corpus of elicited conversation in an experimental situation.

[27] There has been some debate among scholars as to whether the language in corpora is actually real, in particular for learners (see Cook 1997, 1998 and Widdowson 1991, 1996). The

involving actual language use and come to their own conclusions about language patterns and rules. Therefore, the value of corpus-based learning activities can be seen in the direct learner engagement with authentic language materials, and, furthermore, in task authenticity generated by the 'learner as researcher' paradigm. These characteristics have potential to increase learner autonomy and learner motivation. From a teacher's perspective, corpora present a valuable source of authentic materials. Corpora can provide authentic examples for illustrative purposes or for creating exercise materials based on authentic texts.

The concept of authenticity in language learning has stimulated much debate among the language learning research community. Even though authenticity is generally deemed desirable in a language learning context, particularly in the context of communicative language teaching, it is not easily defined and has been attributed to a diverse range of concepts: the learner, learning materials, and learning situations to name but a few. Gilmore (2007: 98) identified as many as eight different, albeit inter-related meanings, and concluded that authenticity "can be situated in either the text itself, in the participants, in the social or cultural situation and purposes of the communicative act, or some combination of these".

The attribute 'authentic', however it is defined, appears to have highly positive connotations such as 'true', 'original', or 'real' while adjectives such as 'fabricated', 'fake', or 'contrived' have negative connotations. In rejection of previous structural approaches to language learning, communicative language teaching has placed much emphasis on the concept of authenticity, and in particular on genuine texts intended for real communicative purposes. Widdowson (1996) described this development as follows:

> If you are going to teach real English as it functions in contextually appropriate ways, rather than a collection of linguistic forms in contrived classroom situations, then you need to refer to, and defer to, how people who have the language as an L1 actually put it to communicative use. [...] Corpus descriptions of English can now make available facts about authentic usage of which we were previously in ignorance. It is an idea, therefore, which is not only appealing in principle, but feasible in practice. The appropriate English for the classroom is the real English that is appropriately used outside it. We now know what real English looks like, so we no longer have an excuse for not teaching it. (Widdowson 1996: 67)

---

authenticity of corpus data in relation to its pedagogical usefulness for learners will be discussed in more detail in Section 4.3.1, Core element: corpus.

As indicated above, the debate on authenticity in language learning is complex and it is not the purpose of this section to resolve the issues related to this debate which is forever striving to define exactly what is meant by 'authentic', or 'authenticity' in the classroom and how it can be achieved. For the purpose of this paper, Morrow's (1977: 13) definition of authentic texts provides a good starting point: "An authentic text is a stretch of real language, produced by a real speaker or writer for a real audience and designed to convey a real message of some sort". These are the texts that corpora are most commonly made of. Widdowson (1979: 80) has described this kind of authenticity as "genuineness" which he states is "a characteristic of the passage itself and is an absolute quality".

However, as is evidenced by the multiple meanings identified by Gilmore (2007), authenticity is not only sought after as a quality in the materials themselves but according to Breen (1985: 61) at least in three other aspects: "the learner's own interpretations of such texts", "tasks conducive to language learning", and "the actual social situation of the language classroom".

Johns (1988: 10) has claimed that corpus-based activities with learners incorporate at least three kinds of authenticity, namely,

(i) authenticity of script,
(ii) authenticity of purpose, and
(iii) authenticity of activity.

(i) Authenticity of script

Authenticity of script, or text in Breen's terminology, is achieved through the use of "unsimplified texts" (Johns 1988: 10) as they occur in corpora which Johns is using for concordancing activities.[28] Johns (1988: 10) conceded that the use of such texts can cause difficulties for learners, particularly if they "believe or have been led to believe that to understand *anything* they should understand *everything*". There is legitimate concern that authentic language may be too difficult for learners. Nunan (1989: 138) has cautioned that "many low-level learners are traumatised when first exposed to authentic samples of language" but in Johns's view it is simply important that the teacher helps "learners to explore the limits of what they can discover at their individual level of ability" (Johns 1988: 10). This can primarily be achieved through task control. Kramsch (1993: 239) had emphasised a positive side to the use of authentic texts when

[28] It is important to note that Johns is working in an ESP context – the corpora he mentions in his 1988 article are all ESP corpora, for example, transportation and highway engineering or plant biology. The matter of corpora for English for general purposes, in terms of achieving representativeness, is a more difficult issue.

she stated that "much of the value of using real-life texts to teach foreign languages may be found in the pleasure it gives learners to poach, so to speak, on some[one] else's linguistic and cultural territory". It is in this role as 'observer' (Gavioli & Aston 2001: 241) that learners can authenticate the language data found in corpora (see also Mishan 2004, on authenticating corpora).[29] Evaluations of learner attitudes have shown that learners do not necessarily share the concerns put forth by researchers on the issue of whether or not language in corpora is authentic. Chambers (2005: 120) reported that her students found the language in corpora "authentic, up-to-date, and relevant" while the language in course books was perceived as "unreal and sometimes stupid". According to Farr (2008: 36), 76% of the teacher trainees participating in her case study regarded the fact that corpora contain "real language use – language in context and cultural insights" as a highly positive aspect of using corpora (see also Amador Moreno *et al.* 2006).

Furthermore, Mishan (2005: 19) pointed out that in light of the rapid developments in technology, "the dichotomy between 'real life' and 'the classroom' which theorists struggled to resolve during the authenticity debate [...] is becoming something of an anachronism". The widespread use of the internet and other related technologies means that "today's learners can reach out and touch 'real life' at the tap of the keyboard" (2005: 19).

(ii) Authenticity of purpose

Concerning authenticity of purpose, Johns (1988: 10) has suggested that "the text [i.e. the corpus] should be of value to the learner quite apart from its use in a language-teaching context". In the context of ESP, this can be easily achieved by analysing specialised corpora composed of texts taken from the respective area of interest; for example, business, computing, and engineering. In more general terms, the concordancing of literary texts – for example, those that are compulsory according to the syllabus – might become the object of analysis. Another example worth mentioning here is the use of texts that the students wrote themselves (e.g. Belz & Vyatkina 2008; Seidlhofer 2000a, 2002). Authenticity of purpose as put forth by Johns also helps to engage the learner with the text which is an important factor enabling learners to authenticate the texts. This engagement is facilitated by authenticity of activity because, in the case of DDL tasks, learners are engaging in 'research'-type tasks which after all is the purpose that both corpora and corpus analysis software were originally designed for.

[29] The discussion on the authentication of corpora features in more detail in Section 4.3.1.

(iii) Authenticity of activity

Authenticity of activity, or task in Breen's terminology, thus relates to the authenticity of the learning situation which can be defined as authentic if it provides learners with an opportunity for acting communicatively as themselves (see Edelhoff 1996: 45). Although dependent on language proficiency level, concordancing with learners has the potential to create such an environment because it focuses explicitly on the main interest of the learner, in this case acquiring the target language, and provides the learner with the means to gain control over that process by trying to discover facts about language in a task environment where the answers are not yet predefined. This is an essential building block for fostering learner autonomy as we will see below in Section 3.3.2. In addition, such tasks are often learner-initiated which means that the students can create their own authenticity. Bernardini (2000: 234) has concluded from a corpus browsing activity with learners that "the joint adoption of authentic tasks and authentic texts has been shown to provide a very rich and stimulating learning environment". Motivation is increased as learners become engaged in activities which they create according to their own intentions, concerns and interests. In particular, this appears to be the case when learners work with their own productions as discussed in Section 3.1.2.

Widdowson (1984) has argued that using genuine materials does not automatically result in authenticity. What is required is a degree of learner engagement with the text which means that the learners need to authenticate the text as they would their own written texts. Widdowson (1998) further stated that learners cannot authenticate genuine texts because they are not the original recipient of that text, which makes it impossible for them to partake in the discourse needed to authenticate the passage. According to van Lier (1996: 128), learners need to engage with the learning materials in order to authenticate them, and he claims that "authenticity is the result of acts of authentication, by students and their teacher, of the learning process and the language used in it". As shown in the discussion above, corpus-based activities have the potential to create authenticity in the classroom. The research character of corpus-based tasks allows learners to authenticate the corpus and the task, because they can become engaged with a corpus of authentic texts in the process of discovery-type learning activities that bear all the elements of text, task, and purpose authenticity.

3.3.2 Learner autonomy

> It is a truism that learning has to be done by the learner.
> (van Lier 1996: 12)

As discussed in Section 3.2.2, the change of the computer's role from 'tutor' to 'tool' and the reversal of the flow of question and answer inherent to this role is an essential characteristic of direct corpus use in the classroom. The underlying assumption of the DDL approach is that "effective language learning is a form of linguistic research" (Johns 1991b: 30) and that the learner assumes the role of the researcher. According to Johns (1988), this approach

> entails a shift in the traditional division of roles between student and teacher, with the student now taking on more responsibility for his or her learning, and the teacher acting as research director and research collaborator rather than transmitter of knowledge. (Johns 1988: 14)

Therefore, direct applications of corpora with language learners provide an ideal environment to foster learner autonomy which Benson (2001: 47) defines as "the capacity to control one's own learning".

The idea of learner autonomy originally emerged in the 1970s and was defined in Holec's (1981: 3) widely quoted report on the Council of Europe's Modern Languages Project for adult life-long education as "the ability to take charge of one's own learning". At the time, learner autonomy was mostly thought of in relation to out-of-classroom situations in self-directed learning settings with no teacher present. This kind of autonomy was seen within the context of "a radical restructuring of language pedagogy, a restructuring that involves the rejection of the traditional classroom" (Allwright 1988: 35).

Learner autonomy is increasingly seen as essential to being a successful learner which has led Little (1995: 175) to conclude that "pursuing learner autonomy as an explicit goal, [will] help more learners to succeed". Further research on learner autonomy in the 1990s led to a shift in focus towards autonomy in the classroom. Smith (2003: 2) has pointed out that the "incorporation of autonomy as a goal in national curricula in European countries and elsewhere" has taken place and recognises the important role of the teacher in 'fostering' autonomy in learners. Benson (2008) has welcomed this development of

> more 'usable' accounts of autonomy from the teacher's perspective – accounts that are based on the assumption that autonomy *is* a capacity that can be developed in the classroom, without any strong implication

of a need for situational freedom in the learning process. (Benson 2008: 23)

Direct corpus applications can be situated within this context of 'classroom autonomy' which Benson (2006: 28) views as "a 'usable' construct for teachers who want to help their learners develop autonomy without necessarily challenging constraints of the classroom and curriculum organization to which they are subject". The teacher's role in fostering autonomy in learners can be seen as creating learning scenarios that allow the learner to take on an active role in the learning process and at the same time to raise the learner's awareness of that process – two important elements of fostering learner autonomy. That learning is an active process, "ein kreativer Konstruktionsprozess" (Wolff 2001: 191), is a key notion of the constructivist paradigm.[30] Learners have to construct knowledge independently from the information they encounter. Wolff emphasises that learners should not simply be confronted with prefabricated knowledge by an expert but that they should rather be provided with the building materials to construct their own meanings. In this sense, constructivism differs from traditional transmission-based models that see the learner merely as the recipient of knowledge. The reasoning of the constructivist model is that constructed knowledge is transferable and memorable as the learner plays an active part in encoding it and placing it into a meaningful context of reference (see Spiro, Coulson, Feltovich & Anderson 1988). The direct use of corpora with learners is thus highly compatible with the constructivist paradigm. Rather than being presented with rules and pre-defined meanings, the learner takes on an active part in a research cycle of *observation – classification – generalisation*. This approach builds the learners' competence by giving them access to the facts of linguistic performance: "we simply provide the evidence needed to answer the learner's questions, and rely on the learner's intelligence to find answers" (Johns 1991a: 2). Concordancing activities thus provide not only a valuable opportunity for learners to take on an active role in the learning process but to literally take control of the learning process as they explore real language use and construct knowledge of the language in the process.[31] Raising awareness in learners of the learning process and fostering learning strategies is an integral part of learner autonomy.

---

[30] It is not within the scope of this study to review the various forms of constructivism and the surrounding debates. The term 'constructivism' is treated here in the sense of 'pragmatic constructivism' as termed by Müller (2001: 3). In this approach, Müller proposes to overcome the seemingly opposite features of instruction and construction in order to arrive at a 'pragmatic' solution for the integration of constructivist ideas in the traditional classroom.

[31] This approach is directly in line with constructionist learning scenarios as proposed, for example, by Rüschoff and Ritter (2001).

Fostering learner autonomy through corpus work can occur to varying degrees according to the learner's level of language proficiency and autonomy. Particularly in the area of error correction, the use of concordances has shown great potential. In their study on error correction with undergraduate students of French, O'Sullivan and Chambers (2006) make a case for the importance of learner error correction based on indirect feedback provided by the teacher. The task of consulting corpora actively engages the learners in the process of improving their writing and in seeking answers to questions based on their productions. In regard to the difficult task of fostering autonomy within the constraints of the classroom context, Little (1995) rightly observes that

> learners do not automatically accept responsibility for their learning – teachers must help them to do so; and they will not necessarily find it easy to reflect critically on the learning process – teachers must first provide them with appropriate tools and with opportunities to practise using them. (Little 1995: 176-177)

Corpora and concordancers provide valuable opportunities and resources for this approach, as is evident in the findings of a study on corpus consultation in academic writing:

> [S]tudents took more responsibility for their language learning as a result of their corpus experience. This is one of the most important roles that corpus technology plays in L2 writing. Corpora are tools that allow students to solve their linguistic and writing problems independently, and they raise students' linguistic awareness through problem-solving with authentic texts. (Yoon 2008: 45)

The crucial role that the teacher plays in applying these tools in the classroom and the challenges inherent to this process will be discussed in more detail in Chapter 4.

3.3.3 Language awareness

> Language Awareness can be defined as explicit knowledge about language, and conscious perception and sensitivity in language learning, language teaching and language use.
>
> (*Association for Language Awareness, ALA*)[32]

---

[32] '*Association for Language Awareness*', website. Available at http://www.lexically.net/ala/la_defined.htm.

Most language learning activities with corpora and concordances are characterised by working with authentic texts, by a focus on lexico-grammatical phenomena and problem-solving analyses that involve the use of linguistic terminology and noticing formal properties of language (e.g. identification of word classes). These activities are regarded to have considerable potential to raise 'language awareness'. In this section, I will discuss the concept of language awareness and the vital role corpora can play for raising language awareness in language learners and teachers.

The concept of language awareness as applied in research literature on corpus use in language learning tends to refer to knowledge about language. The broader definition supplied by the *ALA* is more encompassing and is reflected in Svalberg's (2007) assessment that language awareness "straddles a cognitive to sociocultural spectrum and involves such apparently distinct areas of research and practice as cognitive linguistics (attention and awareness in language learning), language teaching, language use and intercultural communication (cross-cultural awareness)" (Svalberg 2007: 287; this publication provides a comprehensive overview of language awareness).

One of the first to discuss 'language awareness' in the educational context, Halliday put forth a language teaching programme – *Language in Use* – with the aim "to develop in pupils and students awareness of what language is and how it is used and at the same time, to extend their competence in handling the language" (see Doughty, Pearce & Thornton 1971: 8-9). Concerns about falling literacy levels at schools and linguistic intolerance were emerging from a number of studies in the 1970s and 1980s (Bullock 1975; Davie, Butler & Goldstein 1972; ILEA 1980; Rampton 1981) and gave the language awareness movement momentum (see in particular Hawkins's seminal 1984 publication *Awareness of Language* and Donmall 1985). The idea was to introduce language awareness to the curriculum in order to support the language learning process by making learners consciously aware of language structures and phenomena in order to improve their overall language learning capacity (for more detailed information on the historical development of language awareness, see Hawkins 1992, 1999; van Essen 1996, 2008). In this sense, language awareness is not so much a methodology but an approach to language learning and teaching that encourages explicit reflection on language and the language learning process.

By the 1990s, the role of language awareness in language learning and teaching research was gaining more and more significance, as is marked by a number of important publications during that period (Carter 1990; Fairclough 1992; James & Garrett 1991; Mittins 1991; van Lier 1991) and the foundation of the *ALA* in 1992.

The timing is significant as during the same period a renewed focus on form in a meaning-based communicative teaching context was taking hold (Doughty 1991; Doughty & Williams 1998; Long 1991). This was due to the realisation that the virtual exclusion of explicit grammar instruction in the extreme forms of the communicative teaching approach resulted in students failing to achieve high levels in linguistic skill, despite sufficient language input (see Lightbown & Spada 1990; Swain 1998). Hulstijn (1989: 72) concluded from experiments on the processing of natural and partly artificial input that "for implicit and incidental learning of structural language elements to take place, attention to form at input encoding is a sufficient condition". This view is supported by research on noticing and the role of consciousness in learning (Bialystok 1978, 1981; Schmidt 1990).

When learners come into contact with the target language, this is referred to as input. Only when learners can process this input in a way that is facilitative to the language learner, is it referred to as intake. 'Noticing' describes the process of learners paying conscious attention to certain features of language and therefore transforming language input into intake. Finding ways to improve the process of noticing is therefore desirable. The underlying assumption is that conscious or explicit knowledge facilitates language learning and, therefore, consciousness-raising activities that draw the learner's attention to particular aspects of language have an important role to play in language learning (Rutherford & Sharwood Smith 1985; Sharwood Smith 1981; for a different perspective, cf. Krashen 1982). Sharwood Smith (1991: 118) later on abandons the term consciousness-raising and instead proposes input enhancement to describe a "deliberate focus on the formal properties of language with a view to facilitating the development of L2 knowledge". He distances himself from the term consciousness raising and concludes that input enhancement is a safer term since it "focuses on the operation that is carried out on the linguistic material and not on the internal mental process of the learner" (Sharwood Smith 1991: 120). However, despite this, it should be noted that the term consciousness raising is still commonly used.

The role of consciousness in learning and whether conscious learning could become unconscious knowledge has fuelled an intense debate which continues to preoccupy researchers in this field (e.g. Doughty 2003; Ellis 2005, 2008). However, as will become more evident in the discussion below, the language awareness approach integrates both communicative and formal methods, thereby accepting the notion that explicit knowledge about language has a role to play in the acquisition process. The relevance of corpus-based learning activities for language awareness is reflected in five features that Borg (1994: 62) introduces in order to describe a language awareness methodology for language teaching:[33]

---

[33] Note that I have adopted Svalberg's (2007: 291) terms (in italics) to name the five features. Borg (1994) only provided the descriptions but no titles.

(i) *Description*: Learning about language is not the internalisation of a definable body of knowledge but the on-going investigation of a dynamic phenomenon.
(ii) *Languaging*: Learning a language should involve talking about the language.
(iii) *Exploration*: Learning is most effective as a process of learner-centred exploration and discovery.
(iv) *Engagement*: Effective awareness-raising depends on engaging learners both affectively and cognitively.
(v) *Reflection*: Language awareness as a methodology develops in learners both knowledge about language as well as skills for continued autonomous learning.

In the following paragraphs, I will discuss these features and link them to the application of corpora in the classroom.

(i) Description

As part of the first feature, called *description*, Borg (1994: 62) proposes that learners should be given opportunities to "develop an understanding of [language] through processes of continual investigation". DDL activities in the classroom offer such opportunities quite literally and have been described as a "distinctive methodology characterised by the central importance given to the development of the ability of learners to discover things for themselves on the basis of authentic examples of language use" (Johns 1993: 4). Such learning activities are therefore well-suited to provide students with ample opportunity to explore language use and are also very much in line with language awareness in the sense that they are "radically distinct from traditional explicit language instruction" (Svalberg 2007: 291). Concordancing tasks provide a learning environment that facilitates a view of language that is dynamic and fuzzy, governed by patterns of typical use rather than by finite rules and their exceptions. Furthermore, DDL exercises are learner-centred in the sense that the learner takes on responsibility for the learning process. They also provide opportunities for learner-learner interaction when, for example, results of concordance tasks are compared in the classroom or research tasks are conducted in teams.

(ii) Languaging

The second feature that Borg (1994: 62) introduces, *languaging*,[34] involves "talking about language". When working with concordances, students discuss language analytically, a process which helps with the "painless acquisition of the terms needed to discuss grammatical categories" (Francis 1994: 221). In other words, concordancing tasks can provide a meaning context for the teaching of grammatical meta language. In practice, this has shown some promise. A study with primary school L1 learners demonstrated that the students acquired significant levels of metalinguistic competence as a result of a series of concordance activities (Sealey & Thompson 2004, 2007). The process of solving language puzzles, of the kind that DDL tasks provide, engages learners in dialogues with each other and with the language data. This draws their attention to language-related problems, which, in order to solve them, they need to hypothesise, generalise and debate about. These are all processes that can be described under the heading of 'languaging' and contribute to the process of language learning because it is "dialogue that constructs linguistic knowledge" (Swain 2000: 97). Svalberg (2007: 292) comments that "a starting point for languaging about language is noticing" which in turn can be promoted through input enhancement. Input enhancement has been proposed in the form of facial gestures, manipulation of typography or corrective feedback. I would like to suggest that the KWIC format of concordance data can also be viewed as a particularly salient form of input enhancement and could almost certainly serve to promote noticing of particular language features.

(iii) Exploration

At the centre of the third feature, *exploration*, lies the belief that "learning is most effective as a process of learner-centred exploration and discovery" (Borg 1994: 62). Similarly, concordancing activities are defined by the paradigm of the 'learner as researcher'. The learner explores language data in the form of concordances in order to discover facts about language. Often these tasks constitute explicit language study; however, they are generally meaningful tasks, sometimes even learner-initiated. As Johns (1991a: 3) points out, "the DDL approach [...] makes possible a new style of 'grammatical consciousness-raising' (Rutherford 1987) by placing the learner's own discovery to be based on evidence from authentic language use". The process of analysing concordances provides a valuable opportunity for language learners to explore the complexities of the target language in a more transparent way. The exploration of language helps in

---

[34] The term 'languaging' was reportedly introduced by Swain (2006).

raising language awareness and the concordance provides a unique means of visualisation:

> By exploring language, by reflecting on discoveries and previous knowledge, by seeing language in 'different' ways – through visualization, for example – participants can become more *sensitive* to what the linguistic knowledge base represents. (Wright & Bolitho 1993: 300)

It is worthwhile considering the strategies and competencies a learner has to apply in order to solve a DDL task. The learner not only needs to identify the parts of speech but also how they interact and create meaning according to this interaction. DDL presents itself as an approach to implement focus on form in meaning-focused tasks. The positive effects of such discovery-type language exercises are described by a student in Chambers's (2005: 120) study on corpus consultation: "Working out lexical or grammatical patterns on his or her own may help the learner to memorise problematic aspects better than it would be the case when 'spoonfed' with rules". This correlates with van Lier's (1998: 128) assessment that "interactions with learners in classrooms should allow learners to be perceiving, thinking, acting, and interacting persons, rather than passive receivers of knowledge".

(iv) Engagement

Svalberg (2007) summarises the fourth feature in Borg's list with the term *engagement*. In regard to this feature, Borg (1994: 62) emphasises that language awareness "does not assume that learners will be necessarily motivated to participate in language study activities simply because of the cognitive challenge they present". Corpus-based activities should not be introduced merely for the sake of introducing corpora into the classroom. It is moreover important to integrate such tasks in a meaningful context and, ideally, concordancing tasks are even learner-initiated which is thought to increase the learner's motivation. In this context, Seidlhofer (2002) explores the notion of learning-driven data (see also Section 3.1.2). She views learners "not just as perusers and purveyors of textual data, but as participants and analysts in the discourse process of drawing on the potential of corpus linguistics via their own texts and their own questions" (2002: 215). Her study clearly showed that students only became productively engaged in the tasks as "[t]hey discovered that close scrutiny of the language of a text in which they had a personal investment can be a fascinating process rather than a pedantic, tedious affair" (2002: 230). Access to corpora through concordancers can provide an excellent resource for learners to solve problems on how to use language, and Frankenberg-Garcia (2004: 216) concludes that such "learner-initiated concordances are likely to be meaningful, relevant and conducive to successful language learning".

(v) Reflection

In regard to the last feature, *reflection*, Borg (1994: 62) states that within the framework of a language awareness methodology it is important to create "opportunities for learners to think about, discuss and evaluate their own learning with a view to increasing their understanding of how the learning process can be made more effective". In particular, reflection about structural aspects of language during contrastive analyses of the native and second language provides a valuable opportunity for raising language and learning awareness. Studies employing native and non-native (i.e., learner) corpora have shown positive outcomes and proven to successfully engage learners in the process of language analysis (Belz & Vyatkina 2008; Seidlhofer 2002)

As a methodology in foreign language teaching, language awareness has significant implications for teachers and teacher education. Wright and Bolitho (1993: 298) point out that language awareness in the classroom often involves the "need to come to terms with uncomfortable and comfortable discoveries" which commonly challenge "deeply-held views on language, developed in training or over years of experience". It is therefore imperative to integrate language awareness into teacher education in order to enable teachers to use language awareness as a pedagogical tool in the classroom. Raising language awareness in learners depends to a large degree on the teacher. Therefore, it is of great importance that the teacher possesses a high level of language awareness. Wright and Bolitho (1993: 292) argue that "successful *communicative* teaching depends more than ever on a high level of language awareness in a teacher due to the richness and complexity of a 'communicative view'".

The use of corpora and concordances in language teacher education is seen as an important source for language awareness-raising activities (Allan 1999; Amador Moreno *et al.* 2006; Berry 1994; Coniam 1997; Farr 2008; Francis 1994; Hunston 1995b; O'Keeffe & Farr 2003; Tsui 2004). Allan (1999: 57) argues that "the use of corpus data – and concordance lines in particular – has a unique and powerful role to play in raising the language awareness of English teachers". Often, language awareness as discussed in these publications refers to grammatical awareness (e.g. Allan 1999; Berry 1994; Francis 1994; Hunston 1995b) which is seen as essential because "teachers need to be confident in their own knowledge, and not feel threatened by what they may feel to be the intricacies and complexities of 'grammar'" (Francis 1994: 221). However, the significant potential of corpora to "make teachers more critical of how English is described and presented in course materials" (Coniam, 1997: 199) has also been recognised. Francis (1994) aptly sums up the potential of corpora:

> In conclusion, I would like simply to point out that the awareness-raising potentials of observing a corpus are unlimited, provided that learners are given some initial guidance. For teachers particularly, it can give them confidence in their own conclusions and free them from the threats posed by a system that expects there to be clear-cut categories, terminological precision and right or wrong answers. Language is not like this – it is full of indeterminancies, fuzzy categories, and unexpected complexities which no terminology can adequately capture. Above all, however, the activity can be interesting and enjoyable – exciting, even – throwing up insights into language which are beyond the reach of intuition and inspire further exploration. (Francis 1994: 236)

The present chapter has provided a glimpse into the vast array of opportunities and exciting possibilities corpora have to offer for language education. However, as will become clear in the following chapter, transferring these tools and resources into the classroom (beyond the researcher's playground) is not straightforward, and enthusiastic research activities are not necessarily reflected by current practices in language classrooms. For that reason, the following chapter focuses on the apparent gap between research and practice in order to identify crucial factors in the process of advancing the popularisation of corpus use in language education.

4 Adjusting the perspective: from research to classroom

> The fact that concordancing has proved a useful tool [...] by linguists is no guarantee that it can be usefully transferred to the classroom.
>
> (Aston 1995: 260)

Chapters 2 and 3 have introduced corpus linguistic methods and resources and reviewed the impact of corpus linguistics on language education. In particular, Chapter 3 has highlighted the broad spectrum of indirect and direct applications of corpora and corpus analysis software in language teaching and the enormous potential they yield. Furthermore, by analysing three significant concepts in current language pedagogy – authenticity, learner autonomy, and language awareness – it was established that direct applications of corpora in the language classroom are of immediate relevance to these concepts. However, as indicated in the introductory chapter of this study, a gap persists between research activity and enthusiasm on the one hand, and the lack of application in mainstream language teaching practice on the other hand.

The present chapter addresses this gap in the form of a two-staged analysis: firstly, a critical review of evaluative studies on the direct use of corpora in the language classroom is presented; secondly, the core elements involved in the corpus investigation process – the corpus, the corpus analysis software, and the user – will be analysed in light of their transferability from research to classroom. Employing corpora in the classroom usually constitutes a direct transfer of research methods and resources into a pedagogical environment, and Cook (1998: 57) rightly remarks that "the leap from linguistics to pedagogy is [...] far from straightforward". In the present chapter, each of these elements will be analysed in regard to the challenges posed by this transfer. The purpose of this comprehensive analysis is to identify key factors in promoting the use of corpora in language education. This will lay the groundwork for the research presented in the following Chapters 5, 6, and 7.

4.1 The gap between research and classroom practice

When corpora and concordancers were first discovered as useful tools for language learning, the enthusiasm by the proponents of this approach was considerable. This was due to the new and different nature of concordancing as well as the potential value of observing actual language use in corpora made possible by the exciting developments of computing power at the time. In Johns's (1991a: 2) words, what defines the direct corpus approach "is the perception that 'research is too serious to be left to the researchers': that the language-learner is also, essentially, a research worker whose learning needs to be driven by access to linguistic data". Johns saw much potential in the unique way of displaying language 'vertically' in the form of KWIC or concordance lists and in the ability to give learners access to actual language use with just a few keystrokes. According to him, the results of such 'research on the hop' are credible, usable, attainable, and transferable (see Johns 1988: 23-24.). Tribble (1990) also emphasised the distinctive way in which concordancers display results and how that effects the learning process:

> What the concordancer does is make the invisible visible. Patterns that would never be immediately recognizable spring to the eye with a freshness that can be quite astonishing the first time you use such a tool – and which does not lose its fascination even after long familiarity. (Tribble 1990: 11)

The extraordinary potential that many saw in using corpora and concordancers in language education led to very optimistic predictions regarding future developments of this approach. Tribble (1990: 15) believed that "the concordancer will perhaps be the pre-eminent software tool in this next stage in the development of computer assisted language learning". A few years later, Flowerdew (1996: 98) was even sure that "concordancing ha[d] reached the stage where it [was] about to have a significant impact on the organization and practice of language teaching". However, it has since become evident that Fligelstone's (1993: 101) vision of learners being able to "go to any of the labs, hit the icon which says 'Corpus' and follow the instructions on the screen" has yet to come true.

The question as to how corpora should find their way into language teaching practices was addressed quite early on. McEnery and Wilson (1997: 5) believed that corpora would be increasingly used for teaching without specific encouragement from the research community, a process which they described as "percolation of corpora into teaching". However, the desired "ripple effects spreading out from early centres of corpus-based teaching" (1997: 6) failed to appear. As shown in the introduction to this study, many researchers are now coming to the realisation that so far corpora have not entered mainstream teaching practices (Braun 2005; Breyer 2006a, 2009; Kaltenböck & Mehlmauer-Larcher 2005; Mukherjee 2004, 2009; Seidlhofer 2002; Tribble 2000, 2001). Tribble (2000: 31) reflects that "despite the best efforts of people like Tim Johns, Guy Aston, John Flowerdew and myself [...] not many teachers seem to be *using* corpora in their classrooms". In light of the multitude of available publications and corpus resources, this seems indeed perplexing. Clearly, there is an expectation that the extensive research output spanning over more than two decades should have created a natural flow-on effect onto teaching practices:

> At first blush, then, one might readily expect that the multitude of suggestions on how to use corpus data, corpus-based resources and corpus-linguistic methods in the English language classroom [...] has already revolutionised – or is just about to do so – the way in which English is taught and learned as a foreign language. However, in Germany (and probably in many other countries as well) this turns out to be wishful thinking. (Mukherjee 2004: 239)

These observations are so far only infrequently supported by statistical evidence (notable exceptions are, e.g. Mukherjee 2004; Thompson 2006; Tribble 2001).[35] Therefore, one component of this study is to contribute evidence to these claims in the form of a survey of language teacher educators at universities in Germany which will be reported in Chapter 5.

Despite the apparent lack of uptake of corpus-based language applications by language practitioners, a continuing flow of research publications dealing with corpora in language teaching and learning highlights the ongoing interest in the subject which may be taken as tentative evidence for the firm belief in the extraordinary potential of corpora by many researchers (for recent edited volumes and monographs alone, see, e.g. Aijmer 2009; Aston *et al.* 2004; Braun *et al.* 2006; Gavioli 2005; Hidalgo *et al.* 2007; Moreno Jaén, Serrano Valverde, & Calzada, forthcoming; Reppen 2010; Sinclair 2004; also note the considerable space devoted to the topic of corpora in language education in the *Routledge Handbook of Corpus Linguistics*, O'Keeffe & McCarthy 2010). The question then remains as to why corpus tools and resources are not more readily employed by language practitioners. Is it because the approach is less effective than traditional materials? Is the approach too difficult for learners? Or is it that learners perhaps do not share researchers' enthusiasm about concordancing? What have teachers had to say about the use of concordances in the classroom? In order to find answers to these questions, the next section presents a review of evaluative studies on using corpora with learners.

Subsequently, the core elements involved in the corpus analysis process – the corpus, the corpus analysis software, and the user – will be analysed in light of their transferability from research to classroom. Unlike most other materials and technologies designed for the language classroom, corpora and corpus tools were of course originally purpose-built for a research environment. This is one of the unique aspects of the direct corpus approach: it constitutes a direct

[35] These studies will be discussed in more detail in the context of the survey presented in Chapter 5.

transfer of research methods and resources into the classroom, albeit with slight modifications in most cases. The hypothesis deriving from this is that the transfer from research to pedagogical environment is problematic, and it may indeed serve to explain, at least in part, the persisting lack of uptake by teachers. Thus, a thorough investigation is required. As a result, the final section draws together the findings from both analyses and subsequently proposes a range of key factors that hinder or facilitate the use of corpora in language teaching and learning. The outcomes of this investigation form the basis for the research presented in the remainder of this study.

4.2 Evaluations of direct corpus applications

Due to the novelty of the approach, early publications on corpora in language learning tended to focus on showcasing corpus tools (e.g. Johns 1986; Levy 1990), as well as ideas on how to employ corpora for learning activities (e.g. Honeyfield 1989; Johns & King 1991; Tribble & Jones 1997). The majority of these studies are descriptive in nature which led Flowerdew (1996: 112) to point out "the paucity of critical perspectives in a perhaps over enthusiastic concordancing literature".[36] Consequently, he called for more evaluative studies to ensure that concordancing can "be incorporated appropriately into the teacher's battery of reference and teaching resources as the useful additional teaching and learning tool that it undoubtedly is" (1996: 112).

A multitude of evaluative studies on the use of corpora with language learners have since emerged. In order to find answers to the questions posed in the previous section, three areas that have been closely investigated in these studies will be examined: firstly, the effectiveness of the corpus approach based on quantitative studies (e.g. Allan 2006; Boulton 2007b; Chan & Liou 2005; Chang & Sun 2009; Yeh *et al.* 2007); secondly, learner strategies in using corpora (e.g. Aston 1997b; Bernardini 2000; Kennedy & Miceli 2001, 2010); and thirdly, learner and teacher responses to the use of corpora in the classroom (e.g. Davis & Russell-Pinson 2004; Farr 2008; Götz & Mukherjee 2006).

Effectiveness of concordancing

The purpose of this section is to review case studies that have investigated the effectiveness of using concordances in language learning based on empirical analysis. These studies, in which learning outcomes have been quantified by

[36] However, it is worthwhile mentioning here two early and frequently quoted studies, namely Stevens (1991b) and Cobb (1997) which will be analysed in more detail below.

pre- and post-tests, focus mainly on vocabulary learning (e.g. Allan 2006; Chan & Liou 2005; Chang & Sun 2009; Cobb 1997; Lee & Liou 2003; Stevens 1991b; Yeh *et al.* 2007) and to a lesser extent on grammatical language points (e.g. Boulton 2007b; Braun 2007).[37] A number of these quantitative studies also include a qualitative component investigating learner response. These will be discussed separately further below. Research questions put forth by these quantitative studies vary: some compare the effectiveness of concordancing with traditional materials (see Allan 2006; Boulton 2007b, 2008a, 2008b, 2009c; Cobb 1997; Stevens 1991b), while others set out to assess the potential of using concordances to improve on a particular language point (see Chan & Liou 2005; Yeh *et al.* 2007).

Possibly the earliest study on the effectiveness of concordancing is Stevens's (1991b) study on concordances as an alternative to gap-filler exercises. In this stydu, Stevens sets up an experiment in order to investigate whether "exercises drilling the same vocabulary in gap-filler and concordance-based formats can be solved equally well by language learners, and [...] that differences in performance will favor the concordance-based exercises" (1991: 49). Stevens found that the group exposed to concordances achieved slightly better results and that the truncated text typical of KWIC lists did not appear to cause any difficulties for the learners in terms of extrapolating meaning from context. Although cautious about deriving any generalisations from these results, Stevens concludes that the concordance format is superior because "having multiple if disjunct contexts helps [the learners] more in settling on a correct word than do the clues inherent in a passage of discourse with the same words missing" (1991b: 55).

Cobb (1997: 301) set out to "identify a specific learning effect that can be unambiguously attributed to the use of concordance software by language learners". Cobb's participants worked with concordances on the computer, and the goal was to learn new words rather than recall known ones. For this purpose, Cobb developed a program, *PET 200*, that acted as a lexical tutor with a modified concordancer as the main language informant. The corpus used was a very small specialised corpus of 10,000 words from the students' reading materials. For the purpose of the experiment, two versions of the *PET 200* program were developed, one with concordance lines as information source and the other with traditional example sentences and brief definitions of new words. The subjects were 100 first-year Arabic-speaking students, and the project was conducted over the course of one academic year. The class was divided into two groups, each receiving a different version of *PET 200* in order to compare the results from a series of activities (recorded by the software) at the end of the

[37] The list of studies mentioned here is by no means exhaustive and a full analysis of every available case study is beyond the scope of this current research. For a detailed review of evaluative studies focusing on learning outcomes, see Boulton (2010).

year. The results showed that 8 out of 11 students averaged higher on the task when using the concordancing version of the *PET 200* and had acquired 12% more transferable knowledge, which led the author to conclude that "[t]he higher scores appear to result from the subjects' efforts to use concordances to work out the meanings of new words" (Cobb 1997: 313).

Allan (2006) also investigated vocabulary acquisition with concordances in comparison to traditional textbook techniques. The participants of the group were multilingual adult learners studying *English for the Cambridge Advanced English* examination, and the pre- and post-tests were based around 40 selected vocabulary items. The author lists a number of limitations to the study which may have interfered with the final outcome, but she tentatively concludes that "the initial results appear to reflect positively on the uses of concordances" (2006: 40)

The purpose of the case study presented by Yeh *et al.* (2007) was to investigate student performance using an online bilingual concordancer to improve students' use of adjectives. One group of 19 first-year English major students in Taiwan took pre- and post-tests as well as a delayed post-test on 30 vocabulary items selected as relevant by a previous analysis of learner data. The results showed that students' knowledge on synonym use improved significantly. The delayed post-test further demonstrated that this knowledge was retained after eight weeks. The results are seen as encouraging, particularly in light of the fact that "traditional teaching methods [in Taiwan] emphasize deductive teaching" (Yeh *et al.* 2007: 148) which meant that the students were likely to have found the inductive approach of this discovery-type learning with concordances as challenging (see also Chan & Liou 2005; Lee & Liou 2003).[38]

Boulton has been one of a number of researchers (see also Cresswell 2007; Johansson 2009) to argue that "far more empirical research is needed on all aspects of DDL if it is to convince a wider audience and break out of its current research environment" (Boulton 2008b: 595). Consequently, Boulton has presented a series of experiments on the use of DDL (Boulton 2007b, 2008a, 2008b, 2009c). These case studies have similar settings. The participants are lower-intermediate university students who have to pass an English exam in order to successfully complete their degree (architecture or engineering). Boulton's main interest is to investigate whether these lower level learners can effectively interpret concordance data. This is measured against their performances based on traditional materials (e.g. dictionary entries or grammar text book). The participants receive virtually no training prior to their exposure to concordances and, in all cases, the materials consist of prepared and edited concordance printouts. The results from these studies indicate that the experimental groups generally perform better with the exception of the first

38 Further discussion on learner types and attitudes follows in Section 4.3.4.

study (Boulton 2007b) which show that the control and the experimental group performed equally well. Boulton further concludes from comparisons of test results with language proficiency levels within the groups that all learner levels can benefit from the approach. While advanced learners perform better overall, intermediate learners appear to show a higher level of improvement (see Boulton 2008b)

A comprehensive survey of 27 evaluative studies on learning outcomes from corpus consultation has led Boulton (forthcoming b: 17) to conclude that the corpus approach "can be usefully employed for learners of many different language backgrounds and in different situations when appropriately adapted". However, although the results of most studies certainly appear encouraging, it is difficult to derive conclusive evidence from them. This is mainly due to a considerable degree of variability between the individual studies. These variables include: learner profile (age, language proficiency, preferred learning style, purpose for language education), extent of training received prior to the experiment, test settings, and duration of case study. On the other hand, the fact that the approach appears to be effective in such diverse contexts can also be interpreted as extremely encouraging. In other words, the use of concordances appears to lead to successful learning events regardless of the conditions. More empirical studies are certainly needed in order to accurately assess the effectiveness of the corpus approach. For future studies, it would be highly desirable to formulate high quality, reliable guidelines in order to obtain more comparable indications of the effectiveness of the corpus approach.

Learner strategies

Currently, only a small number of case studies have examined the type of skills required for corpus consultation and learner performance in these skills. Early accounts suggested that learners, as novice users of corpora, find it difficult to recognise patterns and regularities in retrieved corpus data (see Aston 1997b). The author attributes this to "their attempt to infer maximally generalized rules from the corpus data, which they felt to be of greater value than mere partial regularities" (Aston 1997b: 209). His further observation that the learners were more concerned with discovering what *could* rather than what *usually* co-occurred (see 1997b: 208), is reflected in Bernardini's (2000) account. She also reports that her learners displayed a tendency to over-generalise from corpus findings and showed a lack of awareness in regard to the representativeness of the corpus. Both Aston (1997b) and Bernardini (2000) propose the use of checklists to help learners refine their search and interpretation techniques. Such scaffolding devices were found to be very effective in more recent studies (see Chang & Sun 2009; Liou, Chang, Chen, Lin, Liaw, Gao *et al.* 2006).

In the context of teaching intermediate level Italian at university, Kennedy and Miceli (2001) systematically evaluated the effectiveness of the students' corpus investigations (see also Miceli & Kennedy 2002; Kennedy & Miceli 2010). For the purpose of their study, the authors developed an apprenticeship programme "intended to promote learning by example and by experience" (Kennedy & Miceli 2001: 79). The corpus was purpose-built for the language course in question and functioned primarily as a reference tool for creative writing tasks given to the learners. The ensuing analysis led the authors to conclude that "while knowledge and experience of the language undoubtedly played a part in how productive the students' work with the corpus was, lack of rigor in observation and reasoning contributed greatly to their difficulties, as did apparent ignorance of common pitfalls and techniques for avoiding them" (2001: 81). These results prompted a revision of the apprenticeship programme for corpus consultation which was then put into place and evaluated in a subsequent publication (Kennedy & Miceli 2010). The authors have declared plans for future refinement of the approach with a particular focus on training learners in looking for patterns, on increasing the corpus component in homework given, and on helping learners become aware of the different characteristics and uses of reference sources.

Observations of learner strategies when working with corpora have highlighted some fundamental differences in perspective by learners and researchers. Learners are looking for easy to obtain, definite (and reliable) answers, something which is to be expected as part of the learning process. As Aston (1995: 259) has pointed out before, researchers "rely heavily upon their intuition as native speakers and their professional training", neither of which is available to the average language learner.

In order to help learners improve their strategies in searching and interpreting data, scaffolding devices have been identified as effective tools (see above). However, in general, there is consensus that learners require relevant training to enable them to take full advantage of the corpus approach. As Estling Vannestål and Lindquist (2007: 344) observe, "It is necessary to spend much time together with the students in front of the computers in order to help them get to grips with the corpus work". The matter of training learners and teachers as corpus users is discussed in more detail in Section 4.3.3.

Learner and teacher responses

Perhaps equally as important as the results from studies that investigate the effectiveness of the corpus approach and analyses of learner strategies are the outcomes from questionnaires and interviews on learner responses to corpus consultation. Questions generally centre on whether learners found the activities useful, interesting, and whether they consider them for future use.

As mentioned above, some of the quantitative studies on the effectiveness of concordancing include questionnaires on learner response. The majority of these studies report positive feedback from learners and indicate a preference of concordance materials over traditional resources such as dictionaries and course books (e.g. Allan 2006). Students in Allan's (2006) study on vocabulary acquisition with concordancing found the concordance tasks extremely useful and, although the students rated their level of interest in this type of exercise as average, the majority of them planned to use concordancing in the future for learning purposes. As part of their study with university students, Götz and Mukherjee (2006: 58) discovered that "the majority of students found working with DDL interesting, productive and motivating". The students' own assessment of the perceived benefits of DDL showed that 79% of the group found the approach useful. Similarly, as part of an evaluation of corpus use with teacher trainees, Farr (2008: 39) concluded that the participants of her case study with teacher trainees "show an overwhelmingly positive disposition towards the use of corpora in terms of their enjoyment and also the perceived benefits". Varley (2009: 145) sums up his study on integrating corpus consultation into an undergraduate EAP context as follows: "Clearly, a majority of the students in this study see that corpus consultation has benefits for them as language learners".

However, there is also evidence that corpora are not always perceived as a positive addition to the language learning repertoire. Based on their experiences from two experiments with university students, Estling Vannestål and Lindquist (2007) caution that corpus work may not be suitable for all learner groups and that some corpus activities may be more suitable at the introductory stage than others. Furthermore, individual learner styles also need to be taken into account (see Boulton 2009a). There is also evidence that technical aspects (e.g. the corpus analysis software) are perceived negatively (e.g. Estling Vannestål & Lindquist 2007; Farr 2008) and that the approach may be perceived negatively when logistical or technical problems occur in the process (see Whistle 1999).

Another issue that is occasionally reported as a negative aspect is that corpus applications are too time-consuming. Concordancing activities typically focus on individual language items and as such often target depth rather than breadth of knowledge.[39] As a consequence, learners occasionally feel that too much time is spent on a single aspect of language (see Thurstun & Candlin 1998). However, as Thurstun and Candlin (1998: 277-278) point out, learners are not always aware that "learning extends far beyond the particular items around which the material is based".

---

[39] Cf. Cobb (1997, 1999). Cobb (1999: 360) presents a suite of corpus exercises with the purpose of "gaining broad word knowledge, in a short time, without sacrificing depth".

Yeh *et al.* (2007) concluded that the majority of students had perceived the concordancing exercises as too time-consuming. At the same time, the results of their case study showed that learners had not only benefited from the concordancing exercises as evidenced in their written assignment but, according to a delayed test, retained that knowledge as well. A closer look at the studies which cite time-consuming as a negative aspect further reveals that individual factors are in play that are not always comparable and thus cannot necessarily be used to come to any general conclusions. Chambers (2005: 118), for example, reports that one of her students "found a number of aspects of the whole activity tedious, tiring, and laborious, in particular counting frequencies, deleting what she considered irrelevant concordances [...], and reading from a screen". She also observes that her students had decided not to take her initial advice and avoid the use of very common words as search terms which may have led the student to view the exercises differently. This example also highlights that learners mostly found the exercises too time-consuming when they were doing hands-on concordancing as opposed to using concordance printouts prepared by the teachers (see Kennedy & Miceli 2001).

One area that has received substantially less attention is the response of teachers to teaching with corpora. There are a small number of studies which deal with teacher or teacher trainee responses on *learning* with corpora (e.g. Amador Moreno *et al.* 2006; Gan, Low & Yaakub 1996). However, these studies do not provide any insights on teachers' perspectives on *teaching* with corpora. Only four studies could be found that in some form deal with teachers' responses to teaching with corpora (Davis & Russell-Pinson 2004; Farr 2008; Mauranen 2004a; Mukherjee 2004).

The study presented by Davis and Russell-Pinson (2004) reports on a training initiative for ESL content-area teachers (as opposed to language teachers) in the United States as a response to the growing number of non-native English speakers in schools. For the purpose of this initiative, a corpus was designed which consisted of 600 oral narratives on topics that were relevant for the subject areas taught by the participating teachers. The authors of the study prepared a range of teaching materials, including concordances, based on the corpus and in accordance with the school's curriculum. As part of this initiative, prospective and practicing teachers were trained in adapting these materials and on how to use corpora and concordances. Further details of the extent of training or the number of teachers participating in the training are unfortunately not mentioned. The authors only provide anecdotal evidence from their observations during the initiative to illustrate the participants' responses to the approach. According to their account, participants found the approach and the materials generally useful, although the technological aspects of using corpora were viewed as intimidating. The other aspect that was perceived negatively was the amount of language data in the concordances and the authors conclude that "upon initial exposure to concordancing, the teachers feel comfortable working with no more than 10 lines and prefer working with 5 lines" (Davis & Russell-Pinson 2004: 157). Finally, it became apparent that the teachers, "without exception", reported that they "wanted to change the language of the narratives to be more like 'standard English'" (2004: 158). No further details are provided; however, the authors subsequently explained that efforts were made in order to increase the participants' awareness of dialects in the community and to encourage reflection on the issue of prescriptive grammatical 'correctness'.[40]

In her study of introducing the *MICASE* into an EAP course at a university in Finland, Mauranen (2004a) reports the comments made by the teacher who ran the course. The teacher was the only one from a small group of teachers who had been introduced to corpora, to agree and integrate the corpus into her class. Although she perceived the approach as one involving risk-taking, her overall impression was that it "had been interesting, exciting, and simply fun" (Mauranen 2004a: 198). However, the teacher also commented that "taking a corpus into the classroom demands that the teacher understand the tentative nature of all knowledge" (2004a: 198). Negative aspects included technical difficulties as well as challenges in using the corpus effectively – particularly in regard to choosing 'corpus-ready' topics. Mauranen (2004a: 199) concedes that "[d]ifficulties of this kind seem inevitable until sufficient experience is accumulated of corpus use".

The purpose of Mukherjee's (2004) study was to investigate the use of corpora by English language teachers in Germany at secondary schools.[41] Survey data gathered from 248 participants of in-service teacher workshops on corpora and concordancing was presented. Two questions were posed to participants after the workshop showed that teachers felt that corpus data was mostly useful for teachers (83.9%) and that, while they were considering teacher-centred activities based on corpora for future teaching, they were much less inclined to undertake learner-centred activities (11.7%).[42]

The study by Farr (2008), discussed above in this section, also included one question for the teacher trainees in which they were asked to reflect on corpora in relation to their future teaching. All participants expressed their intentions to

---

40 For a discussion on corpus language as target language for language learning, see McCarthy and Carter (1995; also Carter & McCarthy 1996) who advocate an increased focus to the spoken features of language based on the findings from the *CANCODE*. A response on the relevance of such an approach is featured in Prodromou (1996a, 1996b).

41 This study will also be discussed in more detail in Chapter 5: Survey: corpora in language teacher education.

42 The issue of teachers' willingness to employ learner- versus teacher-centred activities is discussed further in relation to the results of the case study presented below in Section 6.3.5.

use corpora for teaching, particularly if a relevant infrastructure (corpora, software) was already available at the respective educational institution.

In the next section, the critical analysis of this chapter proceeds to investigate the elements corpus, software, and corpus user in order to identify factors that may hinder or facilitate the transfer of these research tools to a learning and teaching environment. The final section of this chapter draws together the findings from all analyses.

4.3 Analysis of core elements

4.3.1 Core element: corpus

The first element to be investigated is the corpus itself. It lies at the heart of any task, any research project, and any type of corpus-based teaching. Hunston (2002a: 26) rightly states that "[i]t is a truism that a corpus is neither good nor bad in itself, but suited or not suited to a particular purpose". Therefore, this section will investigate the element corpus from the perspective of using corpora for the purposes of learning and teaching languages.

Most commonly, the purpose of corpus linguistic research is to arrive at valid linguistic descriptions by means of investigating language in use, written and/or spoken, captured electronically in the form of corpora and thereby made accessible for computer analysis. Section 2.3.1 on corpus design has highlighted some of the most significant features of corpora for research purposes. These include size, representativeness, content, and corpus annotation. If the purpose of corpus research is to make valid statements about a language or a language variety, then the careful construction and design of the corpus in question will determine the quality of the research outcomes. When using corpora in the classroom, the question must be raised of which criteria are important to make corpora suitable and valuable for classroom use. Even though many publications make use of corpora which have been simply re-purposed for language teaching, the fact remains that most "[c]orpora have been built and annotated to meet research needs" (McEnery & Wilson 1997: 8). This has a number of implications, in particular in regard to corpus size, encoding style, and content, that potentially create unfavourable conditions when these corpora are used by non-expert corpus users, in this case language learners and teachers.

The size of corpora for research purposes, lexicography in particular, is of great importance.[43] Sinclair (1991a: 18) stated that "corpora should be as large

[43] Although it should be noted that more recently the value of smaller corpora for research has been increasingly recognised for in-depth study of "special uses of language, where the linguist can 'drill down' into the data in immense detail" (McCarthy & O'Keeffe 2010: 6)

as possible, and should keep on growing". Their size is a countermeasure to the fact that many linguistic items, in particular lexical items, are in fact quite infrequent. Once initial technical barriers were overcome, there has been virtually no limit to the size of modern super- or cyber-corpora (see Renouf 2007). Such corpora generally aim to cover a very broad range of language use and, ideally, provide numerous instances of as many linguistic items as possible. It is thus easy to imagine that a search of a multi-million word corpus can lead to search results that run into the thousands. The manual analysis of these is very laborious even for researchers. Certain techniques can be employed to cope with such large amounts of data (see Hunston 2002a: 52; Sinclair 1999: 166), and sophisticated software is now being developed to assist in the process of grouping or categorising results (see O'Donnell 2008). It is of course apparent that results lists of this magnitude are not desirable, much less manageable, in a language learning environment. A number of researchers have therefore advocated the use of small corpora for classroom applications. Aston (1997c: 55ff.), a strong proponent of small corpora, lists a number of advantages of these corpora for learning purposes:

- They are easier to manage.
- They are more fully analysable.
- They are easier to become familiar with.
- They are easier to interpret.
- They are easier to construct.
- They are more clearly patterned.
- Their limits are clearer.

Aston has contributed numerous publications on the subject of corpora and language teaching (e.g. Aston 1995, 1997a, 1997b, 1997c 2001a, 2004), and is keenly aware of the vast differences between research and classroom environments. He cautions that classroom concordancing activities with learners "do not permit inferences of similar descriptive reliability to those of corpus linguistics" (Aston 1995: 259). After all, the purpose of using corpora with learners is not to turn them into corpus linguists, but to utilise the full potential of corpora and corpus tools for discovery-type learning with attested language data in order to raise language awareness, foster learner autonomy, and increase language proficiency. Braun (2006) makes the point that, even though small corpora may not be suitable for lexicographical research purposes, in teaching they are still superior to traditional materials such as newspaper articles, individual video recordings, and so forth, because they offer a "more systematic range of material" (Braun 2006: 31). Above all, corpus data for learners have to be relevant and manageable. As a result of this, studies on corpus-based teaching are frequently based on small, custom-designed, and domain-specific corpora (e.g.

Chambers & O'Sullivan 2004; Cobb 1999; Kennedy & Miceli 2001, 2002, 2010). There are also advocates of large corpus browsing, which Bernardini (2000, 2001) refers to as serendipity learning. Johns (1988: 21) first coined this term for an approach which he describes as "a more free-ranging and open-ended type of investigation". However, while Johns bases this task on concordance printouts, Bernardini (2000) gives her learners direct access to a large corpus, namely the 100 million word *BNC*.[44]

Corpora for research on general language use have to be maximally representative of the target language under investigation. In other words, the corpus "must be representative in order to be appropriately used as the basis for generalizations concerning a language as a whole" (Biber 1993: 243). Designing a fully representative corpus is a complex task which involves decisions regarding accurate definition of the target language, choice of texts, and sample size to name a few (see also Section 2.3.1). Representativeness can be more easily achieved in the case of very specialised corpora of finite language subsets.[45] In contrast, general language corpora commonly consist of texts taken from a wide range of genres and topics in order to maximise representativeness. As a consequence, such corpora lack "intertextual coherence" (Braun 2005: 49) which Braun argues is an important aspect of pedagogically-motivated corpus design. According to Braun (2006), learners are more accustomed to working with complete texts and should therefore be able to do the same with corpora.

The content of corpora for research purposes is closely linked to the research objectives. For example, a study on teenage talk (Stenström, Andersen & Hasund 2002) is based on the *Bergen Corpus of London Teenage Language* (*COLT*).

Farr (2010b) bases her research on discourse of teaching practice feedback on a spoken corpus of feedback interactions as well as a corpus of tutor reports from teacher education, and the descriptions of university language in Biber (2006) are based on a spoken and written corpus of academic language (*T2K-SWAL*). The content of corpora for classroom use is directly connected to pedagogical requirements. Corpus data should be pedagogically useful, relevant to learning targets, and in correspondence with the learner's needs. Chambers and O'Sullivan (2004) come to a similar conclusion in their study on corpus consul-

---

44 It is worthwhile noting here that this type of discovery learning falls into the category of autonomous learning activities generally associated with more advanced learners. In fact, in one of her case studies (Bernardini 2001), the author herself is the 'learner' and she details her own experiences with the *BNC*. While English is not her first language, she is of course not only highly proficient in English but also possesses a professional level of research skills.

45 One recent example is the corpus of transcripts from the American sitcom *Friends* (Quaglio 2009). The author investigates television dialogue based on the complete transcripts of the show. This subset is finite and the corpus is thus fully representative.

tation to improve student writing skills. They indicate the one reason that the study returned positive results was "because the corpus, focusing as it did on the very topic on which the students were writing, was able to provide relevant search results despite its very limited size" (Chambers & O'Sullivan, 2004: 170).

Researchers are interested in arriving at accurate linguistic description based on which they can formulate grammatical rules and define lexical behaviour. In contrast, learners aim at mastering these rules and behaviours in order to apply them successfully in communicative contexts. A closer look at the distinction between samples and examples provides a helpful illustration for this discrepancy between expert and classroom user expectations and behaviour. When learners encounter examples in their textbooks and study materials, these are generally presented in order to illustrate a particular grammatical feature, for example. In contrast, concordances are simply the results from a search of a string of characters that require selection, categorisation, and interpretation. These results are referred to as 'samples'. Gavioli (2001) warns of the dangers that arise when learners are unaware of this distinction between 'samples' and 'examples':

> If learners treat corpus data as examples rather than samples, and assume that these will coherently illustrate a generalized principle of the type that they are accustomed to find provided by teachers and textbooks, they are likely to misunderstand and misuse the data in question. (Gavioli 2001: 113)

This observation leads to the question of the pedagogical usefulness of corpus data for language learners. Widdowson (2003: 102) observes that "*samples* of language data do not themselves serve as *examples* of language to learn from". It is the task of the teacher to mediate between corpus and learners and to instruct them on the limitations of corpora.

Pedagogic mediation of corpora is increasingly recognised to be a key feature of successful integration into the classroom setting. Corpora for teaching purposes should be designed "on the basis of theories which belong to applied rather than descriptive linguistics, focussing as much on the learner as the language" (Aston 2000: 16). This approach is in line with Widdowson's (1980) definition of 'applied linguistics' as opposed to 'linguistics applied'. Widdowson is in fact a strong proponent of pedagogic mediation of corpora. In his view, corpora contain language that was taken out of its context and as a result has lost its authenticity. Consequently, he questions whether this language resource can be useful for learners: "It is sometimes assumed to be self-evident that real language is bound to be motivating, but this must depend on whether learners can *make* it real" (Widdowson 2000: 7). Thus, it is of great importance that learners can relate to the texts in a corpus in order to authenticate the task of learning with the corpus. As a consequence, proposals for pedagogic corpora and pedagogically relevant corpora have recently been made.[46]

According to Willis (2003: 223), the pedagogic corpus "is made up of those texts which learners have read or listened to in the course of their studies".[47] He argues that "the best way to exemplify language for learners is to draw their attention to these texts, texts which are familiar to them" (2003: 223). There are a number of uses for pedagogic corpora. Firstly, teachers can use pedagogic corpora to draw attention to a particular linguistic item within the context of familiar text sources. Secondly, they can play an important role in materials design (e.g. Meunier & Gouverneur 2009;[48] Polezzi 1994). Thirdly, pedagogic corpora can be used in order to compare textbook materials with corpora of attested language use (e.g. Biber *et al.* 2004; Chujo 2004; Römer 2005).

Another form of pedagogic corpus is proposed by Allan (2009). The author proposes a corpus made up of graded reader texts which is aimed at intermediate level learners. The selection of these texts helps to "adjust the ratio of known to unknown words for learners with a more limited vocabulary" (Allan 2009: 25). Preliminary results of a comparative study she conducted with the graded reader corpus and the *BNC* suggest that "although some chunks in common usage may be screened out in the grading process and due to text genre, occurrences of chunks in the [...] graded corpus may reflect authentic language use quite closely" (2009: 30).

Pedagogically relevant corpora are designed specifically for and based on learner needs and classroom requirements. Such corpora aim to be relevant to the specific learning context, should be of manageable size, ideally contain audiovisual materials, and integrate well into existing corpora. There are two such pedagogically relevant corpora worth mentioning here: the *Padova Multimedia English Corpus* (*Padova MEC*) (Ackerley & Coccetta 2007) and the *English Language Interview Corpus as a Second-Language Application* (*ELISA*), (Braun 2005, 2006, 2007).

---

46 A note on terminology: in some cases researchers have used 'pedagogic' or 'pedagogical' corpora and 'pedagogically relevant corpora' interchangeably. As will be seen below, there is a difference.

47 Willis (1993) first mentions the concept of a pedagogic corpus in *Syllabus, corpus and data-driven learning*.

48 Meunier and Gouverneur (2009) have recently revisited the idea of the pedagogic corpus and created a pedagogically annotated corpus of textbook materials (*TeMa Corpus*) from a range of international textbooks for English for General Purposes. The purpose of the *TeMa Corpus* is to inform improved textbook design by investigating, for example, collocations presented across different textbooks, the weight of different pedagogical task types, and the use of tasks promoting cognitive processes. The authors argue that "[a]ccess to such type of information helps foster a flexible approach to textbook editing and provides evidence-based guidelines to improving textbooks" (Meunier & Gouverneur, 2009: 197)

Ackerley and Coccetta (2007: 352) rightly observe that "[t]he types of texts found in the corpus affect the kind and quality of the learning materials that can be drawn from it". Based on the *Common European Framework of Reference* (*CEFR*), they propose the design of a pedagogically relevant corpus which "is comprehensive in terms of functions, notions and topics, and that can be used across levels of difficulty" (2007: 352). The *Padova MEC* consists of audio and video recordings of scripted, semi-scripted and authentic texts. For the analysis of the corpus, a multimodal concordancer is employed. The authors argue that this type of information retrieval is superior to traditional text retrieval because the audiovisual component "can give greater access to more of the 'linguistic, situational, social, psychological, and pragmatic factors that influence the interpretation of any instance of language use' (Biber *et al.* 1999: 4) than text alone can" Ackerley & Coccetta 2007: 367).

This approach can also be seen as a successful way of overcoming criticism of corpora containing only decontextualised language. The unique attraction of corpora to language researchers is the possibility of investigating 'real' language use as captured in electronic corpora. However, the language data in corpora is commonly stored as plain text files which means that all previous formatting of the original text sources has disappeared, and any other contextual markers have been lost in the transfer from original to electronic format: "What was a blaring 72-point font newspaper headline appears in the same size and typeface as a medicine instructions leaflet" (Mishan 2004: 220). Some corpora can retain parts of the original format with the help of mark-up language (for example, SGML or XML as shown in Section 2.3.3) while they may also be enhanced by additional information that was previously not part of the original such as grammatical annotation – for example, POS tagging. Widdowson (2000) in particular is concerned with the pedagogical usefulness of corpora for learners. He argues that the "texts which are collected in a corpus have a reflected reality: they are only real because of the presupposed reality of the discourses of which they are a trace. This is decontextualised language, which is why it is only partially real" (Widdowson 2000: 7). Providing learners with the opportunity to access the original context of the data may well effectively counter this disadvantage. In the future, this approach may also prove useful for written language data; for example, by linking the electronic (plain) text with its original format (e.g. the layout of the original newspaper article).

General language corpora include texts from a wide array of topics and genres. This results in a possible lack of relevance for the respective learning context and it also creates lack of coherence because the "texts themselves usually remain an 'anonymous mass' to the learners" (Braun 2006: 26). The *ELISA Corpus* contains 25 video interviews with native speakers from various English-speaking countries. The interviews are about the professional careers of the participants. By focusing on a single topic and using short texts, Braun

(2006) proposes a different way of using corpora in the classroom in order to help learners in the contextualisation process:

> The starting point is a text-based exploration of the corpus content, focussing on the wider social and cultural context of the materials. The analysis on the basis of corpus techniques is intended to support the in-depth study of linguistic means of expression in familiar texts. (Braun 2006: 29)

In other words, non-linear corpus exploitation with concordances should be preceded by full-text exploration (Braun 2007: 309). Braun (2006: 39) also proposes pedagogical enrichments to accompany a pedagogically relevant corpus, ranging from audiovisual materials to ready-made corpus analysis results that can "help learners and teachers who are not familiar with corpus techniques or do not have the time, tools or occasion to apply them to nevertheless benefit from these techniques".[49]

Pedagogically relevant corpora provide a valuable resource for a range of learning activities. They appear particularly useful for low level or intermediate language learners. Indeed, Braun (2007) conducted a case study at a secondary school in Germany with the *ELISA Corpus*. Although the results of the study were mostly positive, the author concluded that more research is necessary for "teacher training and perhaps a better understanding of the pedagogical (as opposed to the linguistic) needs of corpus analysis" (Braun 2007: 326). In the following section, concordancing software, the second element of the corpus investigation process, will be analysed based on exactly that premise – that is, the profile of classroom as opposed to research users.

4.3.2 Core element: software

At the centre of the corpus investigation process lies the second element, the concordancing software. In the process of analysing corpora, the concordancer takes on a central role. It provides the interface between machine-readable corpus and human user. Through the concordancer the user communicates with the electronic text source and can retrieve any given string of characters, count word frequencies, and collect collocation information. Similarly to the other two elements, corpus and user, concordancing software has to be adapted to the pedagogical context in order to be integrated successfully. While the issues surrounding the elements corpus and user have received close attention from

[49] Amador Moreno *et al.* (2006) also concluded from their study of using classroom discourse corpora with teacher trainees that the participants would have preferred a visual component of this valuable resource.

researchers in the past, concordancing software has so far not been thoroughly investigated in relation to transferring it from research to pedagogical context. Therefore, in this section, I will focus on the role of the concordancer in the process of applying corpus technology directly in language education and argue that the prerequisites and requirements of research versus classroom application differ markedly. In order to design truly 'user-friendly' software for learners and teachers, respective user-profiles thus have to be created.

The concordancer is the standard user interface for electronic corpora. As we have seen in Section 2.3.2, basic functions of a concordancer include word search, frequency count, and collocation search. In the past, concordancing software could only process texts of a limited size. With the help of high-speed computers, programs can now process millions of words within minutes or even seconds. The KWIC display is the main feature of a concordancer. It presents the results from a corpus search in the form of three columns: the left context, the keyword itself in the centre, and the right context. This particular display has created a new perspective on language that corpus linguistics has become famous for and which has led to the discovery of patterns in language that were previously not discernable. Tribble and Jones (1997: 3) note that "the real value of the concordancer lies in this question of visibility". Without the powerful search and display functions of the concordancer, the electronic corpus would be little more useful to the user than a traditional collection of text in paper format that can only be searched manually.

The most fundamental difference between research and classroom use of concordancing software lies in the initial motivation of the user to employ corpus technology. For researchers, the concordancer is a tool that allows them to pursue their professional research endeavours. In this respect, the program fulfils a function and aids in the process of achieving a research objective, and, while various products are available, there is little alternative to a concordancer when conducting corpus-based research. In this professional context, the program has to process very large amounts of text, offer extremely versatile search functionality, and statistical evaluation tools. Such tools often come at the price of being rather complex and require researchers to invest time in order to familiarise themselves with the software. As an integral part of their work, researchers may well employ a concordancer over a long period of time and for a variety of research projects. Thus, despite the initial time and effort required in order to master the program, the benefits pay off in the long run. The concordancer is simply the necessary means to an end; as such, the motivation to learn how to use the program is high as it equals the motivation to achieve the user's research goals.

The situation in the classroom context is markedly different. Despite much enthusiasm for the approach and the potential benefits of classroom concordancing, it remains a voluntary component – that is, an addition in an often crowded curriculum where it has to compete for time and attention with a wide array of materials and resources. This significant difference in motivation to use a concordancer has a direct impact on the willingness of learners and teachers to invest time in order to master its functions.

When using a concordancer, whether in a research or classroom context, skills on two levels are required. Firstly, the user has to acquire the technical aspects of the software. This requires general information technology (IT) skills and an ability to master the functions specific to concordancing software. Secondly, using a concordancer requires a certain degree of linguistic knowledge and understanding. In regard to language learners, Aston (1997c: 52) notes that it "is not just a matter of technical skills in using concordancing software. It involves selecting appropriate corpora or subcorpora to interrogate, designing appropriate queries, and appropriately interpreting the results of those queries". It is important to recognise that learners and teachers with no or little prior experience with concordancing software or linguistic analysis face these two challenges at the same time and that "the process of getting to grips with the software invariably shades into getting to grips with the techniques of linguistic analysis" (Leech 1997: 9).

Another point to consider is that unfamiliarity with computer technology continues to play a role in the educational context and therefore needs to be taken into account. In relation to teachers, Tribble (2000: 31) notices "that there is still a high level of techno-fear out there", and, in a report on language learners' experiences with large corpora, Bernardini (2002: 169) reports that she "was surprised to discover how many students are still technophobic and approach new software and tasks involving corpus use with suspicion". Seidlhofer (2002: 216) comes to the same conclusion and, in the particular context of using computers for linguistic analyses, Mukherjee (2004: 249) points out that "[t]his negative attitude towards the computer-based description and analysis of language does not usually change once these students have obtained their degree and become [...] qualified teachers". It is interesting to note that even in very recent studies (see, e.g. Estling Vannestål & Lindquist 2007; Farr 2008) technical difficulties reported by students were reported by learners as a notably negative aspect of using corpora. Thus, it appears that despite the fact that computers are seemingly omnipresent in everyday life, computer proficiency beyond using the internet and email continues to be problematic.

As discussed above, researchers potentially have a high motivation to use a concordancer and may therefore be more willing to invest time and effort into mastering even a complex program because of its long-term benefits. Researchers can be expected to already possess extensive skills in their field of research, and a potential lack in IT skills can be adjusted through their high motivation to master the program. Classroom users, on the other hand, have to overcome difficulties on a linguistic and technological level in order to successfully use concordancers for their purposes. When typical time constraints of the classroom context are factored into the equation, an indication begins to emerge as to why classroom practitioners may remain hesitant about using corpus technology.

Based on the observations above, we can create profiles for the two user groups that will provide the basis for a user-centred software design presented in Chapter 7:

Table 4-1: User profiles for research and classroom

Research user	Classroom user
• High motivation to use concordancer as it is directly linked to desire to achieve research goals and likely to be used for more than one project.	• Concordancer is an optional component in crowded curriculum; motivation to use may initially be low to medium.
• Learning to use the software limited to technical aspects due to prior existing research skills; desire to master these linked to underlying motivation to use for research.	• Particularly learners but also teachers have to acquire skills on two levels: linguistic research and general IT skills in order to operate the software confidently.
• Complex range of features required; for example, sophisticated search functions and statistical tools; must have capacity to process very large corpora and cope with annotation.	• Basic functions including word search and frequency information may suffice; other features more important, such as exporting KWIC-results for materials development.
• Concordancers can be employed for a multitude of linguistic and literary analyses; useful tool for future research projects.	• Concordancer is used as linguistic informant for teachers; for example, to generate teaching materials or as an exploratory tool for learners.

Regarding the use of corpus technology in language pedagogy, Johns, who is otherwise a strong proponent of classroom concordancing, cautions that direct applications of corpora in the classroom present teachers with a multitude of challenges to overcome (see Johns 2002: 107). At least technical difficulties linked to the use of concordancing software can be minimised with software that is designed with the classroom user in mind. Wyatt (1987: 86) points out that successful CALL software design is based on the needs of the user and hinges on "the 'fit' between the computer's capabilities and the demands of language pedagogy". This "closeness of 'fit'" (Levy 1997: 163) is a significant factor in the design process: "If the fit is not good, then the use of technology will probably be rejected; alternatively, if the fit is a good one then the CALL option is probably feasible" (Levy 1997: 164).

While the attraction of classroom concordancing lies mostly in the same functions required by researchers, teachers and learners have a different user profile, and thus user-friendly software for them necessarily differs from user-friendly software for researchers. I propose that the design for a tailor-made concordancer for language teachers and learners has to take into account their motivation to use the program, their IT and linguistics skills, the purpose of use, and the range of functions required for the classroom context. In Chapter 7, I will address this in the form of a blueprint for the software *My Concordancer*, a proposal of corpus technology *for* language pedagogy.

4.3.3 Core element: user

> In view of the range of opportunities they offer, corpora would seem to be powerful learning resources for a user who is able to exploit them effectively.
>
> (Aston 1997b: 206-207)

The transfer of corpora and corpus analysis software from research to classroom practice entails a number of challenges which were discussed in Sections 4.3.1 and 4.3.2. These challenges can be largely attributed to the differences in the user profiles of researchers and classroom users respectively. In particular, the areas of skill, motivation, and time constraints are notably dissimilar. This section will focus on the third element of the corpus investigation process: the user. The challenges, which are present for this group when transferring corpora from a research environment into the educational setting, will be highlighted. Two main groups of classroom users can be identified: learners and teachers. These groups may also include language teacher trainees and teacher educators respectively. It will be argued that the key to a successful transfer from research to classroom for these users is above all appropriate training. In the following discussion, the challenges learners and teachers face when working with corpora will be identified and proposals for solutions will be made. The outcomes of this analysis will provide the rationale and framework for the research presented in Chapters 5, 6, and 7.

4.3.4 The learner as researcher

> Even if we wish to be maximally learner-centred, or construct the learner as a 'researcher', he or she needs skills and guidance in dealing with the kind of data a corpus provides.
>
> (Mauranen 2004b: 99)

When researchers employ corpora for research projects, the ultimate goal in some form or another is to learn more about language. Accurate and reliable descriptions of language use are the ultimate goal of such undertakings. Researchers have to invest a considerable amount of time and possess a high level of linguistic skills in order to produce the desired results. These outcomes should have scientific validity and withstand further examination by fellow researchers. The value of corpora for language learning purposes is not necessarily seen in the outcomes but rather in the processes involved. Language learners generally aim to learn a language, rather than to learn about it (although this happens to be a beneficial side effect of corpus-based learning). As Aston (1997b: 209) points out "[m]ost learners' objectives are to be able to *use* the language, and finding out *about* language is often only of interest when its relevance to potential communicative concerns is apparent". In addition, learners are only in the process of acquiring proficiency in a language, while researchers generally already are highly proficient, if not native speakers of the language in question. In sum, learners and researchers differ greatly in regard to language and research skills, motivation to use corpus tools, and time constraints. Thus, if learners are expected to make use of corpora and corpus tools in any form, they require first and foremost adequate training.

The level and amount of training required depends very much on the type of learning activity one has in mind and the user profile of the respective learner group. On a "cline of learner autonomy" (Mukherjee 2006b: 12), corpus-based activities can range from very basic, fully teacher-controlled exercises to learner-centred, autonomous, and research-like activities that would appear suitable only for the most advanced learners. The issue of training learners has been addressed in a multitude of publications (e.g. Allan 1999; Chambers 2005; Chang & Sun 2009; Estling Vannestål & Lindquist 2007; Farr 2008; Gavioli 1997, 2001; Götz & Mukherjee 2006; Kennedy & Miceli 2001, 2002, 2010; O'Sullivan 2007; Yoon & Hirvela 2004). The following key concerns affecting learner training emerge from these studies:

(i) computer literacy,
(ii) corpus literacy, and
(iii) learner type and attitudes.

While each study has slightly different parameters – for instance, in terms of learner type, educational setting, or teaching goals – some consensus appears to have formed in regard to the best way of training learners. Firstly, a gradual approach, which has been likened to an "apprenticeship" (Kennedy & Miceli 2001: 79), has found widespread support. In particular, for learners who have little or no prior knowledge of the subject, the initial learning curve can be steep (Sun 2003). Corpus-based teaching potentially involves a threefold challenge for the uninitiated: a new learning resource (the corpus), unfamiliar technology (the corpus analysis software), and a challenging new form of learning (DDL). As will become evident below, concordance printouts are now recognised as a gentle way of introducing this type of learning activity to learners (Boulton, forthcoming a). In addition, the use of scaffolding devices has proven to be successful particularly in relation to developing corpus literacy in learners (e.g. Chang & Sun 2009). Finally, the crucial importance of teacher mediation and guidance is more and more recognised (e.g. Charles 2007; Granath 2009; Kaltenböck & Mehlmauer-Larcher 2005). The implications of this for the teacher's role and for teacher training will occupy the following section and the remaining chapters of this study. The discussion below on the key concerns of learner training provides the basis for this.

(i) Computer literacy

Computers play a key role in corpus research, and, as discussed in the previous section, researchers can be expected to invest considerable time and effort into mastering the technological aspects of using corpus analysis software. However, computer literacy among learners and teachers, particularly in the Humanities, remains an issue, despite the fact that computers appear to be omnipresent in many shapes or forms. Indeed, difficulties due to technological aspects of the corpus-based approach have been noted by a number of researchers (e.g. Bernardini 2002; Estling Vannestål & Lindquist 2007; Farr 2008). Estling Vannestål and Lindquist (2007: 344) report from their study with first year English students that "[o]ne of the most negative experiences was the technical problems that the students encountered". Another study with pre-service teachers showed that "the complexity of the software was and continued to be an issue throughout" (Farr 2008: 34). As we have seen in Section 4.3.2 on the core element software, a maximally user-friendly concordancer designed for classroom users is an essential requisite for the successful integration of corpora. However, particularly in the case of low-proficiency-level learners, a simple solution to bypass technology concerns in an introduction to corpora is to use concordance printouts prepared by the teacher. This approach, which Gabrielatos (2005) describes as the "*soft version*" of DDL, has a number of advantages: it is a medium that learners are well-familiar with, no time is lost on setting up computers and dealing with possible technical difficulties, and lastly, concordances can be edited by the teacher and therefore result in easier classroom management. Willis (1998) shows that even learning activities based entirely on hand-written concordances (created by learners themselves) can be extremely valuable. She concludes that "using hand-generated concordances to focus on common words can provide a wealth of effective learning opportunities" (Willis 1998: 62-63).

It is significant to note that using concordance printouts also has some limitations. The number of samples in concordances is limited, and the selection of concordance lines is pre-determined by the teacher. Some may argue that such activities therefore risk losing the explorative, learner-driven character typical of DDL. In addition, the flexibility of changing the order of samples in concordances and to sort the left or right context, in order to make patterns more visible, is lost. However, these disadvantages also have benefits. A limited number of samples can help to prevent learners from feeling overwhelmed, tasks can be much more guided, and at the introductory stage more likely lead to successful learning events. Leech (1997: 10) rightly observes that 'the easy way' "ensures that the maximum number of students are able and willing to participate in this kind of learning experience". As learners get more accustomed to concordance analysis, 'live' concordancing on the computer can be introduced, and the range of tasks requiring more learner initiative can be expanded.

(ii) Corpus literacy

Based on their evaluation of DDL in university teaching, Götz and Mukherjee (2006: 59) come to the conclusion that "the acquisition of some kind of 'corpus literacy' (cf. Mukherjee 2002: 179) seems to be *the* most central prerequisite for a successful integration of DDL activities". The term 'corpus literacy' is still quite new, and "one future research need is the specification of what corpus literacy should include" (2006: 59). Within the framework of language learning environments, it is proposed here that learner corpus literacy should include the ability to

a) read the truncated format of concordance lines;
b) deal with large amounts of authentic text, including potentially unknown vocabulary;
c) conduct successful corpus searches (wildcards, etc.); and
d) interpret results by observing patterns and drawing valid conclusions.

Dealing with truncated lines in concordances appears to be non-problematic for most learners and difficult for some. A close examination of learner studies with corpora reveals that, although there is mention of isolated cases where learners are initially confused or frustrated by this format (Allan 1999; Chambers 2005; Yoon & Hirvela 2004), the majority of studies appear to suggest that truncated concordances either do not pose a significant challenge or that initial difficulties are quickly overcome. In fact, Stevens (1991b: 55) finds in his study on gap-filler exercises with concordance lines that "having multiple if disjunct contexts helps [the learners] more in settling on a correct word than do the clues inherent in a passage of discourse with the same words missing". Furthermore, the truncated format of concordance lines provides other valuable learning opportunities. Learners can be encouraged to finish sentences on both sides of the keyword, complete words that have been arbitrarily truncated in the context, complete a whole paragraph around one concordance line, or guess the genre of this respective line (Honeyfield 1989; Johns 1986).

When working with authentic text corpora, learners inevitably encounter unfamiliar vocabulary. Johns (1988: 10) rightly remarks that this "approach can of course, present difficulties if students believe or have been led to believe that to understand *anything* they should understand *everything*". Very little hard data is currently available to draw on in order to determine whether this actually poses a problem for learners. A notable exception is a study on corpus use in ESL academic writing courses (Yoon & Hirvela 2004). Two courses, with both intermediate and advanced ESL learners, were included in this study, and a survey showed that the majority of the course participants did not perceive unfamiliar vocabulary in the concordances as difficult (Yoon & Hirvela 2004: 270). Teacher-led exercises can help learners to acquire strategies in order to deal with unknown vocabulary which is an important skill when reading authentic texts. The vertical reading of concordances may even support this process, and ideally learners will eventually develop strategies for coping better with texts that contain unfamiliar words. This is important as Dodd (1997: 132-133) believes that in order to benefit from concordancing tasks, learners have to "reach a point at which they are not unduly worried if they do not recognize every language item in the context. But depending on the exercise, this point may come relatively early".

The metaphor 'learner as researcher', which is frequently employed to describe DDL activities, seemingly implies that learners are simulating the researcher's task of producing accurate language descriptions. A more fitting and less taxing metaphor might be the one of learners as 'language detectives' (Johns 1997: 101) as this highlights the true potential of direct corpus applications portraying language as a mystery to be solved (Granger & Tribble 1998) without implying learners act as corpus linguists:

> After all, the major advantage of DDL is that it presents language as 'an intriguing mystery to be explored' (Hawkins 1984: 138). In such a paradigm learners can become active participants in this 'voyage of discovery into the patterns of the language' (ibid.: 150), a voyage which may induce increased motivation for foreign language learning, including some of its hitherto least popular components, such as grammar. (Granger & Tribble 1998: 209)

Typically, the analysis of concordance lines involves categorising the occurrences of a particular linguistic item, identifying regularities, and drawing valid conclusions from the observed data. Gavioli (1997: 109) remarks that "[t]hese processes of observation and generalization may seem banal, but they can pose many difficulties to learners". These difficulties include managing concordances with too many results, identifying different patterns of use, and categorising them correctly (see Gavioli 2001: 110-113). As opposed to researchers, who can be expected to be highly advanced, if not native speakers of the language in question, learners are at a distinct disadvantage due to their lack of language proficiency. Gavioli (1997: 109) rightly remarks that "learners, because they are not native speakers of the language, cannot rely on their intuitions to guide and back up their observations and to suggest and reinforce explanatory generalizations".

As part of their study on *Intermediate Students' Approaches to Corpus Consultation*, Kennedy and Miceli (2001: 87) reported that while language proficiency had some role to play as a cause of invalid findings by learners, they identified "specific problems that seemed to be due to inadequate corpus-investigation skills". It is worthwhile mentioning here that, in the case of this study, Kennedy and Miceli (2001) were aiming at training their students to be able to use concordancing autonomously and outside of the classroom. The authors have since revised their strategies and implementation procedures. In particular, for the initial stages of training their students, they decided to "downplay the learner-as-researcher notion" (Kennedy & Miceli 2010: 30) and "introduce them with 'observe and borrow' mentality first, before progressing to an 'observe and derive rules' approach" (Miceli & Kennedy 2002: 92). The use of scaffolding devices has been shown to be particularly effective in this regard. Kennedy and Miceli (2001) propose a step-by-step learning guide for their students that help them to develop better corpus investigation skills. Each research step is accompanied by questions that help students to make better decisions and improve their interpreting techniques. As part of a study on developing proofreading skills in senior high school students, Chang and Sun (2009) propose a software solution to scaffolding that interjects a series of prompts during the process of concordancing. These prompts supply information regarding keyword selection, concordance analysis, rule formulation, and outcome evaluation. The authors concluded that the experimental group using the concordancer with scaffolding prompts outperformed the control group which used the concordancer without scaffolding.

Such a gradual and guided approach to training learners allows for variance in individual learning styles and gives learners the opportunity "to progress at their own pace towards conducting independent and productive concordance investigations" (Turnbull & Burston 1998: 12). This is of great of significance in order to ensure that different learner types can cope equally well with this learning tool.

(iii) Learner types and attitudes

When Johns (1986) first proposed his software *MicroConcord* for the use with language learners, he had a particular type of learner in mind:

> adult: well motivated: a sophisticated learner with experience of research methods in his subject area [...] with particular needs (fairly closely specifiable in terms of target texts) in a particular learning/teaching situation (in which a great deal of emphasis is placed on developing students' learning strategies and on their responsibility for their own learning). (Johns 1986: 161)

Indeed, the majority of studies on corpus-based teaching involve intermediate to advanced learners in a tertiary context. It is only more recently that studies in a secondary learning environment have been emerging (e.g. Braun 2007; Ciesielska-Ciupek 2001; Johns, Hsingchin & Lixun 2008; Lee & Liou 2003; Maddalena 2001; Rohrbach 2003; Sun & Wang 2003). Similarly, studies with beginners are rare, and in some cases these learners turn out to be false beginners (Hadley 2002) or in one case a highly-motivated linguistics student (St John 2001). Johns (1986: 161) himself cautions that it is not clear whether or not this kind of "research methodology" can be applied with other learners. However, in a later article he is more optimistic and proposes that "most students given the opportunity to show what they are capable of might be (almost) as remarkable" (Johns 1991a: 12). Boulton (2009a) investigated learning styles in relation to learner responses on corpus use. The experiment was a very controlled approach of introducing DDL to a group of French lower-intermediate students studying for an English test as part of their degree requirements. The learners participated in a questionnaire with closed and open questions on their reactions to the DDL activities. The results from this questionnaire were subsequently cross-checked with the results from the Index for Learning Style index. The findings suggested that "DDL should be accessible to learners with a variety of different preferences" (Boulton 2009a, 'Conclusion', para. 3). More studies are needed in order to come to any general conclusions.

In addition to factors like language proficiency, learning style, and educational setting, learner attitudes can also play an important role in the process of introducing learners to corpus-based activities. These can be fundamentally at odds with researchers' beliefs and opinions on using corpora. Learners tend to have a preference for clear rules and definitive answers, while researchers are much more excited about new questions that pave the way for future research endeavours. Granath (2009: 49) reports that speakers at a colloquium on corpora and language teaching mentioned that "corpora ruin students' regulated world. Students want simple, straightforward answers, and are disappointed by the 'blurry' responses they get from corpora". In fact, the 'fuzzy' nature of language, a view that has emerged as a result of corpus linguistic research, can be very unsettling for learners and difficult to deal with in the classroom environment. This issue will be considered in more detail in the case study below in Chapter 6 in relation to teaching the rules of using *some* and *any*.

Another aspect to consider is that learners may not be as enthusiastic about becoming active, autonomous participants in their learning process as researchers may like them to be. Whistle (1999) stresses that in order to

> get students to move from a passive to an active role requires time and effort. When asked at the beginning of the year in a questionnaire how they thought they learned grammar best, 87% of Year 1 and 85% of Year 2 thought it was by having things explained by the teacher. (Whistle 1999: 451)

Furthermore, other factors, for instance cultural background, may have to be considered. Stevens (1991a: 36) points out that "there is a large subset of language learners who through cultural influences or academic immaturity cannot be expected to search automatically for patterns in a welter of linguistic data". However, studies in the educational context of Taiwan have recently shown that these learners, although presumably very used to a deductive learning approach, have performed well on inductive-type corpus tasks (see, e.g. Chan & Liou 2005).

It is becoming evident from the analysis above that training learners to use corpora is not a simple matter but is a process influenced by a number of variables. Kaltenböck and Mehlmauer-Larcher (2005) keenly observe that

> [t]he learners' age, their general level of language competence, levels of expert knowledge and the learners' attitude towards increasing their learner autonomy all have to be taken into consideration when

> deciding on how corpora can be used in a foreign language learning context. (Kaltenböck & Mehlmauer-Larcher 2005: 80-81)

There is a growing recognition that the unmediated use of corpora is not a feasible option in a traditional, curriculum-driven educational setting. Pedagogical mediation by the teacher is thus a key factor in designing successful corpus-based teaching. The following section examines the role of the teacher and resulting implications for teacher training.

4.3.5 The teacher as research guide

As we have seen in the previous section, learners face a number of challenges when using corpora in a formal language learning setting. While these challenges are closely connected to the transfer of research tools and methods into the classroom environment, other factors that play an important role are learner language proficiency, meta-linguistic skills, attitudes towards learning, and their willingness to gain increased (learner) autonomy. When Johns (1991a) suggested the direct use of corpora with learners, his main rationale was to give learners unfiltered access to language data in the form of corpora, so that learners could act as 'language detectives' and conduct 'research' in the classroom. He envisaged that learners become researchers and teachers become research directors (Johns 1988). However, when he defined the DDL method as "an attempt to cut out the middleman" (Johns 1991b: 30) he was not referring to the teacher at all, as some have interpreted this (e.g. Boulton 2009b: 82), but to the edited, didacticised materials that learners are usually presented with. Johns based this proposal on "the underlying assumption [...] that effective language learning is a form of linguistic research" (Johns 1991b: 30).

Johns neither underestimated the key role of the teacher nor the challenges to that role in such a learning environment. Indeed, he pointed out early on that the direct use of corpora in the classroom involves "a shift in the traditional division of roles between student and teacher" (Johns 1988: 14). The teacher "has to learn to become a director and coordinator of student-initiated research" (Johns 1991a: 3). That is a change which Johns concedes "can be difficult for teachers to come to terms with" (1991a: 3). The role of the teacher thus does not become one of less importance or involvement, yet it changes quite significantly. In a later article, Johns (2002: 107) concedes that "[f]or the practising teacher, the direct use of concordance data in language teaching poses a number of challenges: technical, linguistic, logistic, pedagogical and philosophical". At the same time, it must be recognised that the teacher plays a most significant part in the integration of DDL into the language classroom. As Leech remarks, "a corpus enables the learner/student to explore, to investigate, to generalize, to test hypotheses; but it does not itself initiate or direct the path of learning" (1997: 5). This task is left to the teacher.

The previous section has shown that appropriate training for learners is an essential prerequisite for successful integration of corpora, and that teacher guidance is a vital factor in ensuring successful learning events and to assist learners in gaining a sound understanding of how to use corpora. It is becoming more and more evident that this task of training learners is quite complex and challenging for teachers. Indeed, Estling Vannestål and Lindquist (2007: 344) conclude from their study with first-semester English students in Sweden that "introducing the use of corpora to students requires a great deal of time, support, patience, enthusiasm and reflection from the teacher". In particular, three factors add significantly to the demands on the teacher:

(i) the current lack of materials,
(ii) fundamental changes to the traditional role of the teacher, and
(iii) the task of integrating corpora into traditional curricula.

These factors will be discussed in detail below.

(i) Lack of materials

The limited availability of ready-to-use corpus teaching materials is a major contributing factor that increases the challenge for teachers significantly. Kennedy and Miceli (2010: 29), who have jointly run language courses with a corpus component for many years, have concluded that "mastering corpus consultation [is] a gradual, long-term process that needs to be treated as an integral part of the overall language-learning process". Currently, direct corpus applications are neither a standard component in curricula nor in textbooks. This means that not only are corpus teaching materials not readily available but, in addition, teachers have to somehow achieve the task of integration into the learning process by themselves, presuming that their students are unfamiliar with corpora. Of course, most reference materials such as dictionaries and grammars are corpus-based nowadays. Furthermore, there are isolated examples of corpus-informed teaching materials, such as the ELT textbook series *Touchstone* which is based on the *Cambridge and Nottingham Corpus of Discourse in English* (*CANCODE*) corpus (see McCarthy 2004). In addition, a number of stand-alone products comprising corpus-based activities for English are available, for instance the *Collins COBUILD Concordance Samplers* (Goodale 1993, 1995), *Classroom Concordancing* (Tribble & Jones 1997), the concordancing workbook *Exploring Academic English* (Thurstun & Candlin 1997), and, for American English, the recently published *CorpusLAB* series (Barlow & Burdine

2006; Burdine & Barlow 2007). Yet, these materials still leave the teacher with a number of challenges to overcome. The teacher has to assess these materials for their appropriateness in the respective learning context (e.g. language proficiency level, suitable vocabulary) and achieve a meaningful integration into their respective curriculum. Given that so few 'classroom-ready' materials are currently available, chances are high that they do not in fact match the individual teacher's needs. The other option available to teachers is to create their own materials, which, in addition to the above mentioned, adds even more challenges to the list. These include finding or creating an appropriate corpus, acquiring and learning how to work with concordancing software, creating meaningful exercises, and producing worksheets. The process of creating such materials has been reported to be extremely time-consuming (see also Boulton 2008a). In regard to the process of preparing corpus-based teaching materials, Charles (2007) observes the following:

> For the writer/teacher, the use of this approach requires access to a suitable corpus, and a high degree of familiarity with the data is necessary in order to choose searches that prove rewarding. This entails a relatively high cost in preparation time, as each potentially useful search must be carried out in advance, the lines analysed and the value of the concordance data in supporting a given teaching point established before the search can be included in the materials. (Charles 2007: 298)

As part of the case study presented in Chapter 6 below, the challenges and difficulties associated with this process will be analysed during the evaluation of the DDL task created by the participants.

Despite his own enthusiasm for the approach, Johns (1991b: 36) comes to the conclusion that direct applications of concordancing in the classroom "represent a considerable challenge to the teacher's own linguistic sophistication and powers of induction [...] a challenge which has implications for teacher-training which go far beyond the scope and aims of 'computer familiarisation'". He emphasises that this "challenge would be even more severe if we expected each classroom teacher to prepare a full range of teaching materials on the basis of concordance output. Clearly, such an expectation would be highly unrealistic" (Johns 1991b: 36). This emphasises the urgent need for more teaching materials with concrete teaching suggestions, and, perhaps more importantly, corpus-based teaching materials which are integrated into existing textbooks.

(ii) Changes to the traditional role of the teacher

In addition to problems related to the lack of resources, teachers have to possess a certain degree of corpus literacy in order to teach with these materials and integrate them meaningfully into the classroom. One important question to be addressed is just what that level of competence in corpus skills is. Mukherjee (2009) has recently defined corpus literacy in the context of teacher education as the ability to solve linguistic problems independently and competently by using appropriate corpora and corpus software (see 2009: 173). In addition, corpus literacy should also include the ability to compile DIY (do-it-yourself) corpora for specific learning or teaching purposes (see 2009: 175). This definition of corpus literacy is comparable to skills expected of researchers in this area. In order to achieve this (albeit desirable) level of competence in teachers, considerable resources would have to be dedicated to training teachers in corpus linguistics respectively. Evidence provided by the survey of teacher educators in Germany (presented in Chapter 5) suggests that this may prove to be a difficult task, particularly in light of the fact that curricula are perceived to be full already, and that the relevance of this approach may still not be apparent to the majority of educators.

It must also be noted that in order to teach with corpora, the skills required of teachers go beyond mere corpus literacy. Teachers have to successfully guide learners, who will most likely be novice users of corpora, through their training of corpus consultation skills. Especially in the case of non-native speakers, some teachers may not feel competent enough to guide learners through corpus analysis because "once the concordancer becomes an important focus of activity in the classroom, many old certainties start to crumble (e.g. the central position of the syllabus and of the teacher's key at the back of the textbook)" (Johns 1991a: 3). Such issues represent major challenges, both pedagogically and linguistically, to the traditional role of the teacher in the classroom and require more attention in future studies. The following situation described by Hadley (2002) is an interesting example to consider in this context:

> [O]nce a student asked me about a certain frequency of collocations with a phrasal verb. Before I could stop myself, I gave a student a ridiculous rule that I felt at the time would explain the situation. The student looked at me for a moment, blinking in a cool, unimpressed manner. She then went on to produce evidence from the concordancer about why my rule was unsound! Embarrassed but happy that the student made this observation, I congratulated her on her discovery and apologized for my blunder. (Hadley 2002: 119)

Most teachers would most likely rather not experience a situation such as this. Furthermore, Boulton (2009b: 93) points out that "[i]n many cultures, the teacher is not allowed not to know: admitting ignorance is unthinkable". In theory, the direct corpus approach encourages discovery learning and part of the attraction of that approach is the unknown outcome, the discovering of facts side by side, teacher and learner together on the same level. However, in practice, classroom management and traditional expectations about the learner's and the teacher's role are impacted by this rather different approach to learning, and this may be a change that is not readily welcomed by either group. Johns's experience was that the DDL approach tended "to divide language teachers into two camps. Some have reacted with enthusiasm [...]. Others have been puzzled by it" (Johns 1988: 9). He goes on the explain that "[t]his division has little to do with language teachers' alleged fear of computer technology, and a great deal to do with underlying assumptions about the nature of language learning and the role of the teacher in that process" (1988: 9). It is not easy for teachers to change the role of "being the expert in what is grammatically correct and what is incorrect to being a facilitator for creating a learning environment where the student has to reach decisions about appropriateness for themselves" (Bloch 2009: 59). It is argued here that this is a change that requires a lot of confidence supported by high-level language proficiency, sophisticated corpus research skills, and general teaching experience. In the case of non-native teachers, this challenge may be greater again as the language they are teaching is not their own, and they may not be as confident in relying on their intuitions about the language. Seemingly, this has been largely overlooked in the literature so far. Hunston (2002a), for example, points out what appears to be a simple use of corpora as a reference resource in the classroom:

> A teacher wishing to demonstrate to a learner why a particular usage is incorrect can show evidence instead of resorting to tortuous, and possibly inexact, explanations. (Hunston 2002a: 214)

In this scenario of the corpus as a 'sleeping resource' (Johns 1988: 22), at least one computer equipped with a concordancer and a corpus is needed. It basically just sits there until a question arises that requires some "research on the hop" (Johns 1988: 23). Such a question may be "What is the difference between *therefore* and *hence*?" or "When do you say *classic* and when *classical*?". Together with the teacher, the learners can then investigate these features using concordance lines and discover the rules themselves. However, this process is not quite as straightforward as it may sound. The teacher cannot know if the corpus will illustrate the point in question, and the corpus may produce evidence that allows for more than one type of interpretation. The question then is how to handle this in the classroom. It is these kinds of questions that future research on teaching with corpora must address if more teachers are expected to use corpora as part of their teaching practices. This example also shows that teachers require training not only in how to use corpora but also how to teach with them.

(iii) The task of integrating corpora

Once the realisation had set in that the enthusiasm by researchers was not reflected in mainstream teaching, more thought was given as to how to popularise this approach and how to go about integrating corpora in traditional language learning settings. It is important to take into consideration that each time a teacher wants to introduce corpus activities to a new class of learners, this teacher has to fulfil the demanding task of integration. Even if only concordance printouts are used, the process is still a complex one, fraught with pitfalls and challenges to the teacher. As stated above, in particular for low-level and intermediate-level learners, the teacher must be well-trained in these methods and resources in order to "find the right balance, and tailor the methodology to the type of learner and the stage of learning" (Johansson 2007: 26).

In particular, the process of directing learners from "maximum guidance to maximum independence" (Gavioli 2005: 127) is difficult and highly demanding for the teacher. Farr (2010a: 621) rightly remarks that such "[n]ew-found learner roles mean more freedom but also more mediational responsibility for the teacher". It is not a simple task and one that above all requires a high level of skills in terms of familiarity with computers, corpora, and linguistics in general. Johns (1986: 159) points out early on that "it is important that teachers themselves should have experience in using concordance output if they expect their students to make use of it". It is becoming increasingly clear that this experience needs to be quite substantial; that is, teachers need to have a sound understanding of corpus analysis in order to teach with it. This leads to the question as to when and how teachers should acquire this skill set. The context of LTE "has the potential to be the core of diffusion for new ideas and practices" (Farr 2010a: 622), and thus provides valuable opportunities to meaningfully integrate corpora and corpus-based teaching and to devote sufficient time to the subject to allow for in-depth exploration.

A growing number of publications are dealing with corpora as tools in LTE for increasing language awareness in teacher trainees and improving their language proficiency (e.g. Allan 1999, 2002; Chambers 2005; Coniam 1997; Farr 2008; Hunston 1995b; Tsui 2004). Here, corpora are used for the professional development of teachers who in this way experience corpus studies from the learner perspective. Furthermore, corpora of classroom discourse have been increasingly recognised as a powerful resource in LTE (e.g. Amador Moreno *et al.* 2006) because they "can complement more traditional LTE practices of classroom and peer observations, but without the intrusion and time pressure that comes with these" (Farr 2010a: 623).

As we have seen in the previous section, the role of the learner is well documented in research literature on corpus-based teaching. In contrast, the challenges to the teacher in the process of *teaching* with corpora, and the implications this has for LTE have so far rarely been addressed. One of the reasons for this may be that the teachers in corpus studies are often already experts in corpus linguistics, and thus potential difficulties present for the non-expert teacher are overlooked. For example, Yoon (2008: 33) describes the teacher at the centre of their study on corpus consultation in L2 academic writing as "a veteran ESL teacher who had used corpus work extensively in his own teaching". Consequently, the results of this study are not likely to highlight challenges when teaching with corpora.

The present analyses of learners and of teachers as corpus users have revealed that both groups face a number of challenges when corpora are introduced into traditional language learning contexts. More importantly, the discussion has demonstrated that there is a significant difference between learning and teaching with corpora. This provides a strong argument for training teachers with an explicit focus on how to teach with corpora. In order to successfully introduce learners to corpora, a gradual training approach was identified, and the current section has shown that teachers play a crucial role in this training process. It is essential to equip teachers with the required skills in order to enable them to take on that role, and LTE presents a valuable opportunity for teacher trainees to explore the use of corpora from the perspective of learner *and* as teacher. In-depth training can be provided, and teacher trainees can discover the potential of corpora as part of their own training. If they find their learning experience with corpora to be beneficial, then this can be a powerful motivator in their decision to make corpora part of their teaching inventory.

As the discussion in this section has shown, teachers face very specific challenges, ranging from selecting or creating of materials to managing the training process of learners and changes to the role of the teacher in the traditional classroom. Thus, it is argued here that an explicit focus on the task of teaching with corpora is required in order to enable teachers to exploit the potential of corpora in their classrooms successfully. In particular, because corpora are not compulsory items of standard language curricula, teachers may not be interested in using them unless they can "see the advantage of using corpus data in order to solve existing problems" (Mukherjee 2004: 244). It is not sufficient for teachers to read about the benefits of corpora; their own process of discovery is the only motivator powerful enough to achieve this long-term. Boulton (2009b: 86) emphasises the significance of this experience for teachers who "tend to accept or reject particular tools, materials and techniques not on the basis of research evidence, but on their own pragmatic experience – whether it works for them in their particular situation". Thus, creating opportunities for teacher trainees in LTE to learn with corpora and to learn how to teach with corpora, will be a major driving force in the process of advancing the popularisation of corpora in language education.

4.4 Advancing the popularisation of corpora: key factors

> And the goal of bringing the corpus into the language-teaching classroom (though vigorously pursued by a small group of enthusiasts) remains as elusive as ever.
>
> (Rundell 2008: 27)

In order to answer the question as to why the uptake of corpora by mainstream teaching has remained limited, this chapter has presented two critical analyses. The first analysis has reviewed evaluative studies in order to gauge whether the use of corpus data leads to successful learning, to investigate learner strategies in using corpora, and to examine learner and teacher responses to this approach. Subsequently, a second analysis looked at the corpus, the software, and the user in light of their transferability from research to classroom. The purpose of these analyses was to identify key factors that hinder or facilitate the use of corpora in the classroom.

Evaluations of studies on direct corpus use in language education

Although the diversity of studies on the effectiveness of direct corpus use with learners does not provide enough evidence for a definitive conclusion, the overwhelming majority of studies report positive learning outcomes. Not only do experimental groups (using concordances) perform as well as control groups, they actually perform better, even though the difference cannot always be proven to be statistically significant. Thus, the learning potential of the corpus approach should in fact facilitate the popularisation of corpora.

Learner strategies, as observed in a smaller number of studies, appear more problematic. Clearly, learners have (at least initially) difficulties in searching and interpreting corpus data. It must be noted, however, that the studies discussed here represent cases in which learners conducted hands-on searches in very autonomous learning situations. It is evident that tailoring the task to the learner group adequately is absolutely necessary. This also entails devising appropriate introductions for learners, a task likely to fall to the teacher. The discussion will return to the important role of the teacher below.

Learner responses to concordancing tasks are in most cases positive. In general, learners find the corpus activities interesting and useful, although some negative aspects mentioned included that tasks were too time-consuming and that the technical aspects of corpus use caused difficulties. Responses by teachers to teaching experiences with corpora are an area which has seemingly remained unexplored. To the knowledge of the author of the present study, no studies are currently available that systematically report on feedback by teachers on teaching with corpora. Only three studies (Davis & Russell-Pinson 2004; Farr 2008; Mukherjee 2004) were found that provided some data gathered from teachers who had been introduced to the corpus approach and subsequently given feedback on the perceived usefulness of such an approach and on their plans to employ these tools in the future. The analysis of these studies indicates that teachers showed interest in the approach and that they perceived corpora as a useful asset for teaching. However, technology-related issues and aspects about the nature of corpora were causes for concern.

In summary, the analysis of evaluative studies on the effectiveness of the corpus approach, learner strategies in using corpora, as well as learner and teacher responses to learning experiences with corpus resources and tools indicates the following:

(i) Targeted use of concordances for learning activities (especially for vocabulary and grammar) is potentially more effective than traditional approaches.
(ii) Acquiring effective strategies in using corpora is challenging for learners.
(iii) Learners and teachers generally consider corpus-based activities as interesting and useful, although negative aspects include technology-related difficulties and the perception of such tasks as too time-consuming.

These results lead to the tentative conclusion that the use of corpora constitutes an effective learning tool that is generally perceived as interesting and useful by learners and teachers. Thus, neither lack of effectiveness nor appeal can serve as reasons to explain the persisting gap between research and practice. However, negative aspects included difficulties with corpus technology and corpus research strategies. Both of these aspects were addressed in the subsequent analysis of the three core elements.

Analysis of core elements

Subsequently to this critical review of previous research, a second analysis was conducted regarding the transferability of the three core elements involved in the corpus analysis process from research to classroom environment. The purpose of this analysis was to identify factors arising from this transfer to a different context that might hinder or facilitate the use of corpora by language learners and teachers. The results from this discussion demonstrate that the successful transfer of corpus tools, resources, and methods into a classroom environment hinges on a number of closely interrelated factors. These have to be considered in relation to each element – corpus, software, and user – in order to achieve successful integration into a traditional educational setting.

Core element: corpus

The analysis of the core element corpus has demonstrated that design for classroom corpora should be driven by learner needs and classroom requirements. In order to maximise learning benefits, this is of particular importance in the introductory phase and when intending to use corpora with lower-level learners. Furthermore, such pedagogically relevant corpora can successfully overcome disadvantages of large corpora built for research purposes. They should be manageable in size, contain texts relevant to the respective learning context and the curriculum, and ideally be accompanied by pedagogical enrichments, such as learning materials and ready-made concordances. The inclusion of audiovisual materials in these corpora is significant as it supports the process of contextualisation. However, while the value of such corpora designed for the classroom appears great, it has to be taken into consideration that an immense amount of time, effort, and money has been invested into such corpora which may only be of limited use. In the case of the *ELISA Corpus*, for example, the content is mostly restricted to one topic (professional careers), and the question must be asked as to how much use this resource can be put. It seems evident that such elaborate and likely very costly undertakings do not represent a viable long-term solution for mainstream use. Ultimately, the discussion has shown that the more relevant and flexible corpora are, the more readily they can be used for learning and teaching purposes. Thus, the development of pedagogically relevant corpora can be identified as an important key factor in promoting corpus use in the classroom.[50]

[50] The significance of appropriate corpora for teaching is further discussed in the context of the case study in Section 6.3.4.

Core element: software

Despite the fact that concordancing in the classroom seemingly simulates research behaviour, there are fundamental differences in requirements for classroom and research users. The majority of currently available concordancing programs were originally designed for research purposes. The analysis in Section 4.3.2 has revealed, however, that classroom users differ significantly from researchers in terms of motivation to use concordancers, time constraints, research skills, and computer literacy. Furthermore, evidence from previous studies has shown that technical difficulties can be potential deterrents from using corpora with learners. Thus, informing the design of corpus tools for classroom use, in other words tailor-made software for learners and teachers, is another key factor in successfully using corpora in an educational environment with novice users of corpora. The results from both the survey of corpora in teacher education (Chapter 5) and the case study with teacher trainees (Chapter 6) support this conclusion. Chapter 7 discusses the development of such software in detail. This software proposal serves as an example of informing the design of corpus tools by the needs defined by the classroom context.

Core element: user

On the whole, the analysis of the core element user has revealed that appropriate training for both learners and teachers is perhaps the most significant key factor in the process of transferring corpus resources, tools, and methods successfully into the classroom. A gradual introduction to corpora appears to most suitable for training learners, and the use of concordance printouts and scaffolding techniques is closely associated with this approach. Learners can be easily overwhelmed by corpus-based learning activities as they represent challenges on several levels. Consequently, teachers who would like to introduce corpora into their teaching routines are faced with a demanding task. This challenge is disproportionately frustrated by the prevailing lack of relevant teaching materials. Additionally, the inductive, explorative, and research-type character of many corpus-based learning activities entails changes to the learner and the teacher's role which can be as exciting as it is unsettling for both groups.

Key factors in advancing the use of corpus in language education

The analysis of all three elements of the corpus investigation process has comprehensively shown that the transfer of research tools and resources into the classroom presents challenges at several levels. Pedagogical mediation of corpora, designing relevant corpora, and user-friendly concordancers for classroom use were identified as key factors for a successful promotion of corpus consultation in language education. However, if the use of corpora is to become part of mainstream teaching activity in any way, teachers have the most important role to play. Considerations have to include whether the approach is feasible and which conditions have to be met in order to successfully use corpora in the classroom. If the popularisation of corpus use is to transcend the boundaries of the university research context, then it is essential to take into account that the teacher is not likely to be a corpus expert as arguably most of the authors of studies on corpus use with learners are. Teachers represent the main conduit between research and classroom. Until corpora become a standard component of future curricula and textbooks, teachers are the main force behind the decision of whether or not to introduce corpora into the classroom. Teachers arguably play the most central role in the process of popularising corpora and the most productive phase in their professional career for training is pre-service LTE:

> In fact, the strongest force for change could be a new generation of ESL teachers who were introduced to corpus-based research in their training programs, who appreciate the scope of the work, and who have practiced conducting their own corpus investigations and designing materials based on corpus research. (Conrad 2000: 556)

Only if language teachers can discover the corpus approach as relevant and, in addition, receive appropriate training in order to use these tools, will and can they include corpora into their teaching routines. It is of great importance that teachers can discover the value of this approach through their own experiences. Additionally, due to the demanding nature of integrating corpora into the classroom, teachers have to receive training in how to teach with corpora. McCarthy (2008: 564) has recently emphasised how important it is to consider the teacher not simply as a passive recipient of theories but "but as researcher, as reflective practitioner, as someone more actively involved in their own professional development and in what happens in their classrooms".

In order to advance the process of popularising corpora in language education, it is of great importance to learn more about the teacher's perspective of this approach, to gain insight into the pedagogical aspects of introducing corpora into the classroom, and to reassess the role of corpora in LTE. It is easy to perceive the transfer of corpus tools, resources, and methods into the classroom as a one-directional process. However, as Leech (1997) puts it, many

> may well find [his] 'trickle down' metaphor unhelpful, or even offensive. 'Trickle down' implies that research is 'up there' as an élite activity, and teaching is 'down there' in a lower, subservient role. But,

> in the experience of many, there is not a one-way dependence of this kind. (Leech 1997: 3-4)

As the analysis in this chapter has shown, it is of great importance to inform the process of integrating corpora into the classroom by the needs of language pedagogy. Thus, in order to gain much-needed insight into teachers' perspectives of teaching with corpora, a case study is presented in the following chapter that involves teacher trainees in a course on learning *and* teaching with corpora. This case study was conducted at Duisburg-Essen University in Germany. In order to assess the role of corpora in LTE in Germany, the results of a survey conducted prior to the case study will be reported in Chapter 5. Before concluding this study, Chapter 7 presents a proposal for a tailor-made concordancing software for classroom users in response to the findings of the current chapter, in addition to the results from the survey and the case study.

5 Survey: corpora in language teacher education

So far, this study has presented the tools and resources of corpus linguistics and demonstrated the impact this field has had on language education in the form of indirect and direct applications of corpora for language education. In particular, it has illustrated the great potential and wide array of possible uses of corpora for direct classroom application. The analysis in Chapter 4 revealed that in spite of a very active research field that has developed in the area of corpus linguistics in language education, the impact of this research on mainstream teaching practices has remained limited. The critical analyses presented in Chapter 4 demonstrated that corpus tools and resources have to be carefully adjusted based on the needs of classroom users. In particular, the investigation established that teachers are the most important key factor in any effort of introducing corpora to mainstream language learning. Creating opportunities for teachers to learn with corpora and to learn how to teach with corpora is thus a crucial step towards enabling teachers to use corpora as part of their teaching. Pre-service LTE was identified as the most suitable period in the professional careers of teachers to supply this learning experience, and a case study with teacher trainees was proposed. The background for this study is language teacher education in Germany. As will be shown in this chapter, few systematic accounts on corpus use in teacher education in Germany (or anywhere else) are currently available. The current chapter addresses this lack of information in the form of a survey of teacher educators at German universities and a small number of expert interviews. The results of this provide valuable information for the case study presented in Chapter 6 and, furthermore, contribute new aspects to the discussion on the popularisation of corpora in language education.

5.1 Research context: pre-service LTE in Germany

The reviews and investigations of the previous chapters have demonstrated the potential of corpora for language learning and also highlighted the challenges inherent in the process of using corpora in the classroom. After analysing corpora, corpus software and learners and teachers as corpus users, the conclusion was reached that all of these elements need to be adapted according to a framework defined by pedagogy. Most importantly, however, it was determined that in order to advance popularisation of corpora as a tool for language learning, teachers have to be recognised as a key factor in that process. Furthermore, teachers need to acquire the necessary skills and come to view corpus work as beneficial in order to include corpora as part of their teaching repertoire.

Pre-service teacher training plays a major role in providing valuable opportunities for teachers to acquire both skills and motivation through positive learning experiences.

The context of pre-service LTE in Germany for EFL is a suitable environment in which to conduct further research into this matter. English as a school subject is compulsory at both primary and secondary educational institutions in Germany. As a result of this, there is a strong demand for highly qualified English teachers. Thus, teaching degrees for English are offered at all universities in Germany, with the exception of universities that are exclusively technical, medical or part of the military (*Bundeswehr*). In other words, highly qualified teachers of EFL, who in most cases are non-native speakers of English, are in great demand in Germany.

Education in Germany is subject to state law as opposed to federal law.[51] Each of the 16 states governs educational policies independently; however, educational institutions largely operate in very similar systems across the country. Pursuit of a unifying approach is reflected in the 'Standing Conference of the Ministers of Education and Cultural Affairs of the Länder in the Federal Republic of Germany' (*Kultusministerkonferenz* or *KMK*)[52] as much as in the reciprocal agreements of recognition of degrees and school certificates. Since 1999, the European Commission has been seeking to establish a unifying approach across the European Union in the form of the Bologna Process:

> The Bologna Process aims to create a European Higher Education Area by 2010, in which students can choose from a wide and transparent range of high quality courses and benefit from smooth recognition procedures. The Bologna Declaration of June 1999 has put in motion a series of reforms needed to make European Higher Education more compatible and comparable, more competitive and more attractive for Europeans and for students and scholars from other continents. Reform was needed then and reform is still needed today if Europe is

---

[51] The educational and cultural sovereignty of the federal states (*Kulturhoheit der Länder*) is defined in the German constitution (*Grundgesetz*): Art. 70 (1) GG.

[52] From the English dossier of the *KMK* website: In accordance with its official undefined statutes, the Standing Conference deals with "issues relating to educational policy at school and higher education level and research policy, as well as cultural policy of supraregional importance, with the aim of achieving joint opinion and decision-making and of representing joint concerns".
In the framework of the Standing Conference, the Länder assume responsibility for the state as a whole by way of self-co-ordination and ensure the necessary degree of common ground in education, science and cultural matters of supraregional importance. One key task of the Standing Conference is to ensure the highest possible degree of mobility throughout Germany for pupils, students, teaching personnel and those working in the science sector by means of consensus and co-operation.

> to match the performance of the best performing systems in the world, notably the United States and Asia.[53]

This process has impacted on many facets of education across Europe, including teacher education in Germany. The research presented in this study was conducted in 2005. Since then, a number of changes have been made to teacher education in Germany. These changes are mostly reflected by the introduction of Bachelor and Master degrees, the introduction of a credit point system, and the modular design of study programmes (*Modularisierung der Studiengänge*). These changes were only in the first stage of implementation at the time the survey, the interviews, and the case study, presented in Chapter 6, were conducted and therefore had no influence on the results of this research. An analysis of the impact of these changes on language teacher education is beyond the scope of the study. However, as will become more apparent in the following chapters, some of these changes have the potential to create more favourable conditions for cross-disciplinary approaches such as the use of corpora in language learning. Where important, this point will be picked up again at a later stage, in particular in relation to the expert interviews presented in Section 5.3.

5.2 Survey on the use of corpora in LTE

> Surely by now, after twenty-five years of corpus linguistics playing an ever-widening role in language teaching and learning, we no longer need to advocate that knowledge of corpus linguistics and its influence should be part of teacher education? In reality we DO need to discuss the topic because [...] there is still little systematic account taken of what has been called the 'corpus revolution'
>
> (McCarthy 2008: 563)

As McCarthy states in the quote above, very little is known about the actual use of corpora by language practitioners at this point. Even so, the consensus appears to be that the impact of corpora on classroom practices and language education in general has remained limited (see Section 4.1). A small number of publications available on this subject appear to confirm this. Tribble (2001) reports on the results from a survey distributed online via language teaching related mailing lists in the United Kingdom. He comes to the conclusion that "however undeniably important corpus data might be, it is not yet 'central to the daily concerns of language teachers'" (2001: 5).

---

[53] Available at http://ec.europa.eu/education/higher-education/doc1290_en.htm.

The results from this survey, however, may only have limited validity as the target group was only very loosely defined as "technically aware teachers and researchers" whose only common criteria was membership to a specific mailing list. In addition to this, the response rate was very small, approximately 1% based on Tribble's estimations of nearly 8,000 subscribers to the mailing lists he posted his survey to. However, these numbers led Tribble to conclude that "the small size of this return [...] already gives an indication of the endangered species status of corpus aware language teachers" (Tribble 2001: 3).

Mukherjee (2004) reports his findings from a survey conducted among participants of a series of in-service teacher workshops in Germany. Two hundred and forty eight EFL teachers from secondary schools were questioned on their familiarity with and use of corpora as part of their teaching practices. The results showed that only 10.9% of the participants were familiar with corpus linguistics which leads Mukherjee (2004: 243) to conclude that "only a tiny fraction of English language teachers actually know of the existence of corpus linguistics in the first place". However, no information is available on whether or not any of the teachers who had indicated familiarity with corpus linguistics were actually using corpora as part of their teaching.

Thompson (2006) reports on a survey of 75 member institutions of the British Association of Lecturers of English for Academic Purposes undertaken in May 2002. The purpose of the survey was to investigate accessibility and use of corpora for EAP in the United Kingdom. He concludes that the "use of corpora and corpus analysis methodologies at the time of the survey was clearly limited, and in many cases non-existent" (2006: 14). This survey further demonstrates the lack of uptake of corpora in language education, in this case EAP teaching at tertiary level.

To the present author's best knowledge, no information is currently available regarding the use of corpora in pre-service LTE in Germany. In response to this lack of systematic information, the current chapter presents the results of a survey of teacher educators in the areas of teaching methodology and language practice at universities in Germany that offer teaching degrees for EFL.[54] These areas were chosen because they represent those parts of teacher education that provide opportunities for teacher trainees to either learn with corpora or to learn how to teach with corpora. None of the aforementioned surveys investigate these areas. The setup of this survey will be discussed in the next section, followed by an analysis of the results of the survey.

---

[54] Approval to conduct the survey was obtained from Macquarie University's Human Research Ethics Committee.

5.2.1 Research setup and participants

University-based pre-service teacher training for EFL in Germany (*Lehramtsstudiengang Englisch*) takes between four and five years. As part of their teaching degree in English, teacher trainees are generally required to attend courses and lectures from five main areas: linguistics, literature, media studies, language practice (*Sprachpraxis*) and teaching methodology (*Fremdsprachendidaktik*). The purpose of this survey was to explore to what extent teacher trainees of English in Germany encounter corpus-based language learning either as part of their own experience as language learners (i.e., in language practice courses), or as part of their teaching methodology training (i.e., in teaching methodology courses). In order to ensure feasibility of the study, it was decided, instead of attempting to survey the very large body of students, to survey the respective teacher educators instead. Therefore, prospective participants of the survey were defined as teacher educators who either teach 'language practice' and/or 'teaching methodology' at German universities that offer a teaching degree for English.

Examination regulations require teacher trainees to reach near-native competence by the end of their training, and language practice courses are therefore an important component of pre-service teacher training for EFL. Courses offered in this area generally target all four competencies: listening, reading, writing and speaking. These courses offer prime opportunities to introduce corpora as part of language awareness activities, vocabulary and grammar training. Introductory teaching methodology courses familiarise students with various theories and methods of teaching EFL. The aim of these courses is to show trainees how to apply these theories and methods in the classroom. More advanced courses often deal with one particular approach in more detail. Many teaching methodology courses are nowadays concerned with the application of new technologies in the classroom. The use corpora for teaching falls into this category. The reasons for singling out these two areas of teacher education are based on the findings from Chapter 4; namely, the argument that in order to enable teachers to use corpora in their classroom, they need to have had learning experiences with corpora and ideally have had training in how to teach with corpora. Language practice and teaching methodology courses represent two significant parts of teacher training that offer opportunities for both. A survey including linguistics and literary courses was not of immediate relevance and beyond the scope of this study. A follow-up study with this increased scope may be of interest for future studies.

In total, 63 out of 88 universities in Germany offer English teaching degrees (this is based on information provided by the *Hochschulverband Deutschland*).[55]

---

[55] The other 25 universities were either universities of technology, military or medicine only.

Based on the staff information listed on the individual university websites, a total of 414 academics were identified that fit the participant criteria stated above. Two hundred and twenty seven academics were listed under language practice (54.8%), 178 under teaching methodology (43%), and nine were listed as teaching in both areas (2.2%). All of the 414 academics were contacted by a personally addressed letter. In this letter, the purpose of the study was explained and an invitation to participate extended. Furthermore, the details of the survey, how to access it online, dates of availability, and approximate time needed to participate were set out. The participants were all given the generic user login and password in order to ensure security of the data on the one hand and preserve anonymity on the other. The survey was available at the web address http://www.d-dl.net from 25 April to 25 May 2005.

The target group of the present study was identified by reference to the information provided by the universities on the respective staff web pages. Therefore, there can be no guarantee of completeness nor can it be assumed that the information on those pages was up-to-date in all cases. However, as staff directories are generally maintained by an official administrative body of the university, the information will be considered valid and reliable for the purpose of this study. The survey is explorative in its nature and, therefore, conclusions derived from the results can only be indications of the current status quo.

5.2.2 Data analysis

Of the 414 invited participants a total of 217 took part in the survey. Three participants' results had to be disqualified as drop-outs (i.e., the survey was started but not completed successfully). Furthermore, two surveys were answered by linguists who taught neither in teaching methodology nor in language practice. These results were also discounted because the respondents were not part of the target population. It is not clear whether these two participants were part of the total number approached or whether they were colleagues of the original participants.[56] In total, 212 valid responses were evaluated for the analysis below which equals a response rate of 51.2%. Although higher than that of other surveys cited here (see Tribble 2001; Thompson 2006), this response rate shows that the results only reflect the activities and opinions of half the target population. However, there are now a number of publications that challenge the view that low response rates are necessarily a key indicator of survey data quality (see Curtin, Presser & Singer 2005; Holbrook, Krosnick &

[56] There is reason to believe that the latter may have been the case as I received emails from original participants informing me that they had forwarded the letter of invitation to their respective linguistics departments.

Pfent 2007; Keeter, Kennedy, Dimock, Best & Craighill 2006). Therefore, the results are deemed to be a valid indicator of the current status quo.

The survey presented here consisted of 15 questions. There were two junctions in the questionnaire where the answer given by the respondent determines the path the survey follows. Figure 5-1 shows the outline of the survey and illustrates the forks at Questions 5 and 7.

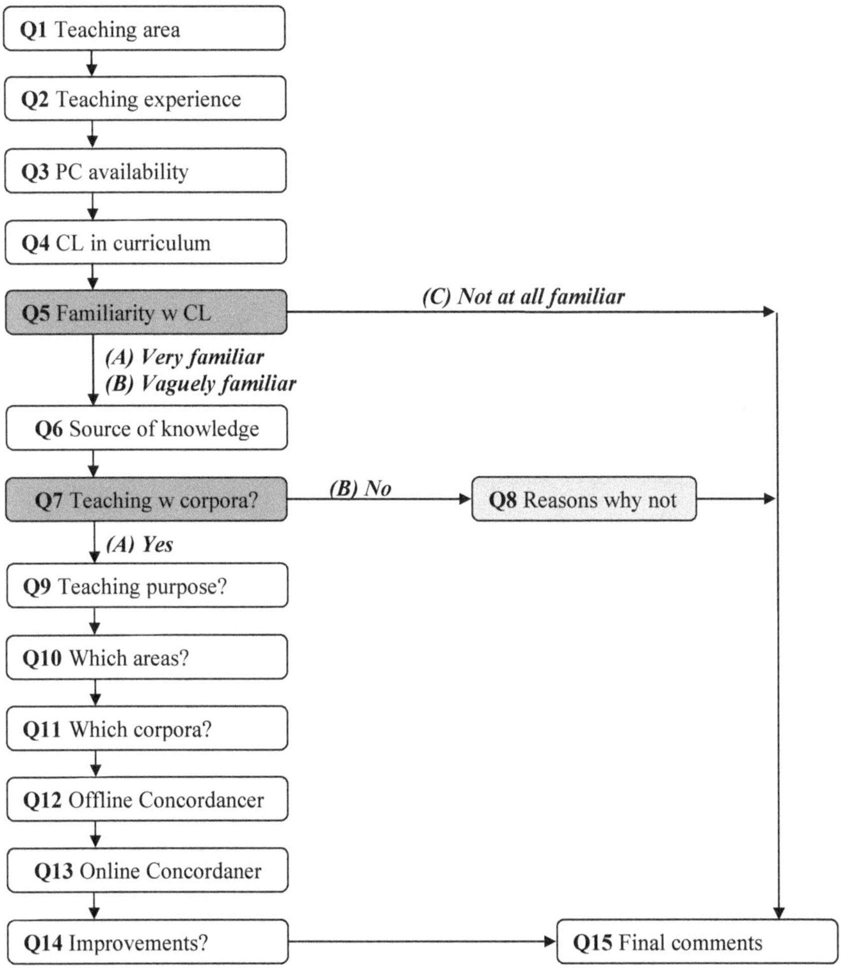

Figure 5-1: CL survey – Outline

For the purpose of the following analysis, each question and the possible answers will be presented, followed by a graph visualising the results, as well as a discussion of the outcomes.

Q1. Please select the area(s) in which you teach classes for EFL teacher training: (*Multiple answers possible*)

(A) Teaching Methodology.
(B) Language Practice.
(C) Language Practice with focus on translation.
(D) Other, please specify:

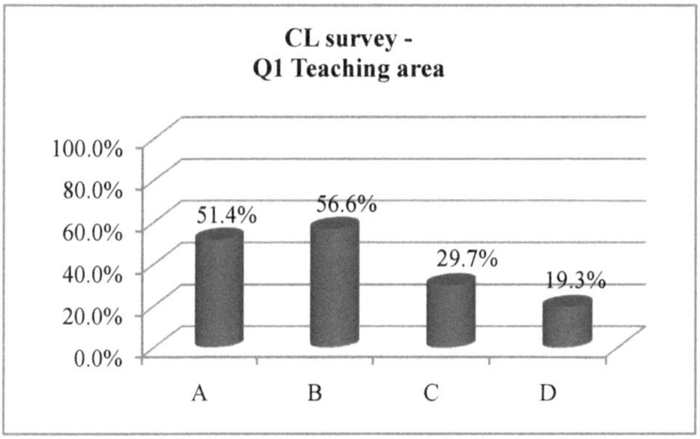

Figure 5-2: CL survey – Q1 Teaching area

During the recruitment process, all participants were identified based on the information provided on the respective university staff web pages. Even though the majority of all participants had been listed under either 'language practice' or 'teaching methodology', the results indicate that many respondents in fact teach at least in both if not additional areas. The results of a preliminary analysis based solely on frequency counts for each answer is visualised in Figure 5-2 which shows that 51.4% of the respondents are involved in teaching methodology courses and 56.6% are teaching in the area of language practice. Just under a third of the group (29.7%) is teaching language practice with a focus on translation and approximately one-fifth of the respondents (19.3%) teach in other areas. These areas include cultural studies, linguistics, literature, and phonetics and phonology. Multiple answers to this question were possible, and a closer

examination of the combinations of teaching areas will provide a better understanding of the group of respondents.
Figure 5-3 gives an indication of the distribution of the combinations of teaching areas as reported by the participants. For the purpose of this analysis, the results listed under "Other" were excluded.

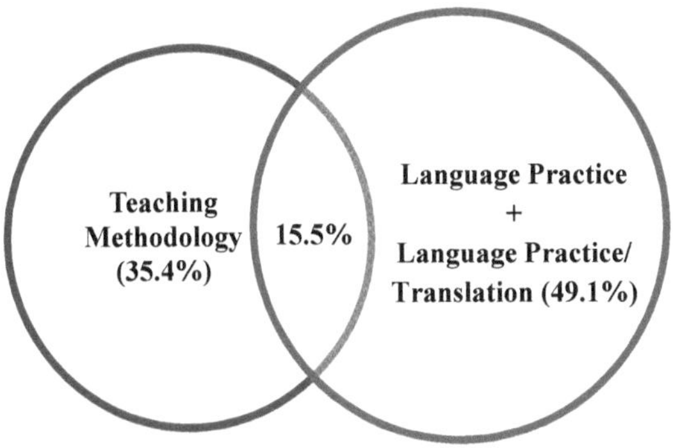

Figure 5-3: CL survey – Q1 Distribution of teaching area

Question 2 also serves the purpose of getting a better understanding of the make-up of the group of respondents. As Figure 5-4 shows, the majority of the respondents had extensive teaching experience with at least five to ten years (14.6%) or more than ten years (44.4%) of teaching experience. Over one-third had been teaching for one to five years (36.3%) and only 4.7% had less than 12 months experience.

Q2. How long have you held a position as a lecturer in university-based pre-service teacher training for?

(A) Less than 12 months.
(B) 1-5 years.
(C) 5-10 years.
(D) More than 10 years.

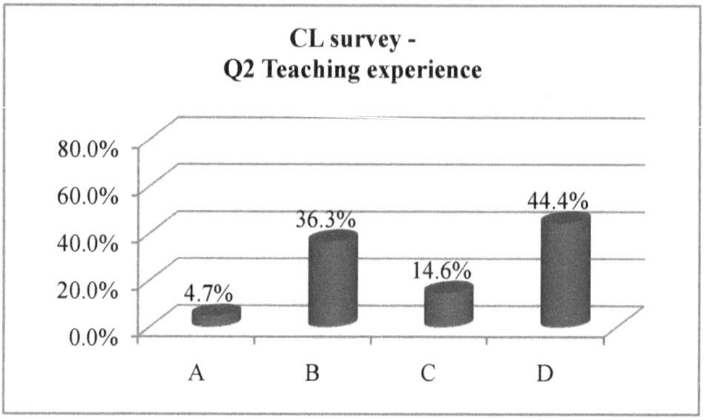

Figure 5-4: CL survey – Q2 Teaching experience

The use of corpora is inextricably linked to the use of computers. Therefore, Question 3 was included in the survey to determine the level of access the participants had to computer equipment for teaching purposes.

As can be seen in Figure 5-5, less than one-third of all participants (31.6%) reported to have access to a state-of-the-art computer lab for their classes. In fact, a larger number of respondents reported to have no access to computers at all (36.8%), and nearly another third (23.6% and 5.2%) reported that they had access only to either one or some, but an insufficient number of computers for their classes. Almost all answers provided under "Other" were clearly identifiable to belong to one of the first four categories, and these numbers are already reflected in the results prsented in Figure 5-5. Only six answers under "Other" differed. Of these, two participants reported that self-access centres for students were available but provided no further information regarding the potential availability of computers for their classes. Four participants stated that they did not require or use computers at all for their classes.

These results lead to several observations. First, the findings indicate that a large number of teacher trainees may not have adequate access to computers throughout their training as teachers. Second, and perhaps most notably, the discrepancy between availability of state-of-the-art computer labs (31.6%) and no availability of PCs at all (36.8%) suggests that teacher trainees across Germany are trained in vastly different environments, at least in the areas of language practice and teaching methodology.

Q3. What kind of computer equipment is generally available to you for your classes?

(A) A state-of-the-art computer lab.
(B) Some, but not sufficient computers.
(C) One computer per classroom.
(D) There are no computers available for my classes.
(E) Other, please specify:

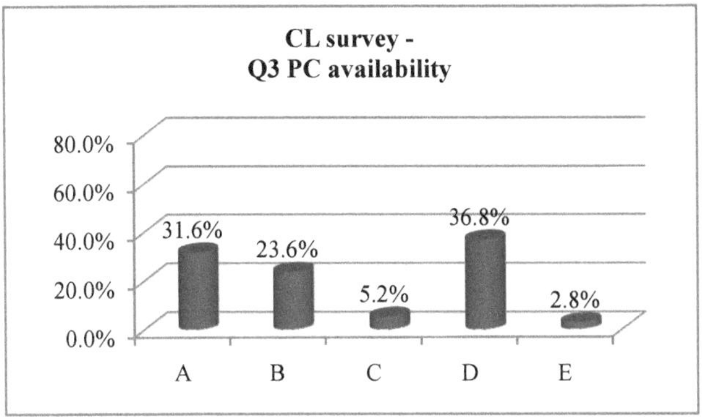

Figure 5-5: CL survey – Q3 PC availability

These results are significant in their potential implications for teacher training. One might argue that these areas of language practice and teaching methodology are of particular importance as they include those courses in which teachers are either taught how to teach with computers (teaching methodology) or where the trainees experience computers as tools for their own language *learning* experience (language practice). In particular, the latter is of great importance as it plays a significant role in their teaching profession later on. It appears that the extensive amount of CALL-related research literature produced over the past 40 years is not reflected in current language teacher training courses at universities in Germany. The results of this survey would certainly encourage a larger survey in order to find out more details about computer availability and computer use as part of pre-service teacher training courses.

In response to Question 4, only a very small number of participants report that corpus linguistics is a compulsory component of the curriculum for teacher trainees. The majority of participants claim that it is an optional component and a quarter of the respondents say that to their knowledge it is not offered at all. Nearly one fifth of the participants (18.9%) state that they are unaware of whether or not it is offered at all.

Q4. Is corpus linguistics part of the curriculum for state exam candidates at your institution?

(A) Yes, it is compulsory.
(B) Yes, it is an optional component.
(C) No, it is not offered here.
(D) I don't know.

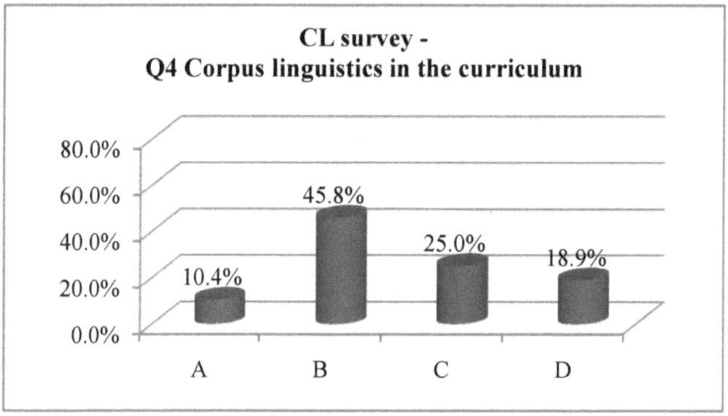

Figure 5-6: CL survey – Q4 Corpus linguistics in curriculum

This question was designed to reflect the participants' awareness regarding the role corpus linguistics plays in the teacher trainees' degree. It cannot represent the actual degree to which corpus linguistics is taught at universities to teacher trainees. However, the results of this question appear to corroborate Mukherjee's (2002; 2004) observation that corpus linguistics in not a compulsory part of language teacher education and that only a minority of EFL teacher trainees in Germany ever encounter corpus linguistics throughout their degree.

Question 5 is the first of two fork questions in the survey. As shown in the survey outline (Figure 5-1), respondents who chose answers A ("Very familiar") or B ("Vaguely familiar") continued on to Question 6 and the remainder of the survey. Respondents who chose answer C ("Not at all familiar") were redirected to Question 15 where the survey ended for them. Only a small percentage of the respondents (15.6%) stated that they were "very familiar" with corpus linguistics. More than half of the respondents (58%) indicated that they were at least "vaguely familiar" and just over a quarter (26.4%) were not familiar at all with corpus linguistics.

Q5. How would you rate your familiarity with corpus linguistics?

(A) Very familiar.
(B) Vaguely familiar.
(C) Not at all familiar.

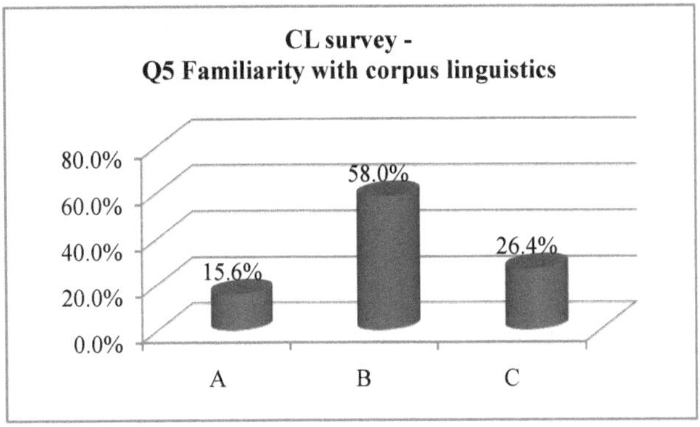

Figure 5-7: CL survey – Q5 Familiarity with corpus linguistics

When looking at these results in relation to the outcomes of Question 3 (Availability of Computers, Figure 5-5), it appears that there is a correlation between familiarity with corpus linguistics and access to computer equipment. More than half of those respondents claiming to be "very familiar" with corpus linguistics had access to state-of-the-art computers for their teaching while a clear majority of those not at all familiar with corpus linguistics had no access at all to computers. Cross-tabulation of the data from both questions showed that there is a statistical significance between them (Chi-square=46.3; *p*-value=0.001).

After this fork question, all respondents who claimed to have no familiarity with corpus linguistics proceeded to Question 15 which was the final question of this survey. Those that stated to be very or at least vaguely familiar with corpus linguistics proceeded to Question 6. This question was designed to explore the participants' source of knowledge of corpus linguistics; for example, whether they encountered corpus linguistics as part of their own university studies, through their own research, or whether they learner about corpus linguistics from conversations with colleagues or at conferences

Q6. What is the source of your knowledge of corpus linguistics?

(A) University-based studies.
(B) My own research.
(C) Conversations with colleagues.
(D) Conferences/Workshops.

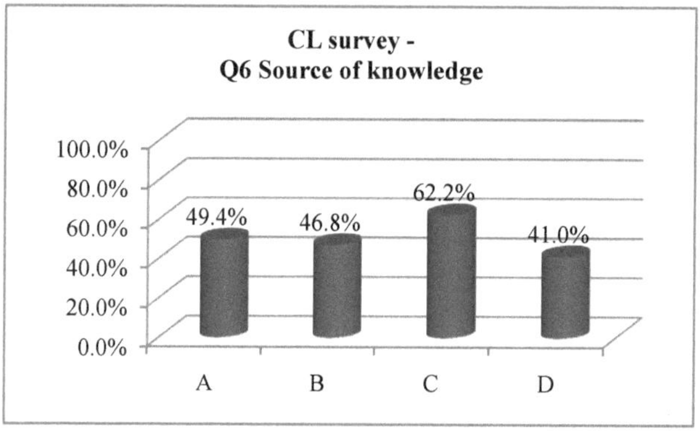

Figure 5-8: CL survey – Q6 Source of knowledge

Multiple answers were possible for Question 6. Figure 5-8 shows that university-based studies, own research and conferences appear to be equally important as sources of knowledge while colleagues play a slightly more significant role. When looking at the various combinations of answers provided (see Table 5-1), four groupings stand out as the most frequently chosen:

Table 5-1: CL survey – Q6 Results; combinations

	Answers	**%**
C + D	Colleagues + Conferences	11.5%
A + C	University-based studies + Colleagues	10.9%
C	Colleagues	10.3%
B	My own research	9.6%

Out of 15 answer combinations that occurred, these four were chosen by more than 40% of the total number of respondents. A closer examination of these respondents shows that 90.9% of this group is only vaguely familiar with corpus linguistics but the vast majority of them (85%) is in fact using corpora for their teaching (as the analysis of Question 7 will show below). In contrast, out of the group of respondents who selected A: University-based studies as their sole source of knowledge (only 8.3%), 92.3% of them were vaguely familiar with corpus linguistics, but only 7.6% of them were actually using corpora for teaching. The numbers are too small to draw any definitive conclusions from these results. However, they give an indication that colleagues not only play a vital role in word-of-mouth dissemination of information on corpus linguistics, but also that those participants who had gained their knowledge through this channel were far more likely to actually employ corpora for teaching purposes than those who had acquired their knowledge through their university studies alone. One explanation for this might be that colleagues can pass on successful teaching experiences, tried and tested with students. The results of this question indicate that, in particular among teacher educators, word-of-mouth and also conferences play a vital role in popularising the use of corpora for teaching purposes. Davis and Russell-Pinson (2004: 157) make a similar observation in regard to the important role colleagues play. They conclude that "hearing about concordancing from their colleagues makes teachers more responsive to later using the technology".

Q7. Do you work with corpora and concordancing software in relation to your teaching?

(A) Yes.
(B) No.

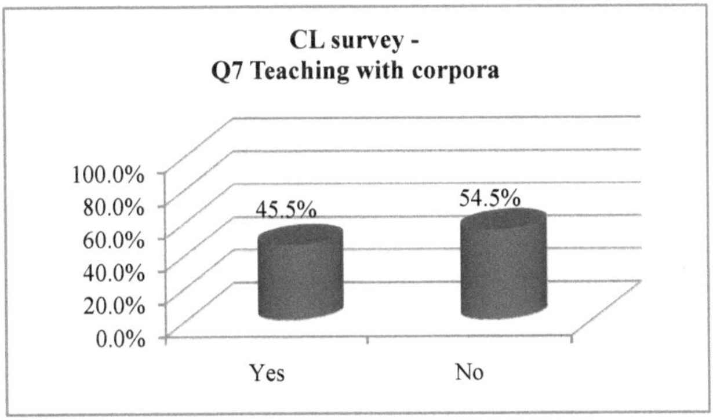

Figure 5-9: CL survey – Q7 Teaching with corpora

Question 7 presented the second fork in the questionnaire. Respondents who answered the question with "Yes" proceeded to Question 9 and the remainder of the questionnaire. Those that answered "No" were taken to Question 15 where the questionnaire ended for them.

When asked whether or not they work with corpora in relation to their teaching, nearly half (45.5%) replied that they did while a slim majority (54.5%) reported that they did not. It is perhaps worth looking a little more closely at these two groups in the form of cross-tabulation with the data results from the previous questions. Firstly, one might expect familiarity with the subject to have an impact on the decision whether or not to utilise corpora for teaching. Indeed, participants who were "very familiar" with the subject were much more likely to teach with corpora than those that were only "vaguely familiar". Nearly three-quarters (72.7%) of the group "very familiar" with corpus linguistics claimed to be using corpora for teaching while this was the case for only just over a third of the group who were "vaguely familiar" (38.2%). Statistical significance tests also showed that these results are significant (Chi-Square=12.5; p-value=0.002). Before moving on to the questions directed at the group teaching with corpora, we will look at the reasons respondents gave for *not* teaching with corpora.

In Question 8, participants were asked to indicates their reasons for not teaching with corpora despite being very or vaguely familiar with corpus linguistics. The reason most frequently cited by the participants for their decision not to teach with corpora was answer B: "The curriculum is already full and corpus linguistics is not relevant enough to include it". The vast majority of this group (81.8%) were only vaguely familiar with corpus linguistics. These results may also reflect a view of corpus linguistics as an addition to the curriculum rather than a tool and a resource to aid in existing components of the curriculum. This includes, for example, using corpus methods in literary studies and corpora for writing classes. Only a very small percentage of the participants (14.3%) viewed corpus linguistics as not relevant at all to the training of EFL teachers. A closer examination of the group of respondents who chose this answer reveals that it is largely made up of instructors of teaching methodology who were only vaguely familiar with corpus linguistics. More than half of all participants (60.7%) chose Answers C and/or D; that is, they would have liked to include corpora but were not doing so either due to a discouraging lack of resources or because they viewed corpus activities as too time-consuming.

Q8. Which of the following statements would most accurately describe your reasons for not applying corpus linguistics in any form in your classes? (*Multiple answers possible*)

(A) Corpus linguistics has no immediate relevance to the training of EFL teachers.
(B) The curriculum is already full and corpus linguistics is not relevant enough to include it.
(C) I would like to include corpus linguistics more but the lack of suitable tools and resources is discouraging.
(D) I would like to include corpus linguistics more but it is too time-consuming.
(E) Other, please comment:

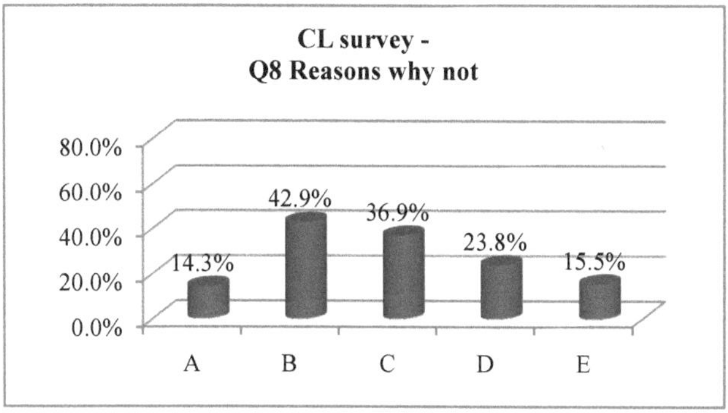

Figure 5-10: CL survey – Q8 Reasons why not

This result is rather encouraging as it indicates that with improved materials and with increasing availability of research on integration, more academics might be willing to use corpora as part of their teaching. The comments provided under "Other" warrant closer examination.[57] Some respondents reported that their lack of expertise was holding them back:

> I don't feel competent enough to apply corpus linguistics in my classes. *(LP; Vaguely familiar)*

> Don't know enough about corpus linguistics to teach with it. *(LP; Vaguely familiar)*

[57] Note that the answers provided are followed by information about the respondents. The information in brackets shows *teaching area* and *familiarity with corpus linguistics*.

> I need to spend more time learning how I could bring CL into the classroom. In other words, my lack of knowledge on the subject is holding me back. *(LP; Vaguely familiar)*

Two participants expressed their intentions to include corpora in their teaching in the near future:

> I am making an effort to include it pretty soon. *(TM; Vaguely familiar)*

> I would like to include corpus linguistics more and I intend to do it fairly soon. *(TM & LP; Vaguely familiar)*

Others felt that there is a general need for more research regarding the integration of corpus use:

> More research is needed before it can be implemented in teacher training courses. *(TM & LP; Vaguely familiar)*

The following comments seem to reveal a certain attitude towards corpus linguistics, one that does not appear to reflect much confidence in a strong relationship between corpus linguistics and language learning.

> We have other courses/departments for teaching methodology and linguistics - I tend to be doing more 'pure' language teaching. *(LP; Very familiar)*

> We have linguistic professors who teach this subject at our university. My courses are of practical nature. *(LP; Vaguely familiar)*

The participant who provided the first response was vaguely familiar with corpus linguistics, teaching in the area of language practice with a focus on translation and reported to have access to computers but didn't require them for teaching purposes. In this case it appears that corpora are not recognised as a valuable tool for language learning. The second comment was made by a participant who was very familiar with corpus linguistics, was teaching in the area of language practice and reported that access to computers was generally not available but at the same time they were also not required for their teaching purposes. The comment does not, however, provide enough information about the courses in order to make any interpretation in regard to the 'practical nature' of them. Other studies have found that while the use of corpora for teacher development is highly useful "it is difficult to envisage time in the programme of study for training in corpus consultation and analysis" (Amador Moreno *et al.* 2006: 100). We will come back to the relevance of these results in the discussion in Section 5.4.

Q9. Please specify how you employ corpora and concordancing software for teaching purposes: (*Multiple answers possible*)

(A) For the preparation of teaching materials.
(B) As an aid for correcting assignments.
(C) For learner-centred activities.
(D) Other, please specify:

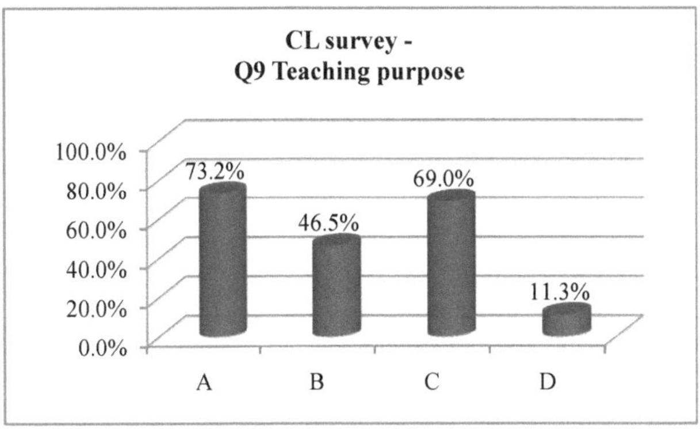

Figure 5-11: CL survey – Q9 Teaching purpose

Question 9 is the first in a series of five questions that were included in the survey in order to take a closer look at how the participants were employing corpora and also which corpora and concordancing software they were using in the process. Nearly three-quarters of all respondents (73.2%) reported to be using corpus resources to prepare teaching materials and almost as many (69%) employed corpora and concordancing software for learner-centred activities. Corpora as an aid to marking assignments were used by 46.5%. Comments under "Other" revealed that one respondent uses corpora to "demonstrate to future EFL teachers how concordancing can be used in the EFL classroom (as part of classes on CALL/TELL/WELL)" while another was introducing corpora as a "resource for learners' self-study (I provide them with *MicroConcord* and we jointly put together a small corpus each term)". The results from this question indicate that the academics who are using corpora and concordancing software as part of their teaching are not only using it as a tool to inform their teaching, but are applying corpora in their classrooms with students.

Q10. Which area(s) do you find corpus work especially useful for? (*Multiple answers possible*)?

(A) Grammar.
(B) Lexis.
(C) Translation.
(D) Stylistics/Literature.
(E) Cultural Studies.
(F) Other, please specify:

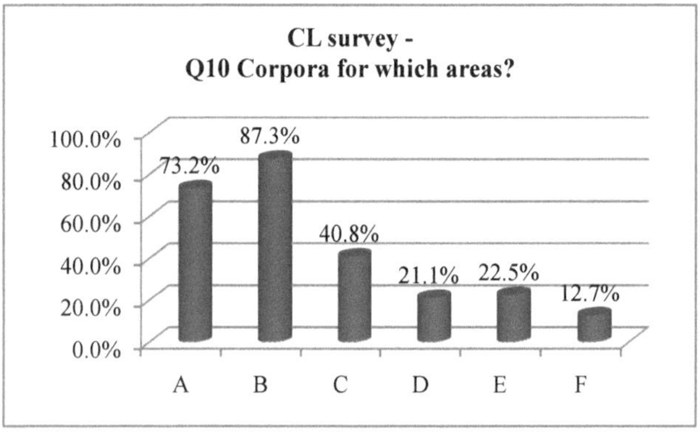

Figure 5-12: CL survey – Q10 Corpora for which areas?

The respondents found corpora to be most useful for the areas of Grammar (73.2%) and Lexis (87.3%). This is not surprising as these are the most common areas of research in which corpora are applied and they are also the areas which are most relevant to language education of the teacher trainees. Translation was also considered to be an area in which corpora are very useful, followed by Stylistics/Literature and Cultural Studies. Under "Other", the participants listed various other fields in which they considered corpora to be useful. They included diachronic linguistics, pragmatics, text linguistics, academic writing, syntax, semantics (collocations), discourse analysis, pragmatics, contrastive studies, and collocations.

One participant stated that corpora are also useful for the improvement of "language learning strategies" while another enthusiastically comments that "corpus work can be useful in almost every area! It's a great tool!!!"

Q11. What type of corpora do you work with for teaching purposes? (*Multiple answers possible*)

(A) Traditional reference corpora (*Brown*, *LOB*, *ACE*, etc.).
(B) Very large corpora (*BNC*, *BoE*, etc.).
(C) Parallel corpora (*Compara*, *ENPC*, etc.).
(D) Learner corpora (*ICLE*, etc.).
(E) Self-made corpora.
(F) Other, please specify:

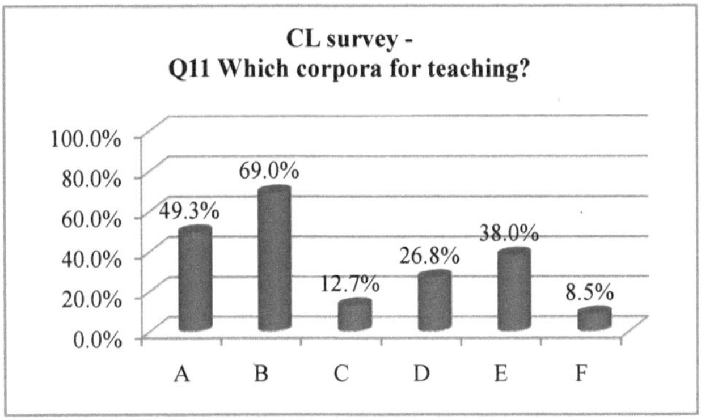

Figure 5-13: CL survey – Q11 Which corpora for teaching?

Very large corpora were the most popular type of corpus for teaching purposes (69%). This is rather surprising but interesting for a number of reasons. Firstly, very large corpora are generally not available to private end-users except through online concordancing interfaces, such as the *BNC Simple Search*, *BYU-BNC*: *The British National Corpus* (hereafter: *BYU-BNC*), or the *Collins Corpus Sampler*. While some online concordancers offer access to such large corpora and a great range of search options, most are restrictive in terms of access to the corpus and output options. Secondly, the advantages of using small corpora for teaching purposes have frequently been pointed out. Small corpora can help to "facilitate interpretation by learners" (Aston 1995: 259) and they are "more fully analysable" (Aston 1997c: 55). Traditional reference corpora were used by nearly half of all respondents (49.3%) while parallel corpora were chosen only by a minority (12.7%). A quarter of these participants are employing learner corpora for their teaching purposes. It is notable that more than one-third of the respondents work with self-made corpora. This large number may indicate a lack of already available resources. It may also point to a need for highly specified corpora. Respondents who stated that they were using self-made corpora were equally "very familiar" and "vaguely familiar" with corpus linguistics. Entries made under "Other" included 'Newspapers', 'Google', and 'WWW'. The last two were chosen by respondents who were "vaguely familiar" with corpus linguistics.

Q12. Please select the concordance program(s) you use for teaching purposes: (*Multiple answers possible*)

(A) *Longman Mini-Concordancer.*
(B) *MicroConcord.*
(C) *MonoConc.*
(D) *Wordsmith Tools.*
(E) I am not sure about the name of the program.
(F) Other, please specify:

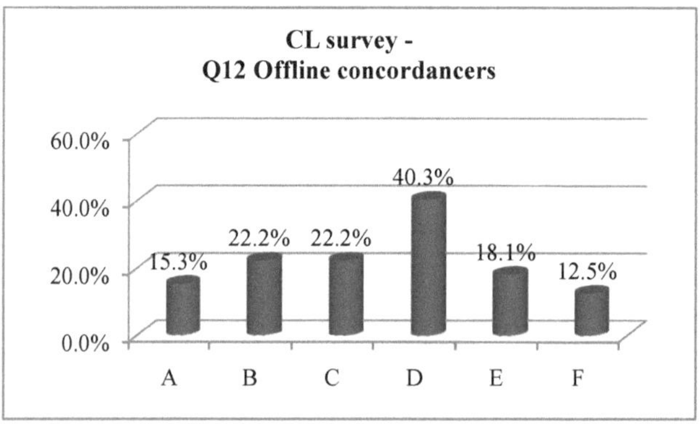

Figure 5-14: CL survey – Q12 Offline concordancers

The most popular offline concordancer was *Wordsmith Tools*. This suite of concordancing tools has dominated the market for some time. Its general popularity is reflected in these results. However, while it offers a wide and complex range of functions, it is not always the software of choice in a teaching context.

It is interesting to note the difference in choice of software when comparing the teaching educators questioned in this survey and the teacher trainees later on in the case study in Chapter 6. The by now very antiquated *Longman Mini Concordancer* (*LMC*) (Chandler 1990) was still used by 15.3% and the DOS-based *MicroConcord* (Scott & Johns 1993) was the software of choice for nearly a quarter of the respondents. These results are rather surprising as both programs are clearly outdated and not even truly compatible anymore with current operating systems. However, one of the comments may shed further light on one of the reasons these concordancers are still in use:

> We are thinking of buying a site license for WS Tools, but money is tight, as everywhere, so the learners can currently only use *MicroConcord.*

Furthermore, from the beginning, *MicroConcord* has been a popular tool to use with language learners – which was also its original purpose. A study published as recently as 2009 (Granath) reported to be using *MicroConcord*, "mainly because it is so simple that students can learn both simple and complex queries in a matter of minutes" (Granath 2009: 55). Other software that was listed by participants was:

> Simple concordance program;
> Learners' dictionary CD ROMs;
> KWiC Concordancer (freeware) and MultiConcord (test version);
> Ball's Web Frequency Indexer; and
> Wordcruncher.

The next question dealt with the participants' preference for online concordancers. As Figure 5-15 shows, the BNC Simple Search and Collins Corpus Sampler were the most popular online concordancers. Surprisingly, a relatively large number stated that they had not yet worked with online concordancers. Participants who stated this were either "very familiar" or "vaguely familiar" with corpus linguistics. Other online concordancers named by respondents included MICASE, BYU-BNC, and WebCorp. The results of this question indicate that there is still a lack of awareness of freely available and easy-to-use corpus tools.

Q13. A number of internet services provide online concordancers. Which one have you worked with previously for teaching purposes? (*Multiple answers possible*)

(A) *BNC Simple Search.*
(B) *Collins WordbanksOnline English Corpus Sampler.*
(C) *KWIC Concordancer* (Business Letters).
(D) I have not worked with online concordancers before.
(E) Other, please specify.

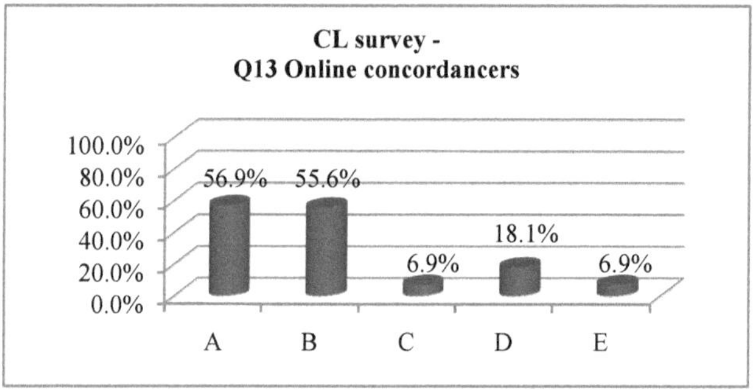

Figure 5-15: CL survey – Q13 Online concordancers

Question 14 was included in order to determine whether there were any areas in particular that those respondents who had some degree of familiarity with corpus linguistics and were using corpora for teaching purposes would like to see improved. Concordancing software and relevant publications were both chosen by a clear majority of the respondents. As Figure 5-16 shows, there is also a high demand for improvements in the area of corpora. These results correlate with the outcomes from Question 8 where those respondents who, despite their familiarity with corpus linguistics, chose not to teach with corpora, gave reasons for that decision. Over a third of these participants had stated that they would like to include corpus linguistics but did not do so due to a discouraging lack of suitable tools and resources. Most answers provided under "Others" were clearly identifiable with one of the first three answers and were therefore counted towards them.

Q14. Which of the following areas would you like to see improved in relation to applied corpus linguistics? (*Multiple answers possible*)

(A) Corpora.
(B) Concordancing software.
(C) Relevant publications.
(D) Other, please specify.

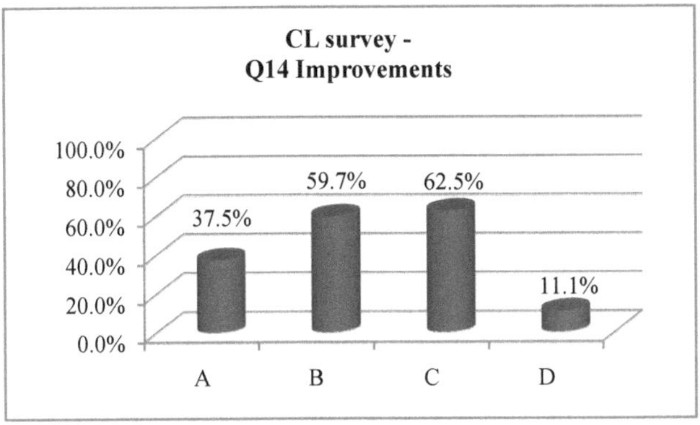

Figure 5-16: CL survey – Q14 Improvements

Two comments given under "Other" stood out in that they were requests for concrete advice on how to integrate corpora and how to use them for language teaching and learning:

> Introductions for teacher training students in particular! Giving future teachers more (and easier) guidelines on how to use a corpus in a foreign language classroom. There is not enough material and research yet!

> More activity resource books like Sinclair's (2003) *Reading Concordances*.

The results from this question indicate that the improvement of tools and resources is of particular importance to the participants.

Q15. The space below has been provided for you in case you have any comments or suggestions either in regard to the discussed topic or the survey itself.

The survey ended with Question 15 for everyone. This open-ended question provided space for the participants to freely comment on the topic or the survey itself. Many respondents took the opportunity and commented more in-depth on the topic. Due to the fact that the question was non-specific and open-ended, the answers can only provide anecdotal evidence for each of the topics raised by the participants. Nevertheless, the comments offer very interesting insights into the issues raised by the participants. In the analysis below, comments are followed by a short profile on the respondent (*familiarity with the subject*; *teaching with corpora: Yes/No*; *desired improvements* (for respondents who were teaching with corpora)/ *Reasons for not teaching* (for those respondents who were not teaching with corpora)). A number of respondents took the opportunity again to express their dismay about the lack of resources, regarding both corpus resources and IT infrastructure, available to them:

> I am dismayed by the lack of free, quality corpora and tools available on-line for student use. *(Very familiar; Teaching: Yes; Improvements: Corpora, Software)*

> Seems as if the most 'interesting' corpora are always either too expensive or not easily accessible, of course because they are owned by publishing houses. *(Very familiar; Teaching: Yes; Improvements: Corpora, Software, Publications)*

> As I said, my classes are too large to fit into the lab. *(Very familiar; Teaching: No; Reason: Curriculum full, CL not relevant)*

As mentioned before in the context of Questions 8 and 14, there is evidently a need for improved, more easily available corpora and corpus analysis software. In a similar vein, many respondents complained about lack of time and lack of funding:

> We find that few students have the time, or the inclination to study independently of their classes. Many work to finance their studies and wish to complete them as soon as possible. The willingness to work outside the prescribed program is limited and since corpus work is not prescribed … *(Very familiar; Teaching: Yes; Improvements: Corpora)*

As EFL trainers, we are expected to be familiar with and use modern media & technology, but, not being 'Wissenschaftler' ['scientists'], the funding is totally inadequate. Germany in particular makes a very clear distinction between language teachers/trainers (usually LfbAs) and Wissenschaftler, the latter tending to look down on the former. Additionally, new cuts in educational funding and the new BA are increasingly occurring at the expense of Language Practice, as Wissenschaft [sciences] tries to lay hold of what little funding there is. Result: too little time, little or no encouragement, no funding. 7 years ago I was really gung-ho to integrate CL in my teaching. Now I am resigned to it being at best a fair-weather hobby. What a shame! *(Vaguely familiar; Teaching: Yes; Improvements: Corpora, Software, Publications)*

It's cuts, cuts, cuts over here – often it's as if it's only just possible to give students the absolute minimum of support, with colleagues' posts cut as soon as they retire and student numbers mounting at the same time. Under these circumstances, time and energy for new approaches dwindles fast (as does motivation, if I'm scrupulously honest). *(Vaguely familiar; Teaching: No; Reason: Lack of resources, too time-consuming)*

We simply have too much routine work to deal with so that, relevant though this may be, it cannot easily be made part of our teaching. *(Vaguely familiar; Teaching: No; Reason: Too time-consuming)*

In our department, the linguistic and methodological aspects of EFL teacher training are pretty well separate – in terms of theory and application. Our English native speakers seem to be on the cultural studies end of the spectrum while the non-native English-speaking teaching staff are linguists. However, the native-speakers are the ones who teach grammar and, to some extent, translation. I suspect this model is not unusual – or am I mistaken? Good luck with this research project! *(Vaguely familiar; Teaching: No; Reason: Different focus)*

A number of structural problems are mentioned in these comments that appear to discourage the integration of corpus work in teacher training by teacher educators. On the one hand, there is the perception that most students' time and willingness to work is limited. On the other hand, it appears that academics feel increasingly under pressure due to insufficient funding, lack of time, and a constant increase in student numbers. However, what all of these comments have in common is a view that corpus work is an extra work load that is not an essential let alone compulsory part of the curriculum. Echoing the comments provided in Question 14, a few respondents made requests for more research on implementation methods:

> I would like some CONCRETE suggestions as to how exactly to apply corpus linguistics in essay or translation homework or class work assignments. Thanks in advance. *(Very familiar; Teaching: No; Reason: Lack of resources)*

> As mentioned before, I think corpora are a great tool (= working with 'real language'!), but they still lack classroom implementation – most teachers either don't have the technical knowledge to use concordance software properly or they simply don't have the equipment to use it in class. Unfortunately there are still many problems to be solved before corpora become an inherent part of (foreign) language teaching. *(Very familiar; Teaching: Yes; Improvements: Software, Publications)*

Encouragingly, a number of the respondents were clearly in favour of using corpora as part of their teaching but some felt that time for further development was needed.

> CL will become more and more important in the future (e.g. with regard to authentic English usage and its relevance to classroom discourse and interaction, integrated lexico-grammatical learning, to learner autonomy, etc.) *(Vaguely familiar; Teaching: No; Reason: More research for implementation needed)*

> I think CL should be part of the curriculum for FL teachers. *(Vaguely familiar; Teaching: No; Reason: Plans to include CL soon)*

> Our *Bundesland* is re-developing courses for teacher training at the moment (I have just been put in charge of it for English), but at the moment we have only one compulsory course (Fachdidaktik Englisch) and obviously time is limited and the knowledge of the students in this area rather basic ... Do another survey in 10 years time and you will get very different results. *(Vaguely familiar; Teaching: No; Reason: Corpora)*

> As I only started working full time at this university not long ago (after having worked as a school teacher for quite a few years), I am still sorting out what I can do in addition to the courses I am offering at the moment. I am really interested in Corpus linguistics and I will

> work with/integrate it more in the future. *(Vaguely familiar; Teaching: No; Reason: Plans to include CL soon)*
>
> Use of corpora should be more widely known as a tool in language learning *(Vaguely familiar; Teaching: Yes; Improvements: Software, Publications)*
>
> The topic obviously has enormous potential in language teaching, but if we as teacher trainers are just learning to use these things it will take a while for the effects to trickle down. Despite all rumours of the younger generation being more and more computer literate, teachers of my generation (early 40s) still seem in general to be far ahead of students, at least here. *(Vaguely familiar; Teaching: Yes; Improvements: Software, Publications)*

In particular these last comments highlight the fact that teacher educators see potential in the use of corpora as part of teacher training. The next section presents the results from expert interviews with teacher educators in the fields of teaching methodology and applied linguistics. Their insights and opinions on the topic will expand on the findings from this survey. At the end of this chapter, the results of both the survey and the expert interviews will be discussed.

5.3 Expert interviews

5.3.1 Research setup and participants

This section reports on the outcomes of five interviews conducted with teacher educators in the fields of applied linguistics, teaching methodology and language practice at universities in Germany. The purpose of these interviews was to expand and to elaborate on the findings of the survey reported in the previous section. In particular, the interviews presented here provide an opportunity to gain more insight into the views and opinions of these experts in regard to the role of and integration of corpus linguistics in language education. According to Bogner and Menz (2009),

> [a]n expert has technical, process and interpretative knowledge that refers to a specific field of action, by virtue of the fact that the expert acts in a relevant way (for example, in a particular organizational field or the expert's own professional area). In this respect, expert knowledge consists not only of systematized, reflexively accessible

> knowledge relating to a specialized subject or field, but also has to a considerable extent the character of practical or action knowledge, which incorporates a range of quite disparate maxims for action, individual rules of decision, collective orientations and patterns of social interpretation. (Bogner & Menz 2009: 54-55)

The expert interview as a methodology to gather qualitative data finds widespread application in social sciences and is a frequently used tool in qualitative research. However, some criticism has been made in regard to its lack of methodological and theoretical background. Trinczek (2009: 203) observes that "purists frequently raise objections to the expert interview on grounds of it being a 'dirty method'", and that these interviews accordingly "operate in a 'no-man's land' somewhere between the qualitative and quantitative paradigm devoid of much profound reflection" (2009: 203). At the same time, expert interviews provide a real opportunity to explore an individual's in-depth experiences in their respective field of expertise. As such, the expert interviews can adequately provide unique insights that no other research method can supply.

The opportunity to interview these experts presented itself after the survey had closed, as contact had been established with the interviewees via correspondence in regard to the survey. The participants of the interviews were deemed qualified as experts in relation to the matter at hand because they are teacher educators at universities in Germany with professional experience in the areas of applied linguistics, teaching methodology and/or language practice. The interviewees have a range of years of experience not only as teacher educators but also as experts in their fields. The interviews were conducted in July 2005, after the survey was closed for submissions. The chosen interviewees had all participated in the survey; however, as the survey was anonymous, their answers in the analysis of the survey were not identifiable.

The individual interviews were conducted face-to-face in three cases and over the phone in two cases. All the interviews were audio taped with the participants' permission.[58] Each interview lasted approximately 30 minutes. For the purpose of subsequent evaluation, the interviews were transcribed shortly after the recordings were made. The interviews were all structured the same way. At the commencement of each interview, the participants were asked to describe their background in regard to their teaching and research experience as part of their position. After establishing the participant's background, the interview then continued with open questions regarding the expert's opinion on the role of corpora in language education, possible reasons for the lack of implementation, and proposals of solutions for bridging the gap. For the analysis

[58] Approval to conduct the interviews was obtained from Macquarie University's Human Research Ethics Committee prior to the interviews. Furthermore, the participants were provided with an information sheet and consent form as per request by the Committee.

below, the transcripts were analysed in detail. By close examination of the transcripts, significant statements were identified which will be analysed in a descriptive manner in the following section. The expert interviews presented in this section serve an exploratory function. They are representative only of the interviewees' views and opinions which may, however, contribute to shed further light on the role of corpora in language education, in this case LTE in particular.

5.3.2 Data analysis

In order to gain a better understanding of this group of experts and also to establish their role in the field, I will first of all report their professional background. All of the interviewees were teacher educators with more than 10 years of experience in their profession. Based on the information supplied by the interviewees in their responses to the first question regarding their professional experience, the following profiles can be drawn up:[59]

> Expert A's professional expertise lies in teaching methodology with a strong focus on the use of new technologies in language education. Linguistics is not part of his/her research profile and his/her experience with corpora in language education is only marginal. Topics of courses taught for teacher trainees include task-based learning, intercultural learning, computer-mediated communication, and language practice with a particular focus on teaching methodology. Furthermore, s/he has a keen interest and past experience in the development of teaching materials.

> Expert B is one of two interviewees to hold a combined position in applied linguistics and teaching methodology (with a special focus on the use of new technologies). S/He has professional experience in the area of corpus linguistics and has a particular interest in corpora for language awareness training. Other major research interests include second language acquisition, learning and teaching strategies, and phonology, to name a few.

> Expert C, who also holds a combined position in applied linguistics and teaching methodology, has a professional background in corpus

[59] Please note that these profiles cannot do justice to the academic and professional accomplishments of the participating researchers. These profiles purely serve the purpose of providing relevant background information on the interviewee that is relevant to their role as an expert teacher educator for this study.

linguistics, functional grammar, intercultural learning and multilingualism. S/He has extensive experience in the area of integrating technology into language learning environments and teaches courses on a diverse number of topics including corpus linguistics and language learning, task-based learning and introductory courses on teaching methodology and applied linguistics.

Expert D's professional experience is mainly in the area of teaching methodology. S/He has a keen interest in literature and teaching methodology, intercultural learning, the use of new technologies in the foreign language classroom, content-based learning and language assessment. S/He developed an interest in corpora for language teaching in the context of language awareness training for teacher trainees and in the potential of corpora to create a natural focus on language in the context of language learning.

Expert E chairs the department of English linguistics at his/her institution. S/He maintains close ties to the teaching methodology department of that university with a particular focus on the application of corpora in language education. S/He has researched and published extensively in the area of corpus linguistics and language education as well as diverse range of other linguistic topics.

The profiles show that this is a group of experts that gives voice to the linguistic viewpoint as much as that of the teaching perspective.
The interviewees were asked to comment on the following three topics:

(i) The role of corpora in language education;
(ii) Reasons for the lack of implementation in language teaching practice; and
(iii) Proposals for solutions to the lack of implementation.

The following three sections describe the comments provided by the experts on these topics. The analysis of the transcript showed that the experts shared similar views on a number of points made. Statements made by individuals are specially marked by the letter in brackets (referring to the experts A-E).

(i) The role of corpora in language education

After having established the professional background of the participants, the first question dealt with the potential the experts saw for corpora in language learning and teaching. The interviewees found corpus applications in the classroom to be particularly relevant in relation to the development of language awareness [A-E], learning strategies [B], and problem-solving skills [A] in learners. They considered this approach to be especially compatible with learner-centred approaches to language learning [C] and task-based learning [A]. Most importantly, as they pointed out, corpus tasks lend themselves to create a focus on language, to talk about language and develop language itself as an interesting topic which means to study language as content. This reflects the assumptions made about the potential of corpora for language awareness in Section 3.3.3. In addition to this, the value of corpus tasks for fostering an understanding of language as a dynamic organism, rather than a predefined system governed by strict rules, was highlighted by the participants [A, B, D].

All of the experts found knowledge of corpus linguistics to be of vital importance for teachers. On the one hand, teachers should be aware of the impact corpora have had on language description and the flow-on effect of this on textbooks and references such as dictionaries and grammars [E]. On the other hand, corpora have great potential for developing life-long learning strategies in teachers [A]. This is of critical importance because research is often no longer part of the teacher's professional life after completing their university studies [D]. All interviewees emphasised the significance of introducing corpora in the initial training phase in order to guarantee successful delivery of a sound theoretical background and to provide sufficient learning opportunities with corpora to enable teachers to create rich learning environments with these tools and resources. According to the experts, the integration of corpus linguistics in pre-service teacher training is a major contributing factor in advancing the integration of corpus linguistics in language teaching practices. In this context, it was also emphasised that language practice courses for teacher trainees should definitely incorporate concordancing activities as they offered prime opportunities to familiarise teacher trainees with corpus tools as part of their own language learning experience [A]. In regard to this, it was further pointed out how important it is to teach about corpora within a pedagogical framework.

(ii) Reasons for the lack of implementation in language teaching practice

After discussing the potential of corpora in language education, the interviewees were questioned in regard to their views on the reasons for a continuing lack of implementation. While the experts' opinions on the potential of corpora largely converged, their observations regarding the lack of application of corpora differed somewhat in their focus on the problem. One of the experts made a number of observations regarding the secondary school system in Germany that worked against an application of corpora in language classrooms [B]. Firstly, s/he commented that in general the acceptance and transfer of insights from research to the classroom is a very slow process. This view was shared by one of the other experts [E]. Purely practical factors, such as lack of IT skills and infrastructure, overburdened teachers and lack of textbooks reflecting such research achievements, significantly hinder this process [A, B, E]. Secondly, class sessions at secondary institutions in Germany are generally limited to 45 minutes which, according to this expert [B], is not conducive to a teaching approach incorporating research tasks. Another important point made by this expert relates to the permanent pressure teachers are under to assess students with grades. There are currently no available guidelines as to how to assess concordance-based activities. This makes it difficult for teachers to integrate such tasks.

One of the other experts emphasised the importance of providing "class-ready" materials to teachers who want to integrate corpus tasks, although he conceded that it is a long way from research idea to textbook [A]. All of the experts highlighted the fact that teachers cannot be expected to create their own materials and that a lack of appropriate classroom materials that are closely integrated with the rest of the curriculum will hamper any serious efforts of integrating corpus tasks. The question that needs to be answered is who should create these materials? According to one of the experts, linguists are not sufficiently interested in language methodology and experts in the latter often lack the necessary expertise in corpus linguistics [B]. Another observation made by one of the interviewees concerns the ageing teaching population in Germany [E]. Once teachers have completed their studies at university, there is generally neither reason nor desire or time to follow new developments in methodology research (*Wissenschaftsferne bedingt durch das System*). In addition to a continued reluctance to use IT in the classroom among many practitioners, the lack of appropriate materials [publications, corpora and software] puts off even those that know of corpus linguistics and are willing to implement these tools and resources [A-E]. This is also reflected in the outcome of the survey presented in this chapter.

Apart from such practical considerations, one of the experts remarked that it is also important as a linguist to keep in mind that what might be interesting or fascinating for linguists may not generate the same interest in the classroom or may even be threatening or distressing for teachers [B, E]. In regard to this, it is also vital to remember that corpora in the classroom serve a different function and have to be used on a different level than from a linguistic perspective.

(iii) Proposals for solutions to the lack of implementation

Two main arguments emerged from questioning the experts on possible solutions to improve the transfer of corpus methods to classroom practices.

Firstly, the experts all emphasised that a solution can only be found from within teaching methodology; in other words it is important to focus on the needs of learners and teachers, not the desires of linguists. It is important not to attempt 'didacticised' linguistics [D], or in Widdowson's [1980, 2000] terms 'linguistics applied', but teaching methodology has to drive and inform the linguistic developments that are relevant to the processes of teaching and learning a language. Therefore, it is important to provide a sound pedagogical framework for the linguistic components – only then will practitioners or trainees become interested in this approach as it is not something that can be dictated from above [A]. Intrinsic motivation can only develop when teacher trainees experience it as a successful tool for their language learning process. As two of the experts point out, in the past the relationship between teaching methodology and linguistics was problematic due to attempts of transferring research directly into the classroom as was the case with structuralism and generative grammar. Secondly, it was suggested that the integration of corpus linguistics into pre-service teacher training would greatly benefit from team-teaching by teacher educators from linguistics and teaching methodology departments [A, B, C]. However, one major obstacle was identified by the participants in the form of the institutional situation at universities as it is reflected in the separation of the disciplines. There was agreement by all of the experts that it is crucial to convince academics from both linguistics and teaching methodology to cooperate. However, at the same time, the participants mentioned that a number of difficulties would likely be associated with such an approach, namely the lack of cooperation and communication between disciplines. While it is deemed to be the right approach, it was also labelled as highly ambitious [A, C]. The process of delivering teacher education as part of a modular design [a part of the Bologna Process described in Section 5.1] may well provide future opportunities for such a cross-disciplinary approach.

Finally, all the experts mentioned throughout their interviews the problematic and prevailing lack of teaching materials, lack of suitable software, and lack of appropriate corpora. The importance of providing these resources is not to be underestimated. Appropriate classroom materials, tangible teaching suggestions, and classroom-ready content are seen as key factors of successful integration.

5.4 Discussion of results

> Even today, it is still perfectly possible for each and every student of English language and literature in virtually all English departments in Germany to take a university degree without ever having delved into corpus linguistics. Thus, it is important to keep in mind that for the time being – and in the foreseeable future – most newly-fledged

> English teachers enter schools with anything but a detailed knowledge about corpus linguistics. (Mukherjee 2004: 244)

The survey presented in this chapter set out to investigate to what extent teacher educators in the areas of teaching methodology and language practice were using corpora as part of their teaching. The results of the survey indicate that corpora still only play a minor role in the teaching practices of teacher educators in those areas. This outcome corroborates the statements made by researchers as detailed in Section 4.1, in regards to the gap between research efforts in applied corpus linguistics and their effects on actual teaching practices. The limited knowledge of corpus linguistics (only 15.6% of respondents were very familiar with corpus linguistics) and the limited use of corpora for teaching purposes (less than half of the respondents with any knowledge of corpora were actually teaching with them) indicate that consequently only a small portion of teacher trainees encounter corpora in language practice or teaching methodology courses.

The main reason respondents gave for choosing to not teach with corpora was that the curriculum was already full and that corpus linguistics was not relevant enough to EFL teacher training to include it. Lack of materials and lack of time were also two major deterrent factors. These results are echoed in Thompson's (2006) report about the uptake of corpora in EAP in the United Kingdom:

> The most common reasons [for not using corpora] given by the respondents were that these institutions lack resources, and they lacked familiarity with both the resources and with potential applications. In several cases, they also claimed that their units were already overworked and did not have time to learn about corpora. (Thompson 2006: 14-15)

From the answers provided in the last question of the survey, Question 15, which invited comments on the survey or the topic itself, a number of structural problems at the institutional level emerge. These comments indicate that the integration of corpus linguistics is hampered by a lack of funding and resources ("too little time, little or no encouragement, no funding") and by a lack of cooperation of the linguistics and teaching methodology departments ("In our department, the linguistic and methodological aspects of EFL teacher training are pretty well separate – in terms of theory and application.").

In particular the last point was echoed by the participants of the expert interviews conducted shortly after the survey had ended. The interviews highlighted the fact that experts see the value of teaching with corpora primarily in its unique capacity of raising language awareness by creating a focus on language as content and in the relevance of this approach for central pedagogical concepts such as learner-centeredness, task-based learning, development of problem-solving skills and life-long learning strategies in learners and teachers. Based on the statements by the experts, pursuing the implementation of corpus use in teacher training is desirable but a number of issues remain to be resolved. In particular, a lack of 'classroom-ready' materials, including user-friendly software and ready-to-use work sheets, as well as a lack of guidelines for the assessment of corpus tasks in the classroom are major factors in the continuing lack of application. Furthermore, regarding the current situation in Germany, an ageing teacher population and a continuing reluctance to incorporate IT in teaching practices contribute to a lack of implementation of corpus tools and methods. In order to advance the use of corpora in LTE, cooperation between departments is seen as essential, yet hard to achieve.

In summary, the results from both the survey and the expert interviews lead to the following conclusions:

(i) Teaching with corpora in language practice and teaching methodology courses for teacher trainees remains limited.
(ii) Teacher educators in these areas have limited knowledge of corpus linguistics and many decide not to use corpora due to a perceived lack of relevance of corpora for ELT, a lack of materials, and structural problems like lack of funding and lack of cooperation between departments.

Three significant factors could be identified from the expert interviews in order to further increase the role of corpora in teaching practices:

(i) Concerns based in teaching methodology must inform the process of transferring corpora into the classroom as a teaching resource and method.
(ii) Integrating corpora into pre-service LTE is a significant step towards training teachers appropriately in the use of corpora for teaching.
(iii) Creating appropriate classroom materials is central to any efforts of popularising the use of corpora for teaching purposes.

But what could this look like in practice? How can more insight be gained into the processes of teaching with corpora from a pedagogical perspective as demanded by the experts? As Mukherjee (2006b: 20) rightly points out, the "gap [between research and classroom application] can only be bridged if [...] corpus-based activities are evaluated under real-time conditions in actual classroom contexts and both from teachers' and learners' perspective". In particular, the role of the teacher in the process of integrating corpora in everyday language teaching is an area seemingly as of yet not fully explored. For this reason, Chapter 6 presents a case study with teacher trainees which highlights their experiences during a course in which they were learning with corpora and learning how to teach with corpora.

6 Case study: learning *and* teaching with corpora

> For publishers, corpora are a given; for researchers, corpora are a given; and it is past time for our future teachers to become actively involved and critically engaged with their use at the first possible opportunity, which, for most, comes during teacher education.
>
> (Farr 2010a: 628-629)

The analysis in Chapter 4 has demonstrated that teachers play a crucial role in advancing the popularisation of corpora in language education. It was argued that teachers require training not only on how to learn but also how to teach with corpora, as the latter can pose significant challenges to the traditional role of the teacher. Language teacher education was identified as the most productive phase to introduce corpora to teachers. Anecdotal evidence from a small number of currently available studies indicates that corpora currently do not play an important role in language teacher education. In response to this lack of evidence, Chapter 5 presented a survey on the use of corpora in language teacher education in the areas of teaching methodology and language practice. The results of the survey confirmed that teacher trainees currently have only limited exposure to corpora in these areas. As a result of this, a case study with teacher trainees was conducted in order to gain more insight into the difficulties teachers might face in the process of teaching with corpora. The case study presented in the current chapter thus acts as an example of a course in LTE that introduces teacher trainees to learning *and* teaching with corpora.

6.1 Learning *and* teaching with corpora

In the context of their study of learner perspectives on DDL, Götz and Mukherjee (2006) observe that

> [t]here is still a general lack of language-pedagogically motivated and, in particular, learner-centred evaluation studies: we think that the learner's perspective has, curiously enough, been notoriously under-represented in applied corpus-linguistic research. (Mukherjee 2006: 50)

However, as was demonstrated in the analysis in Section 4.2, the number of evaluative studies focusing on learner behaviour and attitudes as well as learning outcomes from corpus-based activities has been steadily growing over the years.

In contrast, studies exploring the teacher's perspective are still notably absent. The majority of studies focus on the learner, on learning opportunities, and learning outcomes. Furthermore, these studies are almost exclusively conducted by practitioners who themselves are generally experts in corpus linguistics. Any challenges that teachers who are not corpus experts, face, are therefore unlikely to be noticed and discussed. The critical analysis in Section 4.3.5 has demonstrated that teachers in fact need to overcome a number of challenges when intending to include corpora in their classrooms, and that this may be a major factor that discourages the use of corpora for language learning and teaching. Teachers play a vital role in the process of implementing corpora as learning tools and resources. More recently, the importance of teacher mediation "in the process of recontextualising corpora and any useful findings from corpus-based description" (O'Keeffe & Farr 2003: 391) has been increasingly recognised. Furthermore, the conclusion was reached that teachers are most likely the main conduit through which corpora will enter mainstream classroom practices, short of corpora becoming mandatory components in national curricula. From the observation that "mediation by the teacher is a necessary prerequisite for successful application of computer corpora in language teaching", it is only a natural next step to conclude that this "should therefore be given sufficient attention in teacher education courses." (Kaltenböck & Mehlmauer-Larcher 2005: 81).

Gaining a better understanding and appreciation of the challenges teachers face when using corpora in the classroom, is thus a crucial step to a more widespread application of corpora in language teaching. The stage of pre-service LTE is a valuable opportunity for teacher trainees to explore the use of corpora from the perspective of their role as learner *and* as teacher. In-depth training can be provided, and teacher trainees can discover the potential of corpora as part of their own studies. If they find their learning experience with corpora to be beneficial, then this is likely to positively influence their decision to use corpora for their own teaching later on. Recognising that there is a significant difference between learning and teaching with corpora, as well as providing teacher trainees with the necessary skills, is of great importance. This was the main rationale for conducting the present case study which was undertaken at Duisburg-Essen University, Germany, in the second academic term of 2005.[60]

[60] Approval to conduct the interviews was obtained from the Human Research Ethics Committee, Macquarie University.

6.2 Research design

The aim of this case study was to create a learning experience for teacher trainees from two perspectives: as learner *and* as teacher. The study was conducted with a group of teacher trainees who had enrolled into a course entitled 'Data-driven learning: The learner as researcher'. The goal of the course was for participants to develop a basic understanding of corpus analysis and to learn about using direct applications of corpus-based activities in the classroom. In order to increase their awareness of this learning experience, teacher trainees were encouraged to reflect on their learning process in relation to their future role as teachers in the form of classroom discussions and reflective writing tasks. In the last part of the course, the teacher trainees were given the task to create corpus-based teaching activities as supplemental material to standard EFL textbooks. In this scenario, the teacher trainees had to combine their own learning experiences with their teaching expertise in order to accomplish the successful transition from the role of learner to teacher.

Current research into language teacher education underlines the significance of creating models of reflected learning experiences in order to "allow student teachers to experience themselves the learning process that they are supposed to organize with their EFL students" (Müller-Hartmann & Schocker-von Ditfurth 2004: 16). This approach is part of a model these authors put forth which sees "language teachers as generators of theories based on a reflection of their own language learning experiences and on an ongoing reflection of their classroom teaching" (2004: 9). In a broader context, such an approach is also in line with well-established learning models for adult development such as Kolb's (1984) 'Experiential learning cycle'.

Accordingly, one of the present case study's main goals was to gain insight into the teacher trainees' perspective on teaching with corpora based on their reflections and feedback. The results of the study will contribute to an improved understanding of the process of using corpora in the language classroom and the ensuing challenges to the role of the teacher.

6.2.1 Research setup and participants

The course took place at the English Department of Duisburg-Essen University, Germany, in Semester 2 of the academic year of 2005. As detailed in Section 5.2.1, the study programme for a teaching degree in EFL includes courses from linguistics, literature, language practice and teaching methodology. Completion of the course described here could be counted as credit towards fulfilment of the requirements of linguistics or teaching methodology courses. Successful completion of the introductory courses of linguistics and teaching methodology as well as basic IT competence were set as prerequisites for participation in the course.

The course ran for 11 weeks with one session per week lasting two hours. These sessions took place in the computer lab which was equipped with individual computer stations connected to the internet. Corpus resources available to the teacher trainees included corpora from the *ICAME* CD-Rom v.2 (1999), the concordancing software *MonoConc Pro 2.2* (Barlow 2002), *Wordsmith Tools 4* (Scott 2004), *ConcApp 4* (Greaves 2003), *AntConc 3* (Anthony 2004), and *Concordancer 3.2* (Watt 2004). The choice of resources was dictated by what was made available through the department and any freely available resources found online. The course aimed to convey the following:

- a basic understanding of corpus-based language analysis,
- the ability to work with concordancing software,
- ways of using corpora in the language classroom,
- the production of teaching materials with corpora and concordances, and
- the integration of these materials in future teaching practices.

The introduction to corpus analysis took place through a series of small training units that included presentations followed by related hands-on concordancing activities. These training units formed a major part of the teacher trainees' learning experience. They were designed to gradually introduce the subject matter in a combination of theory and practice; an approach which provided the participants with the opportunity to discover facts and theories while actively taking part in the learning process. This put the teacher trainees into the role of the learner. The purpose of this approach was twofold. First, they were to acquire the necessary knowledge to learn with corpora, and, secondly, the experience was to enable them as teachers to reflect back on this process when deciding how to best teach with corpus tools and resources. After completing each training unit, a discussion was held in the classroom. Often in the form of brainstorming and collecting ideas on the whiteboard, the teacher trainees were encouraged to reflect on their learning experience and discuss it from their perspective both as learner and as teacher. In order to provide a relevant framework for these discussions, the Official Teaching Guidelines for Secondary Education in North Rhine-Westphalia (*Kernlehrpläne*) were introduced early on.[61] As the teaching guidelines are binding for all secondary educational

[61] The Department of Education in NRW describes the teaching guidelines as an essential element of a contemporary and comprehensive concept for the development and quality assurance in education. In particular, the teaching guidelines define the educational goals and detailed requirements for each subject. The guidelines are binding and their relevance is seen to extend beyond school education to ensure the delivery of life-long learning

institutions, they were highly relevant for the teacher trainees' future professional role. The desired target competencies for learners of English as defined in the guidelines served as an important frame of reference during the class discussions. The requisites for successful participation in the course were regular attendance and completion of a number of smaller projects. These projects included writing a reflective essay on one of the training units, reviewing concordancing software, and producing a language exercise with concordances for learners. The fulfilment of these requirements led to a participation credit (*Teilnahmenachweis*) for the course.

Eighteen teacher trainees (14 females and four males, aged between 19 and 33) of EFL participated in the course. The participants were all studying to become teachers of English at secondary educational institutions in Germany. All participants had an advanced level of English language proficiency arising from their secondary school education and their studies at university. According to their own assessment as part of a questionnaire, their computer skills ranged from basic (50%), to intermediate (39%) and more advanced skills (11%). Except for one student teacher, the participants had no previous knowledge of corpus linguistics. All participants had previously gained teaching experience (*Schulpraktikum*) as part of their study programme.

6.2.2 Data collection

The approach adopted for this case study is essentially qualitative. Data was collected in the form of (i) questionnaires and materials produced by the participants. These included (ii) a reflective essay, (iii) a software review, and (iv) teaching materials the trainees designed towards the end of the course.

(i) Questionnaires

The teacher trainees were asked to complete a questionnaire at the beginning and at the end of the course. During the first session of the course, the teacher trainees were informed that participation in the questionnaires was not compulsory and assured that all names and comments would remain anonymous for any subsequent use for publication. The purpose of the first questionnaire was to determine the teacher trainees' previous knowledge of corpus linguistics. The second questionnaire gathered information on computer proficiency and its rele-

strategies and competencies to cope with future challenges of personal and professional life. In regard to individual school subjects, like 'English', the teaching guidelines formulate skills expectations and binding content. They also deliver criteria for performance evaluation (see Department of Education, NRW, website).

vance to teaching, course content, concordancers, feedback on the DDL task and questions regarding the use of corpora in language teaching. The questionnaires were filled out in class in the first and last session of the course respectively. Therefore, the return rate was very high as all teacher trainees were present and agreed to participate in the questionnaires.

The questionnaires were made up of closed, semi-open and open questions. Closed questions were asked to limit the respondents to a range of fixed answers on particular points to gather quantitative information; for example, about their pre-existing knowledge regarding computers and corpus linguistics. The semi-open questions provided the opportunity to combine quantitative and qualitative measures. Open questions were deemed particularly useful in this case study as they encouraged the participants to elaborate on their learning experiences and provided them with the opportunity to give feedback on a number of relevant issues.[62]

(ii) Student teacher reviews of concordancing software

One of the aims of the course was to familiarise the teacher trainees with the use of concordancing software. For this purpose, the participants explored and subsequently reviewed a number of concordancers in groups of two or three. The reviews consisted of a template which detailed the specifications of the software. In addition, each group wrote a short review of the software in which they made statements on user-friendliness and suitability for classroom use.

(iii) Reflective essays

As part of the process of reflection, the teacher trainees were asked to write a reflective essay. These reflective essays proved to be a particularly rich source of information on the teacher trainees' thoughts regarding teaching with corpora.

(iv) Student teacher project: DDL task

Towards the end of the course, the teacher trainees were asked to create a DDL task based on EFL textbooks and present them in class. The purpose of this task was to provide the participants with the opportunity to utilise their knowledge gained throughout the course and write a learning activity. Finally, the outcomes

---

[62] Note that the course was held in English. The questionnaires were also administered in English as were the answers provided by the teacher trainees.

from the participants' projects – namely the software reviews, the essays, and the handouts from the DDL task – were put together and edited into a small booklet called 'DDL Guide'. This booklet also included a section on the advantages and disadvantages of online and offline concordancers, a list of text resources (corpora and text archives online), and a bibliography of publications on DDL and other topics discussed throughout the course. An electronic copy was distributed to the course participants at the end of the course. The purpose of the DDL Guide was to provide the trainees with relevant materials to encourage them to make use of corpora in the future.

6.3 Data analysis

6.3.1 Questionnaire I

The only prerequisites for enrolment in the course were successful completion of the mandatory introductory courses for linguistics and teaching methodology and basic computer skills. Credit for the course could be counted towards the degree requirements for linguistics or teaching methodology. Knowledge of corpus linguistics was not a prerequisite; therefore, it was expected that the group consisted of teacher trainees with varying background knowledge and experience. In Session I, the participants were asked to fill in a short questionnaire in order to gain some insight into the makeup of the class. Questions 1 and 2 were designed to gauge the teacher trainees' state of progression of their degree and to find out the focus of their English degree. Question 1 revealed that the majority of participants (76.2%) had already finished the first half of their degree (*Grundstudium*) which usually entailed that they had done teaching experience courses, finished all introductory courses, written substantial term papers and passed an exam in their main area of study.

As the results of Question 2 show, most participants were focusing on literature as the main area of their study programme. Only 22.2% had elected linguistics for in-depth study and even less, only 11.1% had chosen teaching methodology.

Q2. What is the main focus of your English degree?

(A) Linguistics.
(B) Literature.
(C) Teaching Methodology.

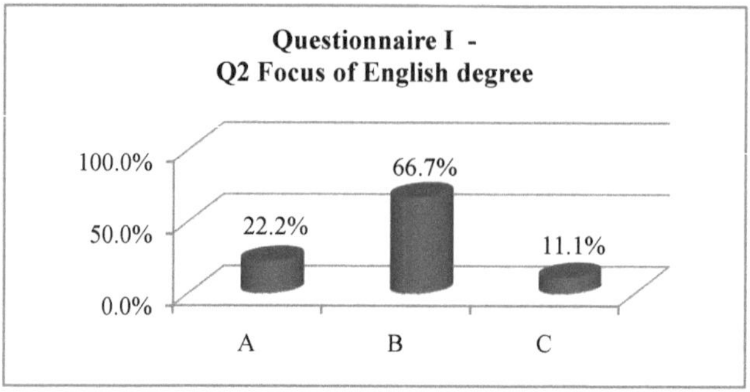

Figure 6-1: Questionnaire I – Q2 Focus of English degree

Question 3 was set in order to determine the participants' knowledge of corpus linguistics. None of the teacher trainees indicated that they were very familiar with corpus linguistics, only one was vaguely familiar and the remaining participants stated that they were not familiar with corpus linguistics:

Q3. How would you rate your familiarity with corpus linguistics?

(A) Very familiar.
(B) Vaguely familiar.
(C) Not at all familiar.

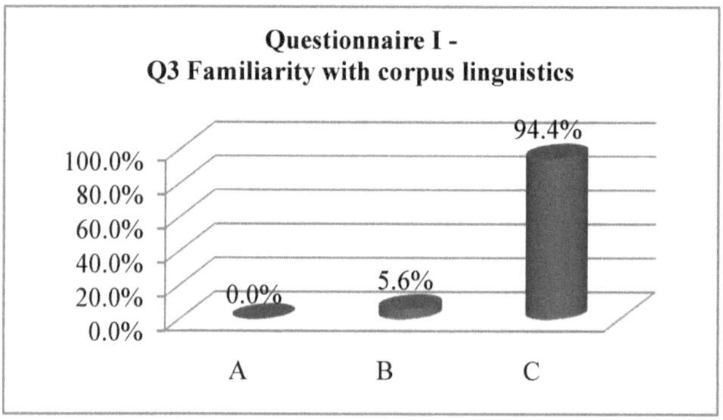

Figure 6-2: Questionnaire I – Q3 Familiarity with corpus linguistics

Question 3 led to a fork in the questionnaire. Respondents who chose answer A or B were taken to more questions regarding the extent of their knowledge of corpus linguistics and their use of corpus resources. The questionnaire ended here for those that indicated that they were not at all familiar with corpus linguistics. The remaining questions inquired about details regarding the participants' use of corpora; however, as only one participant completed the second part of the questionnaire, the results cannot offer any significant information for the analysis here.

6.3.2 Reflective essays: findings and discussion

The training unit 'Analyzing concordances' was part of a sequence of units which were designed to gradually introduce the teacher trainees to the basics of corpus analysis. In this unit, the teacher trainees were given a paper handout, Worksheet (1), with a concordance of *any*. This list was created based on a very small ad-hoc compiled corpus of dialogue transcripts (approx. 29,000 words) from two EFL textbooks (*Green Line*, Ashford, Aston & Hellyer-Jones 1995, 1996) commonly used in secondary schools in Germany. All 19 occurrences of *any* in this corpus were listed on Worksheet (1):

1	ing to the shops for her .... Robert: Do we need	any	bread, Mum? Mrs Croft: Yes, we need some bread, a
2	hocolate biscuits, please. Robert: We haven't got	any	vegetables, Mum. Mrs Croft: Get some carrots, the
3	beans, too, if you like. Robert: O.K. I won't get	any	fruit. We've still got some bananas and apples. M
4	e bananas and apples. Mrs Croft: No, there aren't	any	bananas. Look! Robert: Oh, I forgot. David was he
5	we made milk shakes. Mrs Croft: Milk! Have we got	any	milk? Robert: Let's look. – Oh, there's some milk
6	rs Croft: It'll be enough for today. So don't get	any	milk. Your list is long enough already! Revision
7	ee without cream, please?" "Sorry, we haven't got	any	cream. Would you like it without milk?" "Doctor
8	, dear!"Robert said. "I don't think they'll want	any	more rabbits." They went in and asked. "No, sorr
9	've got a terrible stomach-ache. But I don't want	any	nasty medicine. Doctor: Hmm. Have you got a tempe
10	: Well, don't look at me, Sarah. I can't lend you	any	money. I want to buy the new 'Ghosts' CD today. S
11	was always the only young person there. It wasn't	any	fun for him. "Mum, it's so boring," Robert said.
12	id. "Well," his mother answered, "he doesn't know	any	other children. His birthday parties were fun whe
13	ht. "Great Uncle Arthur is lucky. He doesn't need	any	haircuts because he hasn't got any haid." Robert
14	e doesn't need any haircuts because he hasn't got	any	hair." Robert met Becky and Simon at the shopping
15	e? Oh, I see. Yes, they're great. But I can't see	any	T-shirts. Sarah: Well, there aren't any in the wi
16	can't see any T-shirts. Sarah: Well, there aren't	any	in the window, but I'm sure there are some inside
17	Becky are inside the shop. Sarah: Have they got	any	T-shirts here? Becky: Yes, there are some lovely
18	for a hundred years! Shop assistant: Do you need	any	help? Becky: Er – no thanks. We're just looking.
19	d for the milkshakes? Mrs Richars: We don't need	any	sugar. Only two or three spoons. 2. Mrs Croft: H

Figure 6-3: Worksheet (1): Concordance of 'any' (Corpus: Textbooks)

To begin with, the group discussed the various features of the layout of a concordance. The teacher trainees noted, for example, the centred layout which is inherent to KWIC lists and that words and sentences appear incomplete on either side. The truncated appearance did not appear to be of any concern to them. Looking at the language content, the teacher trainees then continued to list characteristics about the use of *any* according to the KWIC list. They discovered that the samples were apparently all taken from spoken texts, that *any* was almost always directly preceded by a verb, followed mostly by a noun, and that *any* was used either in negative statements or questions. In particular, this last observation piqued their interest as it confirmed the rule as they had learned it in their secondary education. The teacher trainees expressed enthusiasm for this type of language exploration, but also discovered that they were not always sure about using the correct grammatical terminology to express their thoughts about the use of *any*. This led to a further discussion of what this implies for their future role as teachers but also how this kind of activity in turn might be extremely valuable for language learners. They noted that an exercise like this might be of great value to familiarise their students with grammatical terminology – not as an end in itself but as an integral part of the exercise. Furthermore, the trainees felt that while the exercise might be time-consuming, the time was well-spent as the exercise dealt with a high frequency grammatical item, the mastery of which the trainees regarded as significant.

Afterwards, a second handout, Worksheet (2), with a random selection of 20 occurrences of *any* from the *ACE* was distributed:

1	will hang. Plain fabrics look good with almost	any	heading tape but with patterned fabric you need to think
2	g painting in adjoining studios than you would in	any	identifiable philosophies in the City Art Institute and the
3	oot six people on stage and make them look unlike	any	other six people performing." Armstrong said they avoi
4	s. "Gillian approached the concert as she would	any	other film project – that's what will make the differene."
5	before shooting the following night's concert or	any	of the close-ups. Armstrong covered herself well by sho
6	of a sudden you wouldn't be receiving the channel	any	more. It was critical stuff. John went from Racal
7	note advis+ing him that if he thought I could be of	any	asistance to him, to give me a ring. I actually had no int
8	'The trick for	any	customer, no mat+ter what they're buying, is to put their
9	rst, 'that's why we offer a money-back guarantee on	any	product we recommend - that we've chosen for a custom
10	prove who could drive up a hill fastest rather than	any	display to skill or general driving ability. Bearing in m
11	forethought with the type of conditions expected by	any	keen four wheel drive enthusiast. Australia was top sc
12	be meeting you there. He kindly offered to carry	any	letters or messages. Would you like me to have P
13	s strong than a curiosity at the complete lack of	any	trace of these people in my mother's few enough b
14	sure you didn't. There is nothing I much care for	any	longer. Should I like all this? What did the qu
15	ation (IVR) model. The second model asserts	any	absorption must occur into an eigenstate of the c
16	munity Libraries. The Committee does not foresee	any	further school/community libraries being built, e
17	that at this stage it would be premature to make	any	judgment about the levels of freight charges beca
18	hing else. 'The ten commandments do not contain	any	creed to which men are answerable for their crime
19	ere was actually nothing there. No life, not even	any	trees or grass, just dust. And craters. That's al
20	Horton. 'Your sobriety has tipped the balance.	Any	children on the way?' he added. 'We're hoping

Figure 6-4: Worksheet (2): Concordance of 'any' (Corpus: *ACE*)

Upon examination, the teacher trainees noticed that the use of *any* on this handout was much more varied than on Worksheet (1) and could no longer be defined by the simple rules that had applied to the previous example. They worked through the list in groups and tried to formulate tentative rules for the use of *any* based on Worksheet (2). In the next step, the teacher trainees compared their results with definitions from the *Longman Dictionary of Contemporary English Online* (*LDOCE*).[63] The discrepancies between the simple rules of usage as they remembered them from the early stages of their own secondary education, and as evidenced in Worksheet (1) on the one hand and the use of *any* in the authentic language material from the *ACE* on the other, were of great concern to them. A lively discussion ensued in which the teacher trainees debated the implications of this for teaching the use of *any* and *some* to foreign language learners. They were particularly concerned about issues such as whether to teach the complete rules as listed in the *LDOCE*, or the simplified rules as provided in many textbooks. As a follow-up task from this training unit, the teacher trainees were given the task to write a short essay (350-500 words) in which they were asked to reflect on their views on 'Teaching the use of *some* and *any*'. A careful analysis of these essays reveals that the teacher trainees made certain assumptions about their future learners, reflected on their own role as teachers, and dealt with the issue of authentic versus textbook language. In sum, from the 11 essays that were returned, reflections on four main points emerged:

(i) Teaching methodology;
(ii) Language content – Teaching 'real' English;
(iii) Using concordances; and
(iv) Definition of the teacher's role.

In the following, a selection of quotes from the essays will be provided and discussed in order to illustrate these points.

(i) Teaching methodology

During the classroom discussions, the teacher trainees had come to the conclusion that learners should be taught the complete rules of use for *some* and *any*. In their essays, they had to tackle the problem of how to realise this in the classroom. Generally, the teacher trainees felt that it was of great importance to provide beginners, in particular, with clearly defined and reliable rules. Below is a selection of quotes that illustrate this point:[64]

---

[63] The *Longman Dictionary of Contemporary English Online* is available at http://www.ldoceonline.com.

[64] For reasons of space, only anecdotal evidence from the 11 essays can be presented here. The number in the brackets provides information on the essay number in order to enable the reader to compare remarks taken from any one particular essay.

> I think for beginners it is very important to learn grammatical rules. [Essay 02]

> I would say that it is important for foreign language learners, especially for beginners, to have strict rules, which they can follow. Language learning is a difficult thing, anyway. [Essay 05]

> On the one hand pupils perhaps need rules to understand the language, get along with it and use it correctly.[...] I do believe that it is very important for children to have certain rules on which they can rely. [Essay 06]

> Language learners in general – not just at the beginner level – need some clear and structured rules they can learn, repeat and practice in a first step. [Essay 08]

> When pupils first encounter new grammatical phenomena, didactic reduction is inevitable. With too many [sic.] information at once, we would certainly discourage the pupils. [Essay 11]

The assumptions the participants make about their future students are worth noting here. During classroom discussions, the teacher trainees often drew on their past learning experiences in school. Relating back to their own experiences as learners, they felt it was important to provide a 'safe environment' for beginners – in other words to teach clearly defined rules, to provide easy-to-digest information, and to not overwhelm learners with the complexities of language. This attitude, although not in line with the characteristics that generally define direct corpus use through concordancing, is not uncommon. In fact, the comment from Essay 08 about rules that the learners "can learn, repeat and practice" provides a vivid reminder of the traditional present-practice-produce teaching sequence. Their concerns show that successful classroom management and their authority as teacher are of primary concern to them. In her study on corpus linguistics, language variation, and language teaching, Conrad (2004: 68) also observes that "teachers and students seek only definitive answers – such as being able to identify what is grammatical and ungrammatical". Furthermore, in their desire to present the grammatical rules appropriately for beginners, the teacher trainees were faced with the problem of how to avoid error fossilisation:

> I suppose it could be a problem if they just learned the general rules and then, eventually, are confronted with sentences which do not fit into the system they were taught. I assume this is very confusing and it

> is hard to look beyond the rules, which one has once learned. [Essay 05]

> If they do not learn it at an early stage of their language learning, they probably will not learn it at all and will limit their knowledge and language use only to the rules they have learned at school. With this they cannot really become good speakers of English. [Essay 06]

This in turn led them to recognise the potential for over-simplification at the cost of teaching authentic language use:

> The point is, however, that over-simplification leads to incorrect portraying of authentic language use. [...] Pupils are taught only a part of the rule in a bid to keep it straightforward and simple. What troubles me initially is how something can be taught that is quite obviously wrong. As welcome as it may seem, I am astonished at such a misleading and confusing attempt to make learning easier for EFL students. [Essay 01]

In the weeks following this exercise, the issues of authentic texts and vocabulary difficulty were discussed frequently. Various options of dealing with authentic texts in the classroom (e.g. varying the task rather than the text; see Nunan 1989; Prabhu 1987) were consequently explored. The purpose of this simple training unit was to gradually introduce the teacher trainees to concordances and provide the opportunity to experience learning with such an activity. It quickly led the participants to reflect on this learning experience from the perspective of their future role as teachers and to evaluate their newly gained knowledge in light of this. Furthermore, the stages they went through during this task clearly demonstrate the relevance of such an exercise for the raising of language awareness as discussed in Section 3.3.3:

(i) *Description*: The participants described language use of any as attested in the two concordances.

(ii) *Languaging*: They were engaged in discussions about a particular language feature, making use of linguistic meta-language.

(iii) *Exploration*: The trainees explored language use, in this case the rules that govern some and any, and discovered new (to them) facts about these rules.

(iv) *Engagement*: They actively engaged with language and, even though the exercise had the purpose of introducing them to concordancing, the trainees quickly realised the relevance of the exercise to their own interests (teaching of some and any)

(v) *Reflection*: The exercise provided ample opportunity for the participants to reflect on their own learning process regarding the use of some and any.

In addition, the debate on textbook versus authentic language use led the trainees to discuss the merit of two approaches to teaching a foreign language to beginners, and most certainly led them to be more critical in their future evaluations of textbook language, a discussion which is at the centre of the next topic.

(ii) Language content – teaching 'real' language

The direct comparison of textbook language samples from Worksheet (1) and samples from naturally occurring language from the *ACE* on Worksheet (2) appears to have demonstrated to the teacher trainees not only the significance of using authentic language but also the discrepancies between textbook and 'real' language. As one of the participants observed:

> The material at school is based on rules which are regularly broken by real world's [sic.] English. [Essay 03]

In the first part of their essays, the teacher trainees had dealt with the immediate problem at hand – how to teach the use of *some* and *any* – but they quickly engaged in a wider debate on important issues such as what language to teach. This led to an increase in their critical awareness of the textbook materials.

> Also with regard to the curriculum it is very important to confront pupils with authentic written and spoken language [...]. [Essay 02]

> On the whole, I think that it is very important that it becomes clear to our pupils that authentic language use very often differs from the rules we learn and teach at school. [Essay 06]

Even though the teacher trainees generally felt that it was important to teach authentic language use, the task made them aware of the difficulties that this might entail. This is reflected in the conflict they displayed between wanting to teach appropriately for beginners but not at the cost of teaching 'real' English. Should pupils learn English as it is represented by their school books or as it is spoken by native speakers? This question echoes the debate among researchers (see, e.g. the exchange between Carter & McCarthy 1996; McCarthy & Carter

1995; and Prodromou 1996a, 1996b); however, the trainees clearly approached this question from their immediate perspective of feasibility for teaching purposes. Rather than questioning the authority of language from the corpus, the trainees appeared to view the language taken from the *ACE* simply as authentic native speaker English, which appeared to be the most crucial aspect in their minds.

(iii) Using concordances

After addressing the question of what to teach, the teacher trainees focused their attention on how to teach it. For the most part, the teacher trainees regarded it to be the teacher's task to introduce the learner to the basic rules governing the use of *some* and *any*:

> I would suggest that the teacher teaches the simple rules [...] by explaining the rules to the learners. [Essay 03]

> It could be the easiest and maybe best way to teach pupils that *some* has to be placed with statements and *any* with negative sentences and questions. [Essay 10]

Once those simplified rules are learned, the concordancer comes into play as a means of helping learners to discover the extended rule set for themselves.

> From the third year of English the pupils know many vocabularies [sic] and grammar rules as a basis. Then they can discover rules on their own. One possibility is the concept of data-driven learning. [Essay 02]

> Another way to teach *some* and *any* is to start with a concordance-exercise, so that the pupils directly learn about any possibility to use some and any. They can formulate the rules themselves [...] [Essay 03]

> It would perhaps be a nice idea to let the pupils discover these common exceptions on their own, by using a concordancer with chosen texts. [Essay 06]

> Language learners in general – not just at the beginner level – need some clear and structured rules they can learn, repeat and practice in a first step. But in a second step they have to get prepared to transfer

> these rules into an authentic context and language use. DDL offers a wide range for creating such authentic and exploratory tasks and activities for language classes [...] [Essay 08]

The teacher trainees recognised the value of the corpus and concordancer as tools for the learner to explore the complexities of language and also to create credibility by allowing the learner to explore authentic texts and discover language use at their own pace:

> Since they are able to work with authentic texts, the differences become even more plausible. [Essay 10]

> If we as EFL teachers are to help our students to develop language awareness, we have to be extremely careful to supply them with adequate teaching material. [Essay 01]

This inductive approach to learning or 'learning by discovery' lies at the heart of classroom concordancing (Johns 1988: 14). The observations made by the teacher trainees also reflect Bernardini's (2002: 166) view of corpora as pedagogical tools that enable learning by discovery and their significance for "engaging the learners' interests, developing autonomous learning strategies, raising their language consciousness, etc.". The comment on working with authentic texts (Essay 10) also emphasises the trainees' perception of corpora as sources of authentic language use and the significance the trainees obviously placed on authentic language.

(iv) Definition of the teacher's role

Finally, an increasing awareness of the shortcomings of available teaching materials, and the recognition of the responsibility as teacher to introduce learners to adequate language content, prompted the participants to reflect on their own role as teachers. Just as the trainees had found it challenging to reconcile their desire to teach authentic language use and to find appropriate ways for teaching beginners, they were torn between their willingness to take risks in the classroom and their fear of losing control of the learning process:

> One of a teacher's greatest tasks is to trust in his pupils and also to challenge them sometimes, at least in my view. [Essay 06]

> The question is, how teachers should handle those exceptions of rules and if they should teach the rules at all when they are not reliable in class. [Essay 02]

Through working with the concordance handouts the teacher trainees not only honed their own language skills, but they started to reflect on the language content they would be teaching later in their profession. Through their learning experience with the concordance handouts the trainees turned their attention towards complex and central issues related to their future teaching practice.

The analysis of the essays on 'Teaching the use of *some* and *any*' has revealed that the teacher trainees see a strong link between linguistic aspects and pedagogical implications of using corpora in the classroom. The training unit 'Analyzing concordances' not only provided the teacher trainees with a basic introduction to concordancing but also led them to reflect on several important issues in regard to their role as teachers – that is, to language as content, to teaching methodology and to the role and potential benefit of using concordances as a tool for teaching. The essays demonstrate that to them this tool not only provides opportunities but also poses challenges. Furthermore, the training unit alerted them to the difficulties of trying to teach authentic language use in a way suitable for beginners for maximum long-term learning outcomes. The discussion in this section has shown that this simple exercise led not only to an increase of language awareness but teaching awareness as well. This is a significant outcome that highlights not only the challenges teachers have to overcome in teaching with corpora, but also the very useful role such a course can play in language teacher education.

6.3.3 Reviews of concordancing software

The first four weeks of the course were spent introducing the teacher trainees to the basics of corpus analysis and the concept of DDL. During the first few sessions, the teacher trainees were either given prepared concordance handouts or they consulted online concordancers such as *BNC Simple Search* or *Collins Corpus Sampler*. The aim of this session was to familiarise the teacher trainees with a variety of stand-alone concordancing packages (see Section 7.1 for an overview of concordancers). For this purpose, the teacher trainees were divided into five groups. Each group was given the task of reviewing one particular concordancing software allocated to them based on the supplied review template:

Software Name http://www.web-address.com/	
Developer:	
Platform:	
Size:	
Cost:	
Look & Feel:	
Features:	
Review:	

Figure 6-5: Template for software review

The software packages chosen for review included: *MonoConc Pro 2.2* (Barlow 2002) and *Wordsmith Tools 4* (Scott 2004), *ConcApp 4* (Greaves 2003) and *AntConc 3* (Anthony 2004), and *Concordancer 3.2* (Watt 2004). All of the above are stand-alone offline concordancers which were not purpose-built for any particular corpus. *MonoConc Pro* [Review 1] and *Wordsmith Tools* [Review 2] are very commonly used concordancers and were included on the grounds of their popularity; both *ConcApp* [Review 3] and *AntConc* [Review 4] are freely available plain text concordancers and are therefore an attractive option for both learners and teachers. *Concordance* [Review 5] is also a plain text concordancer but is an indexing rather than streaming software and was included in order to present the teacher trainees with an alternative concordancing software solution.[65] All packages were available for download online and the teacher trainees were provided with the respective website addresses in order to obtain the software. The teacher trainees were asked to present their results to the rest of the group in the following week. This way the whole group would be introduced to five programs rather than just a single one and the individual groups were provided with the opportunity to explore the programs by themselves in their own time. The reviews will provide insight into the teacher trainees' opinions on concordancing software. The outcomes have been integrated into the design of the student concordancer detailed in Chapter 7.

The first half of the review template is largely descriptive. As Figure 6-5 shows, the participants were asked to fill in the following fields:

[65] Tribble and Jones (1997: 9) describe streaming concordancers as "those that 'read' a text line-by-line in real time and produce concordanced text" and text indexers as "those that initially create an index of your text in one (sometimes lengthy) operation and then permit a large variety of text retrieval activities including concordancing".

- Name of Developer
- Platforms
- Size of the Program
- Purchase Price
- Look & Feel
- Features

The template was used in order to obtain comparable results from all groups and at the same time served the purpose of providing similarly structured and informative reviews for the DDL Guide. The second half of the template – 'Review' – provided the teacher trainees with space to assess the program for its 'classroom suitability'. The analysis below will focus on this section as it represents the teacher trainees' perspective on the software in question in regard to its value for classroom application.

The analysis of the reviews shows that 'user-friendliness' was the predominant theme and all reviewers related this feature directly to their own motivation and that of their future students to use the software. Great importance was placed on a quick download and simple installation process:

> [...] it does not take long to download the programme and to get used to the functions. [Review 03]

> [...] it is a great advantage that this concordance software is easy to download and it is quickly installed. [Review 05]

This initial contact with the software was seen as an important requirement for the future use of the software. Problems during the installation process were viewed as a strong deterrent:

> As we had problems with the installation and with putting in a text, Wordsmith seemed a bit too complicated for us and didn't promote our motivation. [Review 2]

The reviewers favoured those packages that were easy to understand and that produced results instantly. Failure to do so was perceived as a potential problem that might discourage learners from using concordancers altogether:

> It simply takes too much time to get familiar with the complex functions of *Wordsmith.* We see the danger that pupils lose their enthusiasm, motivation and interest in working with a foreign language before they have a chance to realize the advantages of concordancers at all. [Review 2]

> If a programme is very difficult to understand and the pupils have to work on it for hours without having a result, they will not be motivated any longer. But in the case of *AntConc*, we are sure that every pupil would have at least one result within minutes, because you do not have to open several extra windows, everything is compact and understandable at once. [Review 4]

An intuitive interface also played a significant role. This is attributable to the fact that the teacher trainees generally perceived their learners as novice and not advanced users. Complex and confusing buttons in the taskbar were viewed negatively:

> Most annoying is the fact that the symbols [icons] are very confusing and don't reveal their functions. Some of them are rather superfluous, nothing really happens when clicking on them. [Review 2]

> But there are several reasons why this program may be suitable only for more advanced users with previous experience in concordancing. For example there is not only a vast choice of features and options, there is also a lot of concordancing vocabulary. Therefore at the beginning the user needs some time to get familiar with this program and its specific functions and at first glance it seems rather confusing. [Review 5]

While a wide range of linguistic functions was not necessarily required, features that would aid the teacher to produce learning materials were considered important:

> Teachers can, among other things, prepare tests. [Review 1]

> What we liked about the program is the function 'blanked out' to create tasks for learners. [Review 2]

> For teachers it is a good help, because it is possible to create own tests. [Review 3]

The absence of such editing features was noted negatively. It is particularly interesting to note here that the teacher trainees relate this directly to their future role as teachers.

> On the other hand one has to admit that the programme is very restricted. There is no way to delete single lines, to write comments

> into the lines or to delete the searched word to make a test for your pupils. [Review 4]

> Unfortunately – if I am not mistaken – you cannot copy and paste lines into Word to develop teaching material. [Review 5]

In her article on user perceptions of corpus-based instruction, Farr (2008: 34) finds that, while her students overcame linguistic challenges related to concordancing relatively quickly, "the complexity of the software was and continued to be an issue throughout". Although initially the participants had found the task of having to download and familiarise themselves with a new software package rather daunting, in the end the exercise produced excellent results. As part of the process, the teacher trainees reached a sound level of understanding regarding the various functions and features of five different concordancing packages. Furthermore, the reviews helped to emphasise the kind of features teacher trainees were looking for in software packages for classroom use. The results of the student reviews were integrated directly into the design of the proposed student concordancer discussed in Chapter 7.

6.3.4 Teacher trainee projects: DDL task

Towards the end of the course, the teacher trainees had been introduced to corpora, concordancing software, and to various applications of corpora in the language classroom. They had discussed and reflected on their learning experiences throughout the course, as well as having analysed them in regard to their future role as language teachers. With this in mind, they were asked to put theory into practice and create an exercise with concordances on a topic of their choice. The activity was intended to simulate a situation they might find themselves in as teachers; for example, wanting to supplement existing teaching materials with a hands-on concordancing exercise. Therefore, the task was set leaving the teacher trainees with the freedom to make decisions on the choice of topic, which corpus to use, and so forth. The purpose of this activity was twofold: on the one hand, the teacher trainees gained practical experience in creating such tasks, and, on the other hand, their feedback afterwards provided insight into the practical issues arising from the material creation process. As a starting point, the teacher trainees were given EFL textbooks that are commonly used in secondary educational institutions in Germany (e.g. *English G*). The textbooks were intended for beginner and intermediate learner levels. Based on the textbooks the students were asked to choose a topic and create a corpus task based on this topic. For this purpose the teacher trainees were divided into seven groups. The groups chose to produce DDL tasks on the following topics:

- Adverbs;
- *Some* and *any*; *have to* and negation;
- Phrasal verbs;
- Concordancer as writing aid for essays;
- Comparison of adjectives;
- Adjectives & false friends;
- Reading task with dictionary work & concordancer.

All teams presented their exercises to the class and afterwards the results were discussed. In the following section, I will present three examples of the tasks the teacher trainees produced and discuss the outcomes.[66] The selection of these tasks was driven by two factors. Firstly, they are the only tasks for which the students had created the actual worksheets. The other groups had produced the concept for the lesson but failed to include handouts. Secondly, the tasks chosen for analysis each take a different approach: one provides concordance printouts lists, one requires learners to do hands-on concordancing, and one combines the two approaches. The tasks provide valuable insights into the design of the materials created by the teacher trainees.

[66] Please note that the formatting has been slightly adjusted for the purpose of uniform presentation; however, the content has remained unchanged.

Example 1: Phrasal verbs (*English G*, Vol. C3; Unit 2: Grammar: 32)

Target group: Year 9

Phrasal verbs: look • take • put

Task 1:

Look at the concordances of the verbs *look*, *put*, and *take* you have been given. How are these verbs used? Which words follow them? Make a list.

Concordance of "take"

```
ent that would be impossible because it would take time. People don't understand that.
    two ways you could go about it. You could take the average nominal interest rate the average
  it's a good second house for people to just take a step back and look at things maybe with
 wanna leave yours here? [F0X] I might as well take the lot back to Worcester 'cos I don't know
  out all the pronouns take out all the modals take out any that are followed by and or to and ou
 [F01] Yeah. [F02] so I might as well let them take it away. [F01] Yeah. Well it save you having
   Yes. [M01] and erm I wasn't quite [M02] You take up you take twenty-four hours to get over it
 s some sort of millionaire saviour waiting to take over Birmingham City from the Kumars are
  it will become judgemental. But you've got to take in on face value. If you start thinking well
you for calling MX [M05] Thanks Anna. Bye [F03] Take care. Bye-bye now. You have a proverb in the
  out all the pronouns take out all the modals take out any that are followed by and or to and
 question which [ZF1] we should [ZF0] we should take up er earlier on later on. So it became clear
  Hi. [M0X] Hiya.  [tc text=pause] [F01] [ZGY] take care. [M0X] And a bit of [ZGY] [F01] Mm. [M0X
  she was going to wear for the day and you'd take them out and sort them out and see that they
to be careful about the number of commitments I take on [M01] Mhm. [M02] and focus my energies
  it out but [F01] Mm [F04] I probably I won't take it I said to myself I won't take it up as a
[F05] er a lot of people I mean a lot of people take the mickey out of FX 'cos she's sort of well
```

Concordance of "look"

```
   office. Don't use a number on their card but look it up in the `phone book. [p] If your are
haze. Smart aviator design Night Vision Glasses look like stylish aviator sunglasses, but with
the Birmingham area, until the end of December. Look out for this symbol as you read through the
      [c] price [/c] [c] diagram [/c] [p] How to look forward to driving abroad [p] When driving a
 more considered, but their trick is to make it look as though they haven't given their appearance
Rosy pink and pinky brown shades of lip colour look best with fair hair. [p] Emphasise brows-they
  bright yellow clash,but sharp citrus yellows look surprisingly good against honey-coloured
     be at around pound; 20 a bottle. Names to look out for are Krug, Pol Roger, Veuve Clicquot,
   and yet, at the season's end, that did not look like being sufficient. [p] The thing that
 foyers thick with spivs and hookers, unable to look another nestling doll in the face, and shocke
   for an instrument or monitor you do need to look at. This is a nice bit of lateral thinking,
 discriminate in favour of other Muslims and to look to Iran for guidance and protection instead o
  schools. In Africa women or children usually look after the poultry So children at school could
         [p] I know. Go on." [p] I bent down to look at her although I knew she was dead.  Then I
 [p] Now all the south coast strugglers have to look forward to is a long hard Premier League
  68585. [p] [f] S. from Newry on Forkill road. Look out for signs to the right to [f] Killevy Old
 I am Middle Class. Corbett: I know my place. I look up to them both. But I don't look up to him
```

Concordance of "put"

```
 that you are gland they are there. [p] Don't be put off by thinking that there are deep
      A short list of nearby restaurants will be put up at the party, and you can decide where to
cast on one side alone. this is because they are put to different uses, as inlays for furniture or
Bogart, Nature, Mr Allnutt, is something we were put on this Earth to rise above Indeed we do. But
    kit, and the two-piece lamphouse is quick to put together; although for even illumination it i
 at Children's Television Workshop after she had put the project together Without him Joan Cooney
a week, and occasionally there's just no room to put any of them up [p] Nevertheless, he doesn't
 the reform package and predicted that if it was put to the vote now in a national referendum it
  there can be any compromise over the proposals put forward by his economic team and that of Mr
     s whole drama is that she's not prepared to put up with the fate that would be hers normally.
 hellip; ` [p] They're not [f] all [f] dead," I put in. `You aren't, not legally anyway, although
 He uncapped his pen, wrote his conclusions and put the sheet on his facsimile machine and
 broken it can take months to heal before we can put any stress on it again. Part of our psyche,
  that she'd become a treasured plate or goblet, put safely on a shelf where none could harm it.
       Obtaining one and flying it out had almost put us in the red - now I learned the anchor chai
 Her heart was pounding fearfully as she slowly put it to her ear again. Whoever you are, I know
 least of the three main grapes, cabernet franc, put in an oustanding performance on the Right
```

Task 2
On Worksheet 1, find out the meanings of these phrasal verbs

Phrasal verbs - Worksheet 1
Please mark the correct answer

1. look for
a) try to find s.th.
b) take care of s.o.
c) to watch

2. look after
a) try to find s.th.
b) take care of s.o.
c) look behind s.th.

3. put on
a) add s.th.
b) make nicer
c) lose

Task 3
Worksheets 2 to 3 provide you with exercises of increasing difficulty. First, you are asked to pick the right preposition to go with the verb. On Worksheet 3 you will find gap exercises – You have to choose the correct phrasal verb from a list.

Phrasal verbs - Worksheet 2
Please mark the correct answer

1. Look _____ the geography of your area.
a) for
b) at
c) in

2. Look _____ Fidel Castro and his cigar.
a) after
b) at
c) for

3. Look _____ the answer in the next issue.
a) in
b) for
c) at

Phrasal verbs - Worksheet 3
Please insert the 15 words or word groups correctly

look after • look at • look at • look for • look forward to • look forward to • look in • put off • put on • put out • put up • take after • take care of • take off • take up

____________ [1] the geography of your area.
____________ [2] Fidel Castro and his cigar.
____________ [3] the answer in the next issue.
When I ____________ [4] your eyes I'm absolutely lost.
Will I have to ______________ [5] children if they are ill?

Task 4
Finally, translate the following sentences into English, using phrasal verbs. Write the answers into your exercise book.

a. Michael muss sich um seine Katze kümmern.
b. Das Flugzeug hob nach wenigen Sekunden ab.
c. Warum ziehst Du keine Jacke an?
d. Sie freuen sich schon auf den Urlaub.
e. Susan hat mit Fitnesstraining begonnen.
f. Schaut Euch die Übung auf Seite 84 an!

____
____
____

Figure 6-6: DDL Task, Example 1: Phrasal verbs

In Example 1, the teacher trainees chose the topic 'Phrasal verbs' for a Year 9 (intermediate level) class. Rather than giving their students direct access to a corpus, they decided to use printouts of concordance lines. These lines were taken from the *Collins Corpus Sampler*. This online concordancer provides access to the *Collins WordbanksOnline English Corpus* (see Section 2.3.2) which consists of 56 million words of contemporary English written and spoken text. Searches can be limited to any or all of the following three subcorpora:

- British books, ephemera, radio, newspapers, magazines (36m words);
- American books, ephemera and radio (10m words); and
- British transcribed speech (10m words).

However, it is important to notice that this is only a demonstration version of the concordancer and therefore results are limited to 40 lines of concordances, each with a maximum width of 250 characters. Although the 40 lines are selected randomly, they are always the same 40 lines. In addition, no sorting can be done, and the wider context is not accessible.

To begin with, the teacher trainees had designed an explorative task, in which their pupils were asked to observe the use of three phrasal verbs based on the given concordances. In their presentation, the teacher trainees argued that they preferred the use of concordance printouts for this task in order to avoid any of the potential problems related to providing online access to a corpus. The teacher trainees felt that there were a lot of reasons that would at least initially motivate them to restrict this kind of exercise to paper printouts. These included logistical problems such as having to provide computers, software, and access to a corpus; pedagogical challenges such as training the learners how to use the concordancing software and maintaining the focus on the task rather than digressing into individual computer training.

However, as the group discussed the exercise with the rest of the class, it began to emerge that the concordance lines presented on the handout were not entirely suitable for the given task. While the teacher trainees' intention was to focus their learners' attention on a particular list of phrasal verbs, the concordance lines did not actually match that list. For example, 'look for' does not appear in the prepared concordance lines. Upon closer examination, there is indeed a discernible mismatch between what the concordance lines show as a result for the search word 'look' and the goal of teaching *look* as a phrasal verb. The teacher trainees agreed that, when intent on producing concordance lines for the purpose of a particular teaching goal, a considerable amount of effort has to be put into the editing of these lines. They also felt that such a high level of interference with the corpus data took away from what they perceived as the interesting factor of unexpected discoveries from DDL tasks. Furthermore, the teacher trainees realised that their intention to remove perceived difficulties regarding the process of 'live' corpus consultation with their learners opened up another source of problems. There were also clearly not enough samples in order for prospective learners to detect any kind of patterns of usage. Again, in their attempt to keep the exercise simple and by wanting to avoid 'overloading' their learners, it became apparent that linguistically the exercise was not successful. This example reveals their inexperience with this approach and how this affects their pedagogical knowledge and experience.

Two important conclusions can be drawn here. Firstly, designing corpus-based tasks is not an easy undertaking and many factors determine a successful outcome. Secondly, the combination of a lack of experience in teaching and in corpus analysis presents a double challenge to teacher trainees. However, at the same time it provides a prime learning opportunity for trainees regarding materials design for future teaching purposes.

Example 2: Comparison of adjectives
Target group: Year 8

Comparison of adjectives

1) Have a look at the adjectives which you already know from the previous units. Find the opposites and combine them with a line!

good	***quiet***
long	***small***
fast	***slow***
big	***expensive***
cheap	***interesting***
boring	***bad***
noisy	***short***

2) Now imagine you want to compare means of transport (for example, a car and a bus) by using the words above. Your task is now to find out how you can build the forms in English to compare things. For this task you can work with a computer. Aim is that you become experts in comparisons.

Instructions:

- Work with a partner and share one computer
- Open the programme 'ConcApp' on the desktop
- Go to the function 'Concordance' → *Search*
- Type in an adjective from the list above and press *Enter*. You will get a list of sentences in which this word is used. Try several adjectives of the list.
- Try to find out which forms of these words are possible.
- How do you use it when you want to compare things? Take a guess!
- There are two possibilities to compare adjectives. Which ones do you find?
- Two of the adjectives do not follow a rule. Can you guess which ones? Why?

VERY IMPORTANT
You don't have to understand the sentences!! Only look at the forms of the adjectives and the words directly before and after them!

- Make notes about your results.
- Present the results in class.
- Now compare your results with the grammar part in your exercise book. Did you find the same rules?

3) As you're all experts in comparisons now, look at the pictures in your textbook on page 90 and compare the *bike*, *coach*, *plane*, *train* and *car* with each other. Use the words from the list above.

Homework
Write 10 comparisons of the means of transport into your textbook!

Figure 6-7: DDL Task, Example 2: Comparison of adjectives

The group that designed the worksheet in Example 2 (Figure 6-7) decided to start out with a task type their students would likely be familiar with: finding opposites and connecting them with a line. For the following tasks, their students were directed to use the concordancing software *ConcApp*. On their handout, the group provided instructions to their learners on how to access the concordancer and how to execute a search. However, they failed to mention which corpus the learners were to use (and how to load the corpus into the software). Upon questioning, they reported that the task had not been written with a particular corpus in mind. In addition, they also neglected to instruct their students on how to formulate the search queries correctly in order to ensure that learner would find the results the group had in mind. For example, if the students were expected to find ways of writing comparisons with *good*, then they would have to have previous knowledge of irregular adjectives. A corpus search of 'good' will not show this, as it will only result in a concordance of that particular string of characters. Even in the case of regular adjctives, at the very least learners would have to be aware of the use of wildcards.order to find *long**er*** or *long**est***. However, a search for 'long*' would of course not only result in results showing *longer* and *longest* but also *longing*, *longs*, *longevity* and a multitude of other words with the stem 'long-'. A further problem is posed by the choice of adjectives. Firstly, *good* is a high frequency item and therefore result lists will likely be long. Secondly, *good* could occur as a noun or even as an adverb (e.g. if the corpus includes informal spoken language). These examples provide a glimpse into the list of problems that might occur when using 'live' corpus searches for what is designed to be a traditional learning exercise. They also show that corpora are not easily transformed into useful and appropriate learning tools for lower-level learners and within traditional curricula.

Example 3: Adjectives (*English G*, Vol. C1) Target group: Year 7

Corpus: online; for example, *Brown* (1 million words), UK news (84 000) or US TV-talk (2 million words

Exercise 1:

Aim of the exercise: Assign adjectives to people and things
(86, "Red woman" and "Happy pens"? That isn't right.)

Put the words into the online concordancer. Which nouns do these adjectives describe? Then decide to which of the following three groups they belong:

1. adjectives to describe people
2. to describe things
3. to describe people and things

red	***happy***	***careful***	***dangerous***	***empty***
favourite	***green***	***small***	***young***	***difficult***

Then add more adjectives to the groups. Use the concordancer again; for example, type in a noun like 'sea' or 'teacher and look at adjectives which describe these nouns. Copy and paste all results into WORD.

Concordances for *happy*

```
4    .    He rode in at the head of sixty trigger-happy and liquor-crazed desperadoes and took ove
5     believes that every man can and ought to be happy and satisfied. Fromm also cites a poll on
6    , said, "'Ello", and then more slowly, "I am happy". And they sat down and began their little
7    owing cannot be taken seriously. "Are people happy, are they as satisfied, unconsciously, as
8       I knew what was happening".    "Pressure-happy", Artie said, and climbed in.    "That's r
9    f this in his lively and humorous poem, "The Happy Artists". "I scanned the world through pri
10   e stills of a costume movie. McKenzie was as happy as a clam. "That's authenticity", he said.
11   t some of those people who enter are just as happy as can be. They've worried, they've lain a
12   icion removed. Still, I don't wish to appear happy at somebody's else's misfortune".  A21 015
13   erous than high explosive bombs. They seemed happy at the delay in unloading, glad at the cha
14   contented cows give more milk, why shouldn't happy ball players produce more base hits?    Th
15   nuine pleasure to tell you about an entirely happy bodybuilder who has never had to train in
16   ercise at all, because Henri de Courcy- the "happy" bodybuilder- looks as though he were havi
17   et salamander, Alicia. It is not an entirely happy book, as Mrs. Fink soon becomes jealous of
18    going  N12 0750  8    to"-    "Your trigger-happy brother isn't in the house. About now he's
19      them said. "We have good times".    This happy bulletin convulsed Mr. Gorboduc. "You do"?
20   note. Thereafter the audience waxed applause-happy, but discriminating operagoers reserved ju
78   low, if less sharp, than some of the fortune-happy syndicates which back him, he feels what h
79   se  L23 1000  9    ...    Haney went to bed, happy that at least he was rid of that lousy lan
80   he did not ask B'dikkat when he, Mercer, was happy, the answer would no longer be available
```

Figure 6-8: DDL Task, Example 3: Adjectives

This exercise on adjectives, targeted at Year 7 (lower intermediate) learners, instructs learners to use an online corpus. Three corpora are listed as suggestions: *Brown Corpus*, *UK news* or *US TV-talk*. This approach is problematic for a number of reasons. Firstly, there is no mention of how or where exactly these corpora are accessible. The trainees failed to include the name of the website

(*Compleat Lexical Tutor*) and the web address.[67] Secondly, the proposed corpora differ greatly in language variety (American versus British English), register (news versus TV-talk), domain (general versus specific), and size (1 million words versus 84,000 words). A search for the keyword 'red' in the *Brown Corpus* and in the *US TV-talk Corpus* shows the following results for immediate right collocations:

***Brown Corpus* (218 results)**

and=15	River=12	wine=10	wines=6	cells=5	Bridge=4	cross=4
hair=4	was=4	china=3	McIver=3	or=3	with=3	army=2
bank=2	captain=2	circle=2	clay=2	coats=2	district=2	face=2
glow=2	had=2	Hogan=2	in=2	men=2	road=2	Sox=2
the=2	white=2					

***US TV-Talk Corpus* (118 results)**

drapes=14	and=7	corvette=7	curtains=5	suit=5	neon=4	room=4
chair=3	hair=3	wine=3	building=2	convertible=2		curtain=2
draped=2	dress=2	flowing=2	lips=2	pumps=2		stain=2

A close analysis of these results goes beyond the scope of this discussion; however, a quick glance at the immediate right collocations of 'red' in these corpora show that they differ significantly. Moreover, in particular, the results from the *Brown Corpus* (e.g. *Red River*, *Red Bridge*, *Red Cross*, *Red Sox*, *Red McIver*) reveal that a significant amount of cultural knowledge is required in order to interpret these correctly. This could provide the starting point to a fascinating serendipity task with advanced learners, and may also generate further questions regarding the use of red in its literal sense as a colour or figurative or symbolic uses. However, these results may be less appropriate for lower-intermediate learners. In this case, a pedagogic corpus as discussed in Section 4.3.1 may be of more use. Similarly, the task set for these learners – that is, to group the results into three given categories (adjectives to describe people, to describe things, to describe people and things) – is a difficult task, likely to exceed their skill level. Given the number of adjectives (10), the task might also prove too time-consuming.

Even though the group chose the *Compleat Lexical Tutor* website, which is an excellent resource for corpus-based activities, they failed to exploit this resource effectively. For example, the trainees did not instruct their target

---

[67] '*Compleat Lexical Tutor*', website. Available at http://www.lextutor.ca.

audience to make use of the collocation summaries available with each search, nor about using the sorting options provided by the search interface.

It is important to view the results of this exercise in light of the fact that this was the teacher trainees' first exploration into creating corpus-based tasks on their own. During the evaluation of the three examples above, it became apparent that the teacher trainees had focused very much on the technical aspects and perceived difficulties of corpus-related issues which led them to neglect the pedagogical aspects of the task. Furthermore, the results highlight the difficulties teachers, particular those who are not corpus experts, face when creating such tasks. Firstly, it is evident that the trainees have a predetermined teaching goal in mind when creating the tasks. However, corpus-tasks are mainly explorative in character and thus often uncertain in their outcome. This mismatch between expectation and actual results becomes apparent in the worksheets above. Furthermore, there was great uncertainty as to which corpus is appropriate for which task and whether it was best to present learners with edited concordance lines or to give them 'live' access to corpora.

The analysis of these tasks, created by the teacher trainees, has highlighted some of the challenges that the design of concordancing activities likely entails. It has certainly added weight to the argument that more classroom-ready materials are desperately needed. It has demonstrated that teachers require substantial training, as much experience as possible, and readily available resources and tools in order to meet the challenges of this task. The results of this exercise have also brought into focus the need for training prospective teachers specifically in certain aspects of how to teach with corpora. However, the task was also a valuable learning experience for the teacher trainees as the evaluation of the final questionnaire will show in the following section.

6.3.5 Questionnaire II

At the end of the course, the participants were asked to fill in a final questionnaire. This questionnaire was subdivided into five sections with the following topics:

(i) computer proficiency and its relevance to teaching;
(ii) course content;
(iii) concordancers;
(iv) feedback on the DDL task; and
(v) questions regarding the use of corpora in language teaching.

All of those who participated in the course filled in the questionnaire. The respondents were not required to provide their name but for the analysis each returned questionnaire was assigned with a letter (A-R). Whenever examples of responses are provided for illustrative purposes below, they are marked with the responding letter in brackets.

(i) Computer proficiency

In this section the teacher trainees were asked to provide an assessment of their computer skills and to make a statement as to whether they consider these skills to be important regarding their future role as teachers. Throughout the course, the participants' computer skills, or more specifically the lack thereof, emerged as a significant factor in completing the tasks set for them. The participants demonstrated a much lower level of computer skills than anticipated.

Q1. How would you rate your computer skills?

(A) **Basic**: I can produce basic Word documents, surf the net and write emails.
(B) **Intermediate**: I can do almost anything with Word, an internet browser and other authoring tools.
(C) **Advanced**: I am very proficient and can handle any program that comes my way.

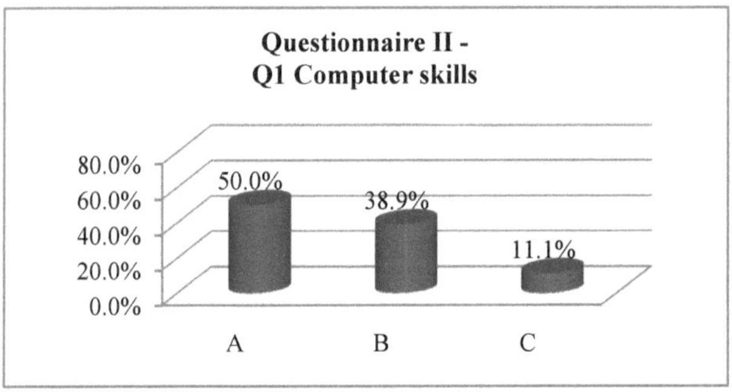

Figure 6-9: Questionnaire II – Q1 Computer proficiency

It seems evident that, despite the prevalence of computers, technical skills cannot be regarded as a given. Seidlhofer (2002) made a similar discovery in a course on corpus linguistics and language pedagogy she teaches for teacher trainees:

> For one thing, it became clear to me that – contrary to the commonly held belief that some degree of computer literacy is a matter of course for school-leavers nowadays – most of our undergraduates are genuinely technophobic. (Seidlhofer 2002: 216)

Figure 6-9 shows that half of the teacher trainees rated their computer skills as basic only. Just over a third of the participants rated their skills as intermediate and only a very small minority claimed to have advanced skills. These results correlate with the experiences from the course. The teacher trainees were often hesitant about using the computers and required a lot of instruction and reassurance.

Q2. Do you consider your computer skills to be vital for your future role as a teacher?

(A) **Yes**, because…
(B) **No**, because…

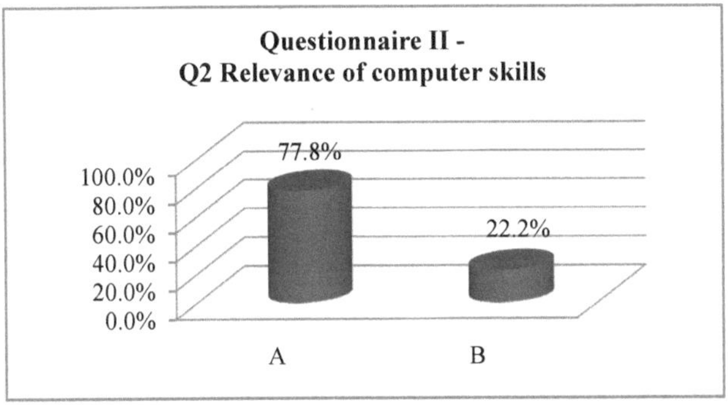

Figure 6-10: Questionnaire II – Q2 Relevance of computer skills

As Figure 6-10 shows, the majority of the participants believed their computer skills to be of significance to their future profession as a teacher. Some respondents clearly felt that this is due to the increasingly important role computers play in general and the resulting demand for computer use by students:

> Yes, because computers are a must-have already and they offer infinite possibilities. [A]

> Yes, because it gets more and more important. [C]

> Yes, because there is high demand [L]

> Yes, because students like computers ... [O]

> Yes, because in future times the computer will play a much more important role as an instrument of the learning process than today. [P]

These respondents had indicated in the previous question, Question 1, that they rated their computer skills as basic, except for respondent [A] who rated her/his skills as advanced. Others considered their computer skills to be important because they saw benefits in using computers:

> Yes, because working and learning with computers supports the pupils' motivation, the PC can help to prepare the lessons. [E]

> Yes, because the PC makes the work easier and faster [J]

> Yes, because working with a computer can be interesting for pupils and this motivates them to do certain tasks. [N]

Four teacher trainees did not consider computer skills to be a vital component of their profession as a teacher. These respondents had rated their proficiency as basic. Their answers to Question 2 indicate that there may be a direct correlation between their computer skills and their intention to use computer technology for their teaching practice:

> No, because I feel not so proficient with dealing with computers, that I would use them very often. [D]

> No, because computer technology is developing too fast for me to keep up with it. [G]

> No, because I am not very good with computers and using them in the classroom is too difficult and takes up too much time. [Q]

> No, because I am not so good with PCs and I don't need to use them in class when I teach English. [R]

(ii) Course content

In this section the teacher trainees were asked to define the concept of DDL, to explain what a concordancer is and describe its functions. This section was included in the questionnaire in order to get insight into the teacher trainees' understanding of crucial parts of the course content.

Q3. In your own words, please define 'data-driven learning'.

The responses to Question 3 can be grouped into four categories. The number in the brackets shows the amount of times responses in this category were provided. Sometimes more than one aspect was provided in a single response. Each occurrence was counted.

I. Learning with computers/computer-generated materials (11)
II. Learning based on data/corpora (6)
III. Learning with authentic texts (6)
IV. 'Research'-type learning (2)

The answers show that the teacher trainees viewed the use of computers as a central aspect of DDL. The majority of responses defined DDL as learning with computers, as the examples below from Category I show:

> Data-driven learning is based on computer learning. [D]
>
> Working based on computers, authentic texts. [M]
>
> With data-driven learning students can learn with the computer and authentic texts. [Q]

Only two answers addressed the 'learner as researcher' paradigm that lies at the heart of the DDL approach:

> DDL is an active and autonomous process which enables the learner to research and thus get authentic material and interferences about language, its linguistic features, grammar skills, rules, teaching material and the use of language itself in an English-speaking country through concordance lists. [N]
>
> DDL is an approach where the learner's attention to a certain vocabulary or linguistic topic is drawn to by providing him/her with concor-

> dance data. The learner is guided to make a hypothesis, verify and prove it. [O]

The results indicate that the technological aspect of DDL played an important role in the perceptions of the teacher trainees. A possible reason for this is the teacher trainees' lack of confidence in their computer skills. One could argue that only once any computer-related problems are eliminated can the subject matter itself attract the central focus. This underlines the importance of adequate computer skills in order to ensure successful integration of any kind of computer-assisted learning approaches.

Q4. What is a concordancer?

Accurate definitions of a concordancer were provided in 13 responses; for example:

> A program to examine a text corpus. [A]

> A concordancer is a program which can scan a chosen corpus. [C]

Although not entirely wrong in the strictest sense, some answers were less accurate:

> A special program that works as a 'native speaker'. [H]

> Basically a tool that makes language to a lesson's content by researching and discovering. [K]

> A concordancer is a research tool of computer-assisted language learning. [N]

> It is a computer-software with certain features. It is an instrument, which collects and which is able to select. [P]

> Research software that shows authentic language use. [R]

The answers show that the participants of the course had largely reached an accurate understanding of the concept of concordancing software.

Q5. What kind of functions does a typical concordance program have?

The responses to Question 5 can be grouped into the following categories:

V. KWIC display (12)
VI. Word search (9)
VII. Frequency / Word list (7)
VIII. Collocations (6)
IX. Sorting (2)

The most frequently mentioned function was the KWIC display which, combined with word search, is arguable the most important characteristic of concordancers. The results of Questions 4 and 5 show that the majority of the class had gained a good understanding of concordancing software.

(iii) Concordancers

As the software reviews written by the teacher trainees and the tasks they had produced had shown, the role of the concordancer was not only very important but so too its functionality. Therefore a number of questions regarding the use of concordancers were included in the questionnaire.

Q6. Do you prefer an online or an offline concordancer for classroom use?

Although this question required only a single answer, two respondents ticked both and two didn't answer the question at all. As a result, 10 respondents indicated that an online concordancer is the preferred choice and another 10 chose an offline concordancer.

Reasons provided for preferring an online concordancer included the following (Note: Respondents often provided more than one reason in their answer; therefore, the number of responses does not correlate with the number of reasons given):

I. Corpus available (4)
II. Corpus is bigger (3)
III. Texts are more recent (2)
IV. Easier to use, less preparation required (3)

The majority of the answers (categories I-III) show that the teacher trainees saw the main advantage of online concordancers in the availability and quality of texts:

> The corpus is bigger and more recent. [I]

> A lot of texts, a huge corpus is already there. It is lexically always right. [P]

The answers show that the teacher trainees consider online concordancers as reliable tools provided by professionals. Their answers are also an indication of their attitudes towards acquiring corpora themselves which is strongly reflected in their feedback on the DDL task discussed in 6.3.4. Interestingly, only three respondents preferred online concordancers for their obvious convenience:

> It is easier to handle in class. [K]

> No time in class to explain offline program, online is simply there with the texts. [Q]

> For beginners it is easier to use and less organising. [R]

This is rather surprising, particularly considering the teacher trainees' initial struggle with the offline concordancers and their general hesitancy towards computer use in general. However, the reasons provided by the respondents who preferred offline concordancers may shed some light on this. The respondents who had preferred an offline concordancer provided nearly all the same reason, namely that the teacher has more control over the corpus (eight answers out of 10). Below is a selection of the responses:

> You can specify a corpus and, hence, the output. [A]

> You can choose a corpus (e.g. for younger pupils), depends on the aim of the teaching unit and skills of the pupils. [B]

> You can choose texts being not too difficult for pupils. [H]

> The teacher can choose suitable texts before. [M]

> It is often necessary to put in an own text with selected concordances. [N]

These answers emphasise the teacher trainees' evident desire to have some form of control over the corpus itself and the results it would likely produce in class. On the one hand, teacher trainees show concern about vocabulary difficulty which might create problems, particularly for beginners. On the other hand, it appears that teacher trainees are unwilling to relinquish control over possible outcomes of learner tasks [A, N].

Q7. Which offline concordancer do you prefer for the preparation of classroom materials? (Multiple answers possible)?

(A) *AntConc.*
(B) *ConcApp.*
(C) *Concordance.*
(D) *MonoConc.*
(E) *Wordsmith Tools.*

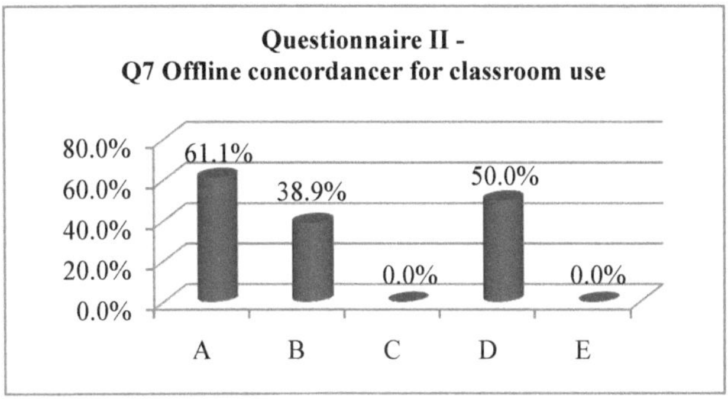

Figure 6-11: Questionnaire II – Q7 Offline concordancer

The results from this question correlate with the software reviews prepared by the teacher trainees. The two most popular offline concordancers, *AntConc* and *MonoConc Pro*, had been described as "very good and appropriate for usage at school" [Review 4] and as "appropriate for a first contact with a concordance programme" [Review 1]. Both *Concordance* and *Wordsmith Tools*, more sophisticated programs designed for research, were ignored. The evident difference in user requirements between the classroom user and research professional was highlighted in the discussion of user profiles for classroom versus research in Section 4.3.2.

Q8. Which online concordancer do you prefer for the preparation of classroom materials? (*Multiple answers possible*)

(A) *BNC Simple Search.*
(B) *BYU-BNC.*
(C) *Collins WordbanksOnline English Corpus Sampler.*
(D) Other:

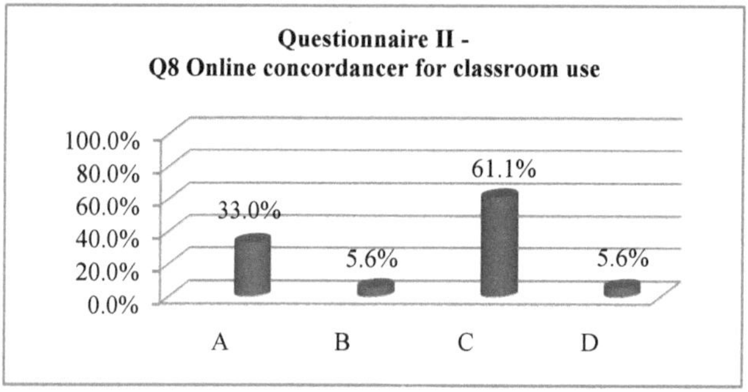

Figure 6-12: Questionnaire II – Q8 Online concordancer for classroom use

The *Collins Corpus Sampler* was the most popular online concordancer. It has a simple and user-friendly design which likely contributed to its popularity. The second most popular online concordancer was the *BNC Simple Search.* In contrast, the *BYU-BNC* concordancer was much less popular. Its interface offers many more options for corpus searches but evidently a simpler user-interface was more appealing to the participants than a bigger range of search options. This again corresponds with the findings from the previous question, Question 7, and the software review conducted with the trainees.

(iv) Feedback from DDL task

Feedback from the DDL task was sought from the participants. Questions 9 and 10 were open-ended questions, set in order to record commentaries on the choice of corpus and task design of the DDL task.

Q9. During the process of creating the exercise, did you find suitable corpora? Please describe your choice and give reasons.

Finding a suitable corpus proved to be the most difficult part of the assignment. The majority of the teacher trainees (61%) reported that they had been unable to find suitable corpora. Lack of suitable texts and level of lexical difficulty were among the most frequently quoted reasons:

> Suitable texts were very hard to find – how can I make sure that the corpus I make includes language that I want to teach?? [Q]

> It was quite hard to find suitable texts which would fit into my exercises. [D]

> It was difficult to find corpora for beginners. [J]

> I couldn't really find a suitable text for a corpus. The texts on the Internet were too difficult (Newspapers!). [O]

When regarding the teacher trainees' feedback it is important to keep in mind that they are novice users of corpora. Issues that are significant from a corpus linguist's point of view, such as the question of representativeness, are clearly not at the forefront of their minds. First and foremost it is important to them whether or not the task will work in the classroom, whether it is suitable for the topic provided by the textbook in use, and whether it will adequately illustrate the learning target in question. Concern was also expressed regarding the accuracy of the chosen texts:

> It was hard to find suitable corpora and took a lot of time searching on the Internet. No guarantee of correctness. [K]

> I couldn't find anything for my corpus. The internet is not so reliable and what if the corpus has mistakes?? [L]

This issue frequently came up during classroom discussions. The teacher trainees believed that it would create a difficult situation for them as teachers if errors in the corpus were discovered during an exercise. They also expressed frustration about a perceived lack of control over the exact content of the corpus because the corpus was originally not intended as a dedicated learning device for the use in the classroom. The participants' answers further illustrate their concern that unknown vocabulary may pose a serious problem for the learners. This point in particular was frequently the focus during feedback sessions after the teacher trainees' presentations. They strongly expressed their frustration at not being able to obtain authentic text material that would suit their individual purposes. Based on more traditional approaches to teaching, the teacher trainees were looking for examples to support their desired learning target rather than language samples that would reflect language use as it naturally occurs. This is in direct opposition to the very core of concordancing and corpus linguistics itself, where the data comes first. This view becomes clearer in the evaluation of Question 10 below.

Q10. Did you encounter any difficulties during the process of creating the exercise – technical or otherwise?

The comments below reveal that the teacher trainees were very intent on creating 'closed' tasks – in other words, tasks they, as the teacher, already knew the outcome of:

> [...] teachers cannot always know the result of DDL exercises. They are also difficult to prepare. [D]

> The concordance lines didn't show the examples I wanted to use for the exercise. [Q]

Hunston (2002a: 171) observes this problem relating to classroom management: "[i]f the corpus is consulted and no answer is apparent to student or teacher, or if further difficult questions are raised, the teacher may feel that a loss of expertise has occurred". It appears that the teacher trainees viewed the unpredictable nature of concordancing activities as a source of concern rather than an asset. A feeling of fear of losing control of the teaching process emerged. In addition to this, the teacher trainees found it challenging to gauge whether or not the task they were creating was appropriate for the target learner group they had in mind:

> I was not sure whether my task was too difficult. It is hard to tell with this kind of exercise. [B]

> Perhaps the task would be too difficult for the students. [D]

> It is difficult to anticipate what the students know. [J]

Such concerns are closely related to the trainees' inexperience with corpora but also with their lack of teaching experience at this early point in their careers. A few teacher trainees experienced technical problems which were all exclusively related to the handling of the concordancing software.

> [...] technical problems: an online concordancer outcome wasn't possible to copy [I]

> [...] I couldn't copy the KWIC lines into Word. The lines lost their formatting. [L]

Despite the reported difficulties which were the focus of this section, the teacher trainees had presented very interesting learning activities and expressed their enthusiasm for the task as such. However, as one of the teacher trainees [O] concludes, "a lot more teachers would use DDL to teach grammar/vocabulary if the teaching materials were already prepared. It takes quite some time to create a proper exercise." This view regarding the need for classroom-ready concordancing activities and materials was echoed by teacher educators in the survey and the expert interviews as reported in Chapter 5.

Throughout the course, the trainees experienced corpus applications in the classroom from their perspective as learners and as teachers – although the transition between the two viewpoints was often seamless. The two components of the course discussed here represent both perspectives. The analysis of the training units has shown how the teacher trainees have transferred their learning experience with concordances to their role as teacher. During this activity the teacher trainees built on their own learning experiences and, based on this, they formulated challenges and advantages of this approach. The analysis of the data presented in this section has shown that pedagogical concerns as expressed by the teacher trainees play a major role when teaching with corpora.

(v) The use of corpora for language teaching and learning

Q11. In which areas do you consider data-driven learning activities as a valuable supplement? (*Multiple answers possible*)

(A) Vocabulary.
(B) Grammar.
(C) Writing Aid.
(D) Cultural Studies.
(E) Translation Studies.
(F) Other, please specify:

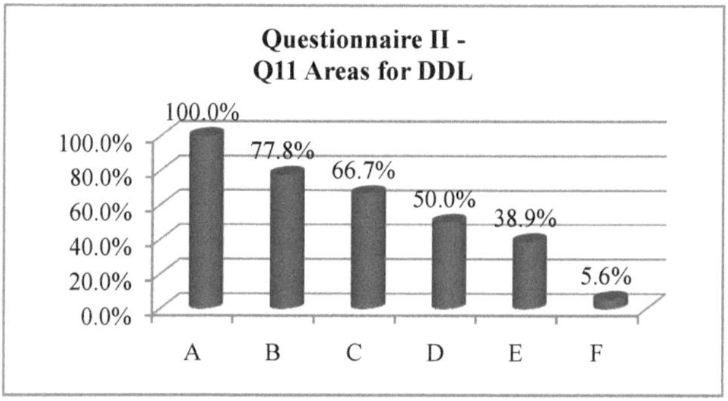

Figure 6-13: Questionnaire II – Q11 Areas for DDL

Question 11 was included in the questionnaire in order too find out more about the potential uses of DDL activities as seen by the trainees. Figure 6-13 demonstrates that the majority of the participants regarded DDL activities as a valuable tool for vocabulary and grammar exercises and as a writing aid. It was considered slightly less helpful for cultural and translation studies. This may also be due to the focus on the first three areas throughout the course; however, it also echoes the trends that can be observed in research literature on the subject. The use of corpora for cultural and translation studies was discussed only on two occasions throughout the course which is likely to have influenced the results for answers (D) and (E). Only one respondent ticked 'Other' and added: 'Motivation'. While clearly not an area of study per se, one might assume that the participant meant that data-driven activities can positively influence motivation.

Q12. Which learner groups do you consider DDL activities useful for? (*Multiple answers possible*)

(A) Beginner
(B) Intermediate
(C) Advanced

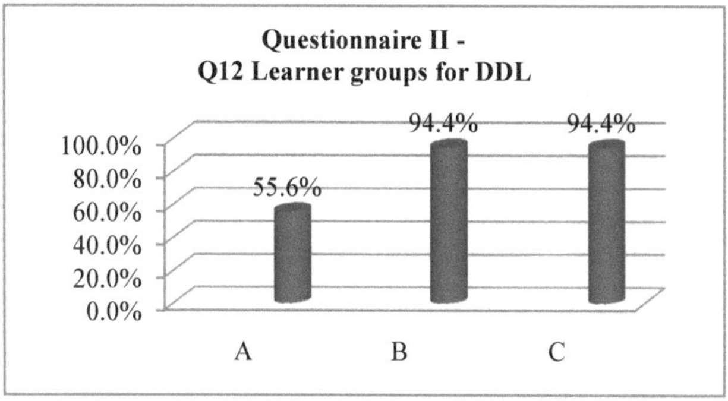

Figure 6-14: Questionnaire II – Q12 Learner groups for DDL

As can be seen in Figure 6-14, most of the respondents deemed DDL activities to be useful for intermediate and advanced learners. Surprisingly, more than half of the participants found DDL to be also useful for beginners. Throughout the course, several ways of adjusting the difficulty level of DDL tasks had been introduced and this may have positively influenced their attitude towards using DDL with lower proficiency learners.

In his evaluation of a series of in-service workshops for language teachers on applied corpus linguistics, Mukherjee (2004: 242) found that "most teachers would only consider making use of corpus data and corpus-based methods themselves"; in other words, there was "a bias towards teacher-centred corpus activities". This tendency was also noted by Estling Vannestål and Lindquist (2007: 339) who report that "most students were positive towards corpus use, especially for answering questions from pupils and marking papers, but also for their own writing. They were more dubious, however, about using corpus methodology in their own classrooms". Question 13 explored the teacher trainees' attitude towards using different applications of DDL.

Q13. In your future role as teacher which DDL activities would you consider using? (*Multiple answers possible*)

(A) Hands-on concordancing with computers (Grammar, Vocabulary, etc.)
(B) Hands-on concordancing with print outs (Grammar, Vocabulary, etc.)
(C) Informing your decisions when marking assignments
(D) Teaching your students how to utilise concordancers to improve their writing

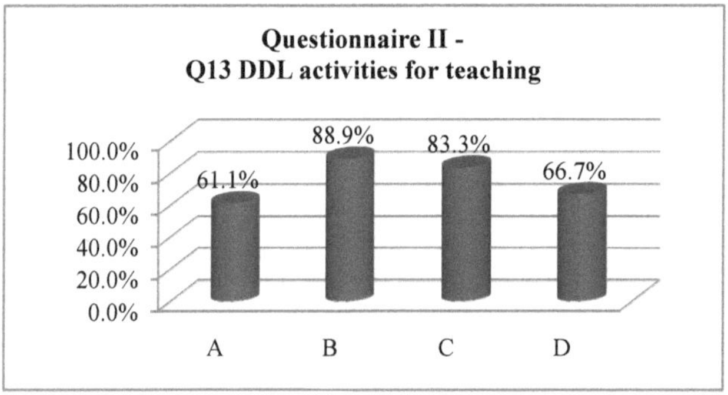

Figure 6-15: Questionnaire II – Q13 DDL activities for teaching

The results from Question 13 as visualised in Figure 6-15 suggest that in the present case study the participants were open to using corpora for learner-centred activities, such as concordancing – with concordance printouts or hands-on with the computer – as well as for teacher-centred activities such as using concordances as an aid to marking.

While there is not enough hard evidence to support any general statements, this may support the assumption that factors such as the amount of training received play a major role in this decision. Furthermore, it is also possible that integration in pre-service training for teachers encourages the use of learner-centred activities more than in-service training. This could be largely due to necessary time constraints of in-service training and also the lack of experience with corpus-based learning activities from the perspective as learner – in other words, to experience the potential benefits of this approach first-hand. Results presented in Farr (2008) appear to corroborate this, as they showed that all the participants, who had experienced corpora integrated into a language systems module as part of a Masters degree in ELT over a two year period, indicated their willingness for in-class use of corpora (Farr 2008: 37-38). These uses included learner-centred activities such as student projects (corpus investigations) and hands-on lab sessions (2008: 38).

In the next question, the participants were asked to provide their assessment of the benefits of the corpus approach in relation to the Teaching Guidelines:

Q14. In relation to what we have found out about the NRW Teaching Guidelines, where do you see the benefits of DDL activities in the language classroom?

In their answers the teacher trainees focused in particular on learner autonomy, authentic language use, and improvement of computer-related skills. The number of trainees who made mention of these points is indicated in brackets:[68]

I. Employs authentic language use (10)
II. Improves computer-related skills (8)
III. Promotes learner autonomy (6)

The use of authentic texts is an elementary part of the Teaching Guidelines. The answers to Question 14 show that the teacher trainees clearly identify DDL activities as a prime opportunity to integrate authentic texts into the classroom. Below are some examples of the responses given to Question 14:

> DDL activities provide the learner with exercises from authentic material, it promotes learner autonomy. [A]
>
> DDL activities help the pupils to work with authentic language and control their own texts (autonomy and self-correction). [B]
>
> Learners are autonomous and use authentic language. [M]

As part of a small-scale survey with a beginner class, Hadley (2002: 118) found that "in the opinion of this group, the main strength of this approach was the exposure to examples of 'real' English (as opposed to the English in textbooks)". The answers given by the teacher trainees above indicate that they also see a strong correlation between the ability to deal with authentic texts and learner autonomy. Therefore, they clearly regard the use of corpora as a valuable tool to achieve target competencies as outlined in the Teaching Guidelines; namely, working with authentic texts and increasing learner autonomy. Despite or maybe

[68] Only a few carefully selected quotes of each category are presented for illustration.

because of the teacher trainees' lack of confidence in their computer skills, it appears that working with corpora and concordancers provided them with a welcome opportunity to use computers in the classroom in a meaningful way:[69]

> It can provide the ability of working with other media which is necessary. [C]

> Promotes media competencies. [E]

> Frequent use of computers is benefit in itself. [P]

> The students use the computer for DDL and improve PC skills. [Q]

The following question was included in order to provide the teacher trainees with the opportunity to freely comment on the negative aspects of DDL activities and at the same time provide solutions as they perceive them:

Q15. What do you consider the biggest disadvantages/pitfalls/ problems of DDL activities? Can you think of improvements in resources and tools that would remedy these issues?

The answers to Question 15 can be grouped into six categories:

I. Training for teacher required (7)
II. Corpus-related difficulties (6)
III. Too time-consuming (5)
IV. Lack of computers at school (2) & potential technical difficulties (2)
V. Training for learners required (5)

The teacher trainees clearly identified the need to train teachers in order to use DDL successfully. It was the most frequently cited aspect they mentioned in their answers. Furthermore, they also drew a strong connection between the training required for the teacher and the necessary computer skills. This seemed to be an important consideration:

> Teachers must be taught to teach it. They don't have (enough) knowledge. (B)

[69] Please note: The translation for 'new technologies' in German is "Neue Medien". As a result of native language interference, the respondents are in fact referring to IT-skills when they make mention of 'media competencies'.

It can be a problem introducing this new method to the school, in particular to older teachers. (F)

Teachers don't know much about computers. Training needed. (J)

Insufficiently skilled teachers (also regarding the computer). (M)

Corpus-related difficulties were again a frequently mentioned problem. This had already come across very strongly in the section collecting feedback on creating the DDL task and is again mentioned here.

Corpora can have mistakes. (B)

It might be difficult to find good corpora. (N)

No guarantee for the correctness of corpora. (K)

There was, furthermore, concern about the practicalities of employing data-driven activities in the classroom: lack of time, lack of available resources, and potential technical difficulties were all mentioned as matters of concern:

It takes a lot of time. (F)

…not enough time … (O)

DDL task takes too much time. (Q)

Examples for responses in category (V):

Lack of equipment (E)

The school might not have any PCs (F)

*txt format for corpora limits user-friendliness (A)

Some of the programs are not that easy to handle (G)

And finally, category (VI), the teacher trainees also recognised that their prospective learners would require training as well, and that, in particular, the use of concordancing software might present an obstacle.

The learners have to be guided before and during their activities. (C)

> Usage of those software programs is not always easy for students. (P)

> Pupils may not understand how to work with concordancer. (R)

The final question was included in order to gauge to what extent the teacher trainees regarded corpus tools and resources as an asset to their studies.

Q16. In relation to your own studies, would you consider the integration of corpus tools and resources to be a valuable addition? Discuss.

Seventeen participants responded to the question and the answers were all positive. The majority of the responses related to corpora as an aid in writing essays. In particular, the trainees regarded the corpus as a 'native speaker' to consult in order to improve their writing:

> Yes, I think it is a valuable addition because we don't have the same knowledge as native speakers and won't reach it. Working with a corpus is a good possibility to make sure whether native speakers use a word in a specific context. (B)

> [I]t is useful if you do not know a native speaker to ask. (M)

The trainees found corpora to be useful to check their own intuitions:

> I reckon it is a valuable addition to make sure that special expressions are correct. (N)

> Yes, corpus tools and resources can be a valuable addition because often there is an uncertainty about using words. (D)

> Corpus tools might be useful to improve your own style of writing by checking certain possibilities of expressing something [...]. (G)

In relation to their study programme, the trainees found corpora to be useful in the areas of language practice and literary studies:

> Yes, it can be a valuable addition. Also, for a discussion of literary texts (e.g. word fields). (C)

> Really helpful for 'Sprachpraxis' [language practice] and also for literature studies (e.g. Jane Austen corpus). (R)

The participants' responses were very positive and encouraging. They clearly saw potential for the use of corpora for their training, and one student pointed out that it is "important to introduce corpus tools quite early to students because they are useful for their studies".

6.4 Discussion of results

One of the goals of the case study presented in this chapter was to create opportunities for teacher trainees to explore the use of corpora from the perspective of their role as learner *and* as teacher. This approach was designed in order to highlight not only the differences but also the links between these two roles and, in particular, to gain insight into the teachers' perspectives of this approach. The observations from the training unit on the use of *some* and *any* serve as a good illustration for this. Furthermore, they demonstrate how the trainees made the transition from their role of learner to teacher.

As part of the learning phase – that is, while they were exploring the concordances from both the textbook corpus and the *ACE* – the trainees learned more about the explicit rules governing the use of *some* and *any*. During the ensuing classroom discussions the participants also realised that they needed more training in relation to formal knowledge about language; for example, in the form of grammatical terminology. As the discussion in Section 4.3.1 on corpora has shown, it is above all important to use corpora for learners with content that is relevant to them. The textbook corpus was relevant to the trainees because it contained language from textbooks their future students might likely encounter. Teacher trainees are in a transitional phase. Partly, they still consider themselves learners, as their experiences as students (going to school) are usually still fresh in their minds. They are also learners again (at university), learning to become teachers. At the same time, they constantly project into their future profession, asking themselves 'What would I do as a teacher?'. As a result, the trainees not only reflected instantly back to their own experiences of learning the use of *some* and *any*, but they also quickly and without further prompting related this to their future role as teacher.

Of particular concern to them was to find adequate ways of teaching authentic language use to their students on the one hand and dealing with their (beginner) learners' limitations on the other. The exploratory nature of the concordance task, first looking at the use of *some* and *any* as used in textbooks, then discovering and analysing the use of these words in a corpus of actual language use, was seemingly very appealing to them. This became evident in the evaluation of the reflective essays the participants wrote. Here the trainees identified this approach as a solution to their struggle to reconcile their desire to teach 'real' English with the limitations of beginner learners.

In brief, it can be concluded that a simple introduction to concordances and very basic concordance analysis has led this group of teacher trainees to reflect on language use, their own knowledge of a specific linguistic item, textbook versus authentic language use, teaching authentic language to beginner learners, employing a discovery-type learning activity with language learners, and teaching methodology. The exercise has furthermore shown that the trainees saw a strong link between linguistic aspects and pedagogical implications; for example, in terms of teaching method or classroom management. Overall, the task has shown great potential for raising language as well as teaching awareness.

The evaluation of the concordancing software by the participants clearly showed that they wanted above all a user-friendly solution. Their experiences in using the programs as learners clearly flowed into their reviews of the respective concordancers. As teachers, they felt that it was important to have a 'simple to install', 'easy to use' solution to produce results quickly and reliably in order to successfully integrate such a program in the classroom. Additionally, many pointed out that exporting and editing features were important to them in order to design teaching materials. Their concerns and ideas have been incorporated into the design of the classroom concordancer proposed in Chapter 7.

The evaluation of the DDL task that the trainees were asked to create towards the end of the seminar clearly showed that a lack of corpus expertise coupled with a lack of teaching experience poses a serious challenge to teachers. In particular, creating a simple task aimed at lower to intermediate learners, that is linguistically relevant and successful, proved to be very difficult indeed. As the discussion in Section 4.3.4 on training learners showed, the use of concordance printouts has been proposed for the introductory stages of learner training. However, the analysis of the DDL task created by the trainees has highlighted some disadvantages and hidden challenges of this approach. It is not a simple matter to generate the 'right' list of concordancers that will successfully lead to the lesson's set goal. In most learning contexts, in particular in secondary education, teachers have a learning target in mind, and the processes in the classroom should ultimately enable learners to reach this goal. Therefore, concordances have to be relevant, they have to include the right samples and also enough samples to show any patterns. The analysis of the task that used hands-on concordancing with learners showed that this particular approach is even more complex. The trainees had evidently not given enough thought to the particular details of the corpus nor could they foresee other variables (e.g. the importance of formulating the corpus query correctly, etc.).

It became further apparent that the trainees had difficulties to judge which skills were needed for a particular task and the extent of prior knowledge required of their learners in order to successfully solve the given task. In sum, it appears that the complexity of designing successful corpus tasks has been underestimated and that corpora are not easily transformed into useful and appropriate learning tools.

Finally, the questionnaire conducted at the end of the course showed that computer skills played an important role and one that these trainees increasingly recognised as such for their future teaching career. Computer-related difficulties that emerged throughout the course were a constant source of worry and discouragement to the trainees. Consequently, the design of (classroom) user-friendly concordancing software is an important step towards successful integration. Consequently, the following chapter presents the design for a corpus analysis software tool for classroom use: *My Concordancer*.

Despite all encountered difficulties, the participants of this case study generally gave positive responses in relation to using corpora in the classroom. While nearly all of the trainees indicated that they would use corpus tasks with intermediate and advanced learners, more than half also thought it to be useful with beginners. Additionally, the majority of the participants considered using concordancing (concordance printouts or hands-on) with their students. In comparison, only 12.9% of the participants of an in-service workshop on corpus linguistics indicated that they viewed corpus tasks as useful for teachers *and* learners (see Mukherjee 2004: 241). This led Mukherjee (2004: 242) to conclude that "most teachers [...] exclusively focused on teacher-centred activities and showed that learner-centred activities would presumably have no place in their classrooms".

These results further lend weight to the argument that pre-service courses are better equipped to prepare teachers for the use of corpora in the classroom with learners than in-service workshops for example. Firstly, teachers can gather first-hand language learning experiences with concordances. If these experiences are positive, and teachers perceive them as valuable, then this in turn may predispose them more positively towards classroom concordancing. Secondly, the present case study has shown that teaching with corpora is a complex matter, particularly with lower-level learners. Therefore, sufficient time and effort has to be dedicated to training teachers appropriately. In-service workshops, for example, are generally by necessity very short and therefore may not be suitable for this task. However, they may well have significant potential in training teachers to use corpora for teacher-centred use (e.g. marking). If that is the desired goal, in-service workshops appear as an appropriate response to an ageing teaching population which one of the experts in Chapter 5 referred to. Such workshops could successfully bring these new developments to this group of practicing teachers who are no longer actively participating in new research developments.

This case study has shown that a course on learning *and* teaching with corpora has great potential in LTE. All of the participants found corpora to be useful for other areas of their degree – for example, language practice courses, an obvious choice, but also literary and cultural studies. It has furthermore emerged from the analysis that some of the characteristics generally considered to be positive features of DDL were regarded with caution by the teachers for reasons of classroom management. The difficulties, as reported by the teacher trainees, regarding the process of creating materials, highlighted the importance of availability of ready-made and integrated tasks.

Beyond this, the case study has highlighted that the role of corpora in LTE is potentially more than just about raising language awareness and improving language competence. Working with corpora provides a context that is very conducive to stimulating discussion and reflection on teaching methodology and raises language as much as *teaching* awareness. The close relationship between language as content and questions regarding teaching methodology make it an ideal playground for teacher trainees. Amador Moreno *et al.* (2006: 100) point out that it is "difficult to envisage finding time in the programme of study for training in corpus consultation and analysis". In light of the results of this study, however, I would argue that such a course on learning and teaching with corpora has much to offer beyond training in corpus literacy. In particular, teacher trainees' reflections about their own learning experience and how to make the successful transfer of this into their teaching practice has proved to have enormous potential. The teacher trainees not only gained better language awareness but naturally created a strong connection between the subject matter of their teaching – that is, language – and how to teach it. The reflective essays particularly displayed their struggle to come to terms with the challenges to their own beliefs and attitudes generated by the work with corpora. This clearly demonstrates the significant role corpora can play in LTE.

Limitations of the study and implications for further research

There are some limitations to this study that need to be acknowledged. Due to the exploratory nature of this small-scale study, generalisations drawn from the analysis presented here must be regarded with caution. In particular, it seems necessary to conduct more longitudinal studies that explore the effect of such a course for teacher trainees on the actual classroom practices of those teachers. More research also needs to be done in order to determine the extent of corpus literacy teachers need to possess to successfully teach with corpora. Finally, the course underlying the case study presented here is situated within the context of pre-service language teacher education in Germany. Therefore, the results are shaped and influenced by the characteristics of this environment. Furthermore, the participants were training to teach a language that is not their native language. While this is an important consideration when regarding the results of this study, it should also be noted that this is a very common situation in language education. Therefore, the main insights gained from this study should be transferable to and applicable in other LTE contexts.

7 Corpus technology *for* language pedagogy: *My Concordancer*

The concordancer plays a central role in the corpus analysis process, as shown in the discussion in Chapter 4 regarding the three core elements – corpus, software, user. The functionality and accessibility of this software is highly important to the classroom user who uses the concordancer either to produce teaching materials or conduct corpus searches for language learning or teaching purposes. Furthermore, the results from the survey presented in Chapter 5 have shown that the majority of teacher educators (61%) who are currently using corpora in some form for their teaching would like to see concordancing software improved (see CL Survey, Question 14). In addition, the expert interviews reported in Section 5.3 showed that they too believe that a lack of suitable materials, including user-friendly software, impeded the process of popularising corpora in language education. Römer (2008) rightly remarks that

> new concordance programs that are appealing and easy to use may have to be written so that teachers and learners are not put off from working with corpora right away because the software is too complex or not user-friendly enough. (Römer 2008: 12)

The current chapter presents the blueprint for concordancing software designed for classroom use based on the user profiles for classroom users as described in Section 4.3.2. This concordancer is proposed as a tool *for* pedagogy with the needs and requirements of language learners and teachers as the key factors driving the design process. The chapter begins with a review of concordancing software and then showcases the proposed software: *My Concordancer*.

7.1 Concordancing software

Concordancing software has been developed for over 40 years. One of the earliest examples is *COCOA – A word-count and concordance generator* (Russell 1965) which was designed for the Atlas system, one of the most powerful mainframe computers in the 1960s (Rojas & Hashagen 2000). Its main purpose was for the analysis of literary texts and it featured a simple frequency count and a concordance function. The author of *COCOA* notes that it also "provides a worthwhile tool for linguists" (Russell 1965). The results of a text search on this mainframe system came in the form of paper printouts, and retrieving the full concordance of Shakespeare's work "would certainly stand higher and would probably weigh heavier than any prospective COCOA user"

(Russell 1965, Outline; para. 4). In 1981, the first machine independent concordancing software, the *Oxford Concordance Program* (*OCP*), was released (Hockey & Martin 1987). The *OCP* was widely used for linguistic research, and *Micro-OCP*, a later version designed for micro computers, was equally popular. In the early 1980s, the *OCP* was employed for teaching purposes with students of linguistics and English (Davidson 1990). The functions of both versions include the generating of word lists, indexing, and concordancing. The increasing availability of micro computers and the development of software like *Micro-OCP* signalled a new era in concordancing which had now become available to individuals. In 1986, Tim Johns published the seminal article on the software *MicroConcord* in which he described the architecture of the program and in addition presented his ideas for applying this software in the language classroom. Increasing availability of personal computers and a continuing interest in classroom concordancing led to the release of a variety of concordancing applications in the 1990s. These applications included simple MS-DOS routines (Stevens 1991c), built-in macros for word processors that emulate basic concordancing functions (e.g. Deeth 1993; Holliday 1993; Low 1992), applications that were written for a specific purpose (e.g. Cobb 1997) and, finally, commercial software both for research and classroom purposes.

In recent years, due to the development of the internet, two distinct types of concordancers have emerged: online and offline concordancers. Offline concordancers can be further subdivided into product-independent (e.g. sophisticated research programs such as *Wordsmith Tools* and *MonoConc Pro*) and product-dependent concordancers (e.g. *XAIRA* which was developed for use with the *BNC*)[70] which are specifically designed for the use with one particular corpus. Furthermore, concordancers can also be purpose-built like *aConcorde* which was designed to deal with Arabic languages in particular.[71] Online concordancers (e.g. *BYU-BNC*; *Collins Corpus Sampler*; *Compleat Lexical Tutor*; *WebCorp*) have become increasingly available over the internet. They offer a quick and easy way of giving an introductory demonstration to the basics of concordancing because they are already attached to a corpus and no installation is required. However, internet access is a necessary prerequisite, and its availability continues to pose a problem in the educational context. Furthermore, online concordancers often provide only limited functions in relation to sorting, editing, and printing concordance results. Thus, independent offline concordancers are more flexible for classroom application as they do not rely on the internet and can be used with any selected text or text collection.

---

70 Although please note that *Xaira* will function with other corpora as long as they are in XML format.

71 Development of the software appears to have halted. The website hasn't been updated since 2005.

In regard to mainstream applications, two programs were designed explicitly for the use in language pedagogy: the *LMC* (Chandler 1990) and *MicroConcord* (Scott & Johns 1993). The *LMC* was very popular for its ease of use and its fast processing but it was limited to 50,000-word text files. *MicroConcord* was very widely used and, despite the fact that it runs only in the now outdated MS-DOS environment, it continues to be used (e.g. Granath 2009; Johns *et al.* 2008).[72] A possible reason for this is reflected in the following statement by Gavioli and Aston (2001):

> [M]ore user-friendly software to interrogate corpora is required. In our experience, the most suitable concordancer for everyday classroom use is still *MicroConcord* (Scott & Johns 1993); more recent programs present a forbidding range of complex options which can easily confuse the learner. (Gavioli & Aston 2001: 245)

AntConc is a more recent example of software designed for classroom use (Anthony 2005). This excellent software was developed specifically for the context of technical writing; however, it is very versatile and not limited to this specific context.

In order to narrow down what exactly a 'suitable concordancer' for classroom use entails, Chapter 4 has provided a detailed analysis of classroom versus research users. This investigation has shown that classroom users have different user profiles to that of researchers. In particular, the differences can be found in motivation to use concordancing software, linguistic and IT skills, time available for learning how to use the software, range of functionality, and purpose of use.

The analysis of the survey in Chapter 5 showed that more than half of the respondents who stated that they were familiar with corpus linguistics, and who were using corpora as part of their teaching, wanted improvements in the category 'concordancing software' (see Q14). Furthermore, during the interviews, the experts emphasised the importance of designing relevant tools and resources for the classroom. In response to this and to the findings of Chapter 4, namely the key role of the concordancing software in the process of using corpora and the different user profiles of classroom versus research users, the following section presents a blueprint for the design of a concordancer tailor-made for classroom use: *My Concordancer*.

---

72 This was also evidenced in the results of the survey (Q12): 22% of the respondents indicated that they were using *MicroConcord* for teaching purposes (see Section 5.2.2).

7.2 Blueprint: *My Concordancer*

This section will explore the approach taken by *My Concordancer*, corpus analysis software that is offered as a tailor-made solution for the classroom based on the projected user-profile of language learners and teachers defined in Section 4.3.2. In regard to the context of CALL software development, Levy and Stockwell (2006: 27) emphasise that "[t]he designer needs to make every attempt to get to know the potential users and the learning context". *My Concordancer* was designed to retain the basic functions of professional corpus analysis software on the one hand and to take into account the special circumstances of the pedagogical context on the other hand. The following sections will discuss the main components of *My Concordancer* and, while by no means exhaustive, they will show how these components add up to a design compatible with the requirements of classroom use.

7.2.1 Intuitive interface

The rapid progress in the development of powerful hardware has allowed for a shift of focus in software design from what is technologically possible to maximum user-friendliness. When Flowerdew stated in 1996 that

> software has become much more 'user friendly' and is now capable of handling large amounts of text very quickly and easily, whereas in the past large amounts of data could only be handled by software which was slow and difficult to use, (Flowerdew 1996: 98)

it becomes obvious that what his use of the term 'user friendly' really stands for is 'technologically possible'. Nearly fifteen years down the track, due to significant developments in computer technology, software design can now focus on projected user-profiles in order to maximise true 'user-friendliness'. For software intended for use in language learning environments, Hémard and Cushion (2000: 41) emphasise the need to "develop a readily recognizable, professionally robust and intuitive interface". The graphical user interface (GUI) of a program is the main point of communication between the user and the machine. It therefore stands at the centre of this user-centred approach. As discussed in Section 4.3.2, the user-profiles for classroom and professional users differ considerably. The main differences lie in IT-proficiency, motivation to use and learn to use the software, time constraints, language skills (including metalinguistic knowledge), and requirements regarding the range of required program functions. These specifications are reflected in the design of *My Concordancer* through an economically designed interface, short navigational pathways, and easily accessible navigational controls. The teacher trainees who participated in the case study presented in Chapter 6 pointed out the significance of user-friendly design in their reviews of concordancing software. According to them, user-friendliness is directly related to the language learners' motivation to use the software. Therefore, this must be of central importance to the design of this software intended for classroom use.

The interface of *My Concordancer* consists of the following main elements: the menu and toolbars, the corpus workspace, the KWIC display, and the context window. The architecture of the interface of *My Concordancer* provides instant access to all the vital functions of the program without requiring the user to navigate through additional menus or settings. When the program is started for the first time, the user can choose to open a file from a selected location or open one of the example text collections that form part of *My Concordancer*. Once opened, these files appear in the corpus workspace. From here the user can rename, add or remove text files and specify a name for the current corpus project through the right-click context menu.

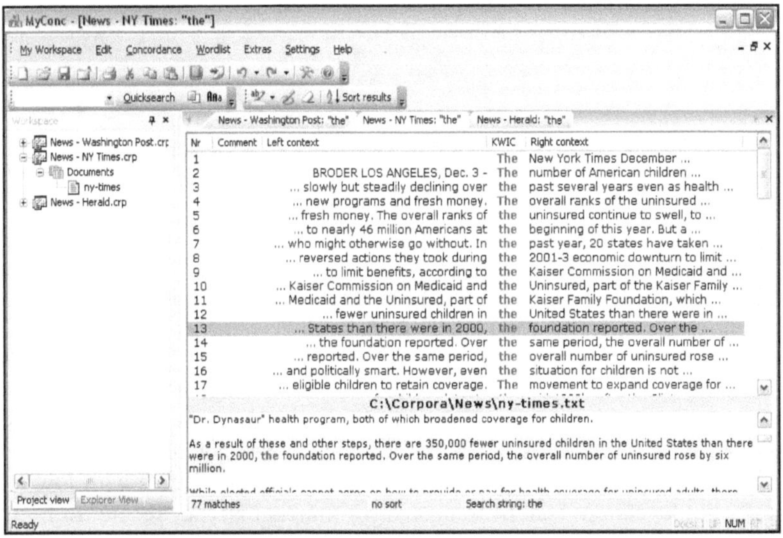

Figure 7-1: *My Concordancer* – Graphical User Interface.

This feature is particularly helpful for teachers or learners who work with self-generated or 'ad-hoc'-compiled corpora. Above the corpus workspace is the QUICKSEARCH toolbar. Here the user can type in a search query and start the search by hitting the ENTER key or clicking on the QUICKSEARCH button. The results are instantly presented in the KWIC display. If the program is used for the first time, a dialogue will appear that asks the user to choose a text file or to pick one of the example text files that are part of *My Concordancer*. If the program has been used previously, it will load the text that was active when the program was closed in the previous session. This function can be deactivated in the program settings. In a classroom setting this allows students to pick up straight away where they left off at the end of the last session. In the menu 'Concordance' a more advanced search option is available which will be discussed in more detail in the next section. This feature is meeting another demand made by the teacher trainees in Section 6.3.3, namely the ability of quick access, and the ability to produce results instantly.

Closely tied to the display of search results is the window management. Each new search is conducted in its own window tab and, depending on the chosen setting, can either automatically open in a new tab, or delete the old search results. Any open windows are organised in the form of tabs. Each tab is automatically labelled with the designated corpus name and the search term:

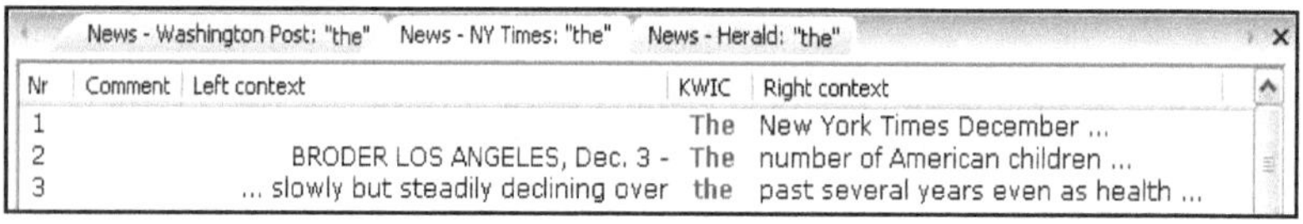

Figure 7-2: *My Concordancer* – Tab navigation

This allows for easy navigation in order to compare search results, clearly marks which corpus each search relates to, and avoids 'losing' windows.

One way of reducing the length of navigational pathways is to operate the program mainly through the use of buttons in the toolbar. The difficulty in operating a program this way lies in recognising the functions of the symbols displayed on the buttons. It is up to the program developer to decide on the design of these buttons and which buttons to display where. Users with low or medium IT skill levels can benefit from an environment that they recognise from other standard applications. Based on the assumption that the use of word processors is widespread, the program buttons of *My Concordancer* were designed to resemble standard buttons for functions such as NEW, OPEN, SAVE, CLOSE, COPY, CUT, PASTE, PRINT, etc. Familiar design of the program buttons allows the user to profit from any past experience with computers and immediately exercise some control over the program's basic functions. The significance of this was emphasised by the teacher trainees in Section 6.3.3, in particular in regard to novice users, which classroom users generally are, at least when first introduced to concordancing.

Figure 7-3: *My Concordancer* – Taskbar

In addition to this, all available toolbars are fully customisable. The location of each toolbar and the buttons can be set up by the user if this is desired. Thus, the interface of *My Concordancer* provides the user with the opportunity to manage corpora or text collections, conduct simple searches, read the results in the KWIC format and view the full context all in one window without having to access any of the menus or open up additional windows.

7.2.2 To find what you are looking for

My Concordancer offers two ways of conducting a concordance search:

(i) the Quicksearch function accessible through the toolbar; and
(ii) the advanced concordance search function in the 'Concordance' menu.

The QUICKSEARCH function is particularly useful in order to give a quick demonstration or to get students started straight away and also allows for quick follow-up searches.

One of the skills that the user has to master is devising successful search strategies. In their report on a concordance project with students of Italian, Kennedy and Miceli (2001: 84-85) point out that students often lack the ability to construct successful search patterns due to a lack of meta-linguistic knowledge and experience in formulating research questions. A carefully guided approach to concordancing can aid in introducing students to the subject slowly and allow them to learn from their own experience. While there are limits as to how the program itself can contribute to this learning process, *My Concordancer* offers a few elements that have been implemented in order to help students to find what they are looking for. A common challenge that learners face when entering the search term is the abstract system of wildcards, Boolean searches or even regular search expressions. In order to reduce this difficult aspect of the software and provide more intuitive access to search patterns, the main search dialogue in *My Concordancer* offers an optional help function with a number of buttons that insert the wildcard characters according to the description on the button per mouse-click. As a result, users do not have to remember any particular wildcard character and can formulate their search query with the help of statements like: 'any number of characters', 'one or no character', 'exactly one character', etc.

Another source of error that often leads to unsuccessful or incorrect results is spelling mistakes. In their concordancing environment, Ahmad *et al.* (1985: 6) had installed a simple failsafe mechanism that prompted the user each time with this comment after the user had typed in the search string:

> The string you asked for is: SEARCH WORD. Providing this is the string you want, press RETURN. However, if you have made a typing mistake, type ERROR and press RETURN, in order to correct it.

This simple feedback gives at least reason to reflect on the formulated search question. In *My Concordancer*, a built-in dictionary will – when in doubt – prompt the user with a comment like "Did you mean X?". At this point the user is given the chance to proceed with the original search or alter the search term. If desired, this feature can be deactivated for future searches. Such scaffolding prompts have been shown to increase learner's confidence and efficiency in using concordancers (see Chang & Sun 2009).

7.2.3 KWIC display and on-screen editing

The KWIC format is the most common way of displaying concordance results. Its main characteristics are the centred display of all occurrences of the search string and the truncated left and right context. In *My Concordancer* the KWIC display is located in the centre of the screen and separated from the context window through a horizontal bar at the bottom. The main window is divided into five columns: line number, comment, left context, keyword, right context. The line numbers are included for easier reference when discussing results in the class.

Nr	Comment	Left context	KWIC	Right context
1		Joseph Conrad	HEART	OF DARKNESS I The Nellie, a cruising yawl, swung ...
2		... the silence of the land went home to one's very	heart	,--its mystery, its greatness, the amazing reality of ...
3		... to the hidden evil, to the profound darkness of its	heart	. It was so startling that I leaped to my feet and ...

Figure 7-4: *My Concordancer* – KWIC display

In the second column, the user can type in words or numbers of up to 24 characters as a comment in the respective line. Other concordancers currently only allow the entering of a single character, either numerical or alphabetical. With the COMMENT function the user can type in full words describing, for example, the function of a word (noun, verb, etc.). Several lines can be selected at the same time by holding down the CTRL key. Entering a comment into one of the lines will automatically fill the remaining selected lines with the same comment. If desired, the results can be re-sorted according to the entry in the COMMENT column. Individual or several selected lines can be deleted either by using the right-click menu or the DELETE key. The user can also choose to 'hide' unwanted results rather than deleting them. Hidden lines are then retrievable later on. This feature is particularly important for teachers when preparing teaching materials with concordances.

For the beginner, the truncated text of concordance results often adds to the difficulty of adjusting to this new way of looking at language. While *My Concordancer* offers the option to adjust the context by entering an exact number of characters, words or sentences in the settings, the user can also simply change the display of the context by adjusting the column width of the left and right context using the mouse on the column bars entitled 'Left Context' and 'Right Context' respectively. This lets the user adjust the context width after the search and without having to look for that option in the settings. This feature is currently set up in a way that truncates the text at the word level, thereby leaving individual words intact. Similarly, the user can perform three simple sorting options by clicking on the column bars. The 'Left Context' column sorts the results by the first word left to the keyword, the 'KWIC' column sorts by the keyword itself and the 'Right Context' column sorts by the first word to the right of the keyword. More specific sorting options are available through the SORT dialogue. The KWIC display options combined with the QUICKSEARCH dialogue described above enable the user to perform a search, adjust context width, perform preliminary sorting of the results, include individual commentaries, and delete or hide selected unwanted results without leaving the KWIC display once and without having to navigate other menus or settings dialogues. Eliminating the need to find functions in menus, such short navigational pathways are an important element of user-friendly design.

Early on Johns (1988: 24) pointed out the need for learners to be trained in "strategies of observation" in order to work successfully with concordances. Acquiring these strategies is part of a gradual and guided training process that many practitioners in this field advocate (e.g. Gavioli 1997, 2001; Kennedy & Miceli 2001; Turnbull & Burston 1998). On the one hand, the user needs to become familiar with a new perspective of language in the form of KWIC concordances and with the program itself, and on the other, he/she faces new challenges that require meta-linguistic and research skills. In relation to learners,

Kennedy and Miceli (2001: 82) note that they require explicit training in these four areas:

1) Formulating the question;
2) Devising a search strategy;
3) Observing the examples and selecting relevant ones; and
4) Drawing a conclusion.

While the computer cannot effectively help in devising a meaningful research question, assistance can be provided in formulating the correct search syntax as described in the previous section. The computer can help little with Step 4 – that is, drawing a conclusion from the observed data. However, what the program can do is make the results more visible and help test hypotheses formulated by the user. Johns (1988: 24) emphasises the importance of "practice in identification and classification" for students and that "multicoloured fibre-tip pens for marking up contents are an excellent auxiliary tool". In *My Concordancer* the user can underline words manually in the left and right context on-screen while in the KWIC display mode by simply selecting the freehand tool. The tool can be used with different colours. With the eraser tool this process can be reversed either for a single word or if desired the whole screen can be cleared. In addition, *My Concordancer* offers an in-text search function that searches the left, right or both sides of the context of the concordance results. On demand, the program will automatically highlight the findings in the context. This feature is particularly useful to make patterns visible that the user may suspect, which means that it can aid the user in testing a hypothesis.

Time constraints often play an important role in the classroom, and activities often cannot be finished within the limits of a single classroom session. One of the experts interviewed in Section 5.3 actually pointed out the difficulty of introducing research-based tasks due to the restraints imposed by the 45-minute class cycle. In order to ensure that the results of an ongoing research project are not lost, *My Concordancer* can save the entire workspace, including edited search results, and if desired, maintains a "search history" that lists previous search queries for each respective corpus. When opened the next time, the workspace is completely restored including selected corpora, search results and edited KWIC displays.

7.2.4 Input and output options

Plain text (ASCII) files are the standard file format in which corpus data are stored. These files are compatible with Windows, Mac and UNIX systems and contain only raw text without any formatting. As soon as formatting is included

– for example, in a standard word processor – the file is stored as a binary file in order to keep the formatting. While plain text files are very commonly used as data storage files for text corpora, learners and teachers may not be quite as familiar with them. Most text files that users encounter these days are MS Word documents, PDF files and HTML files. In the classroom, word documents are arguably the most frequently used files, especially for storing texts produced by learners. Yet, most currently available concordancers can only read plain text files (*.txt) and rich text files (*.rtf) but not binary files such as word documents (*.doc). Many concordancers can read HTML and XML files although not all programs provide adequate tag set handling abilities which often renders the results illegible as the following example shows:

, see and the two sheets there in the middle? now	you	see </OVERLAP1> that Poli Sci one-six
VERLAP1> that Poli Sci one-sixty, when	you	leaf through it, <U2 WHO="S2" NSS=NS"
rs section. so that could be an honors course for	you	<U2 WHO="S2" NSS="NS" ROLE="JU" SEX="F"
re a lot of different ways to do an honors course	you	don't have to do Honors Math to do an honors cour
F= AGE="1" RESTRICT="NONE"> okay </U2>	you	can take, all sorts of other, options for honors
E= FLANG="EST"> now uh one thing i haven't asked	you	, is, eh-whether you took any A-P tests in May.
uh one thing i haven't asked you, is, eh- whether	you	took any A-P tests in May. </U1> <U1 WHO=S2" NS
="NONE"> mhm </U2> now, that will give	you	some credit toward graduation. </U1> <U1
how does that not mean <OVERLAP1> that	you	</OVERLAP1> </U1> - <U1 WHO="S2" NSS="NS" ROLE="J
> and how many credits would i get th-	you	know? or or </U1> - <U1 WHO="S1" NSS="NRN
"F" AGE="4" RESTRICT="NON" FLANG="EST" i think	you	get six actually i don't remember < WU2
T="NONE"> wow </U2> uh, no, excuse me.	you	have to get, a five to get six, but you get three
xcuse me. you have to get, a five to get six, but	you	get three hourse of credit. </U1> = <U1 WH

Figure 7-5: Visible tags in KWIC list (*AntConc*; Corpus: *MICASE*)

For classroom use the concordancer should be able to either read Word documents or at least provide an internal converter that opens binary Word documents as plain text files. This would make it much easier for learners to examine their own texts or for teachers to work with learner texts.

Of equal significance are the output options provided by the concordancer. Especially for the production of teaching materials, such as concordance-based handouts that may require further editing in a word processor, the concordance lines should be exportable in their original format into the Word document. The greatest concern here is that the concordance maintains the KWIC format. In order to achieve this, a number of concordancers currently rely on using fixed width fonts such as Courier while others do not offer any specific output options other than the 'Copy to clipboard' command which results in a total loss of the centred KWIC format.[73] *My Concordancer* offers the option to export the KWIC results as a table with a predefined number of characters, words or sentences in

[73] A fixed width or monospace font is one where each character, symbol, or space has the same width and therefore occupies the same amount of horizontal space.

the left and right context. This has at least two advantages. Firstly, it ensures that the KWIC format can be maintained at all times, and, secondly, it allows the user to alter the line numbers, left context, the keyword, and the right context independently:

Table 7-1: Tabular output generated by *My Concordancer*

1		HEART	OF DARKNESS
2	of the land went home to one's very	heart	,--its mystery, its greatness, the amazing
3	evil, to the profound darkness of its	heart	. It was so startling that I leaped to my
4	to clap my teeth smartly before my	heart	flew out, when I shaved by a fluke some
5	the thump--eh? A blow on the very	heart	. You remember it, you dream of it, you
6	penetrated deeper and deeper into the	heart	of darkness. It was very quiet there.
7	seen the pilgrims stare! They had no	heart	to grin, or even to revile me; but I believe
8	light, or the deceitful flow from the	heart	of an impenetrable darkness. "The other
9	started for the interior with a light	heart	, and no more idea of what would happen

As a table, the exported results are fully customisable within the word processor environment without losing the KWIC format. The user can choose whether or not to display the table frame, change the font type or size and display or blank out individual columns. This allows the user to modify and easily edit and sort the results according to the specific needs of the task at hand. If transferred to Excel rather than Word, the table format even permits further sorting of the left or right context if this is desired. In case the user prefers not to transfer the KWIC results into a word processor *My Concordancer* provides a number of printing options. Apart from being able to choose between various print modes (Print lines x-y; Print selected lines; Print all results; Context width, etc.), the printer dialogue also offers a print preview that calculates an estimated number of pages, which is a helpful feature that prevents unintentionally printing too many pages – for example, in the case of high-frequency word searches.

7.2.5 Help and tutorial options

My Concordancer offers a help file which primarily serves as a source of reference for the operation of the program. Additionally, in order to familiarise the user with some of the functions of the program and furthermore with some significant aspects of concordancing, *My Concordancer* offers a range of simple training units. When using the program for the first time, the user can decide whether to initiate the training sequence or skip directly to the main program. The units can be accessed at a later stage through the HELP menu.

While the main purpose of these tutorials is to familiarise the student with the techniques and pitfalls of concordance analysis, they also aim at stimulating the learner's curiosity about the workings of language. The topics currently covered in these units are 'The value of observation', 'Analysing concordances', 'Hands-on concordancing', 'Finding what you're looking for' and 'Limitations of corpus data'. The units are designed to be adaptable to beginners, intermediate, and advanced levels of language proficiency.

7.3 Corpus software for classroom users

The proposal for *My Concordancer* (Breyer 2006b) originally appeared in an edited volume by Braun *et al.* (2006) with the title *Corpus Technology for Language Pedagogy*. The title of this book and the publications contained in it reflect a growing recognition on the part of researchers that the demands of pedagogy have to be of primary concern in the application of corpora in language education. Both the results of the survey and the case study presented in Chapters 5 and 6 of the current study show that there is a need for more user-friendly software adapted to the requirements of the classroom user. Another key factor that was identified in order to advance the popularisation of corpora is the development of classroom-ready corpus materials. The availability of user-friendly software to produce concordances for this purpose is therefore equally important for publishers and language practitioners involved in that process. Corpora and concordances are competing with many other ideas and approaches in the lucrative market of language education. It is therefore imperative that the tools and resources work well and easily produce impressive results.

In terms of ongoing research in this area, it is furthermore of great importance that concordancing software for the classroom contains a user protocol function. Cobb (1997: 302) rightly observes that "commercial concordance software does not generate user protocols, leaving informal observation the default research tool". User protocols could play a critical role in further empirical research by providing information about the way learners use concordances and should be part of any new software development. This could help to improve training guidelines for learners; for example, by supplying information about search patterns during a specific task.

Concordancers for the classroom fall into the category of computer tools as opposed to computer tutors. Levy and Stockwell (2006: 24) describe the role of technology as an "'enabling' device" in the sense that "the tool might facilitate access to and act as a means of searching a database". The design of *My Concordancer* falls into the trend of "shaping these general-purpose tools, both technically and pedagogically, so as to sharpen their focus and effectiveness for language learning" (2006: 25).

8 Teaching with corpora: serious challenges and great potential

> Teachers should be central stakeholders in the corpus revolution, but, so far, [...] teachers have spoken only with muted voices, and not always been listened to.
>
> (McCarthy 2008: 565)

The emergence of corpus linguistics, driven by the advent of computer technology, has had a resounding and lasting impact on the study of language. Corpus-based research is increasingly gaining significance in nearly all branches of linguistics, and the ramifications of this are yet to be fully explored:

> Major theoretical advances have often come when linguists have realized the significance of different forms of data. Corpora are just data and quantitative methods are just methods, but their combination has led to a major shift in theory, and it is this theory which has to be evaluated. (Stubbs 2009: 117)

Results from corpus-based research have equally impacted on many key areas of language education; these include dictionaries, grammars, syllabus design, and teaching materials. Furthermore, recognising the powerful effect of corpus resources and tools, researchers have attempted to harness that power for the classroom from a very early stage of the development of corpus linguistics itself. A great range of studies have demonstrated concordancing with learners to be a genuinely valuable learning activity: it involves learning with authentic language, it is an effective tool for targeted vocabulary and grammar learning, it creates a natural focus on language itself, and it is highly compatible with current, desirable goals in language pedagogy (e.g. language awareness and learner autonomy). This shows that corpora have an important role to play not only in the study of language, but also in learning and teaching languages.

This study has highlighted the pivotal role teachers play in the process of promoting the use of the powerful resources and tools that corpora and concordancers undoubtedly are. Importantly, this study has given insight into teacher trainees' concerns and views in regard to using corpora for language teaching and has identified key factors to take into account for future development of corpus materials and tools. In the following paragraphs, the outcomes from the research presented in this study are brought together in relation to the main hypotheses underlying this study as outlined in Chapter 1.

(i) *The use of corpus data in language learning and teaching has significant potential; however, in spite of this, corpora do not appear to play a significant role in mainstream teaching.*

Throughout this study, the potential of corpora for language learning and teaching was highlighted. Evidence for this was drawn from a number of different sources. To begin with, Chapter 3 provided an overview of indirect and direct applications of corpora in language teaching, with a focus on the latter. The range of possible uses of corpora in teaching as evidenced in a multitude of publications illustrated the versatility and flexibility of the approach for a broad range of learning scenarios. Subsequently, an analysis of corpora in relation to authenticity, learner autonomy, and language awareness demonstrated the relevance of corpus use for these important concepts in contemporary language education. The statements made by teacher educators during the expert interviews (Chapter 5) provided further support for this; particularly in relation to the potential of direct corpus use in the classroom for raising language awareness. In addition, the evaluation of the reflective essays written by the teacher trainees during the case study clearly demonstrated that the participants had engaged in all the five features of language awareness as introduced previously in Section 3.3.3.

In a search for answers as to why a gap persists between the potential of the approach as evidenced by research publications on the one hand and a lack of tangible impact on teaching practices on the other, Chapter 4 proceeded with an analysis of evaluative studies on the effectiveness of the approach, on learner strategies as well as learner and teacher responses to using corpora in the classroom. This analysis demonstrated that the use of corpus data compared with traditional materials can indeed lead to better learning outcomes. This is particularly true in the context of targeted vocabulary and grammar exercises. The responses by learners and teachers to using corpora in the classroom also appear to confirm the potential of corpora. In general, responses were positive and the approach was perceived as interesting and useful. However, some negative aspects were also noted. These included difficulties with the technical aspects of corpus analysis and the perception that corpus tasks are too time-consuming.

(ii) *The transfer of a research approach into an educational environment is problematic and requires careful adjustments and considerations which should be informed by language pedagogy.*

The analysis of the three core elements of the corpus investigation process – corpus, software, user – in Chapter 4 has highlighted the significant differences between the requirements of research versus educational environments. Specifically, it was demonstrated that research and classroom users have very different profiles in terms of their language proficiency, their research and computer skills, their motivation and intended purposes to use corpora, as well as time constraints imposed by classroom conventions. As a result of this, the user profiles of learners and teachers and the requirements of the classroom context should be taken into account when designing and creating corpus tools and resources for classroom use. This view was also echoed by the teacher educators who had participated in the expert interviews (Section 5.3). Furthermore, the case study highlighted the differences between linguistic and pedagogical contexts. Discovering new facts about language is a central aspect of the corpus approach. Indeed, Sinclair (2007: 157) once summarised his views of the corpus as follows: "A recurrent theme [...] is the attitude I have to corpus evidence; the corpus has things to tell me, and I try to work out where it is heading". However, in response to their given task of creating a corpus-based learning exercise, the teacher trainees had expressed their frustration about not finding 'suitable examples' for their exercises in the corpora they had consulted. In other words, the trainees were clearly guided by set teaching goals in their minds, defined by the task at hand and were looking for examples accordingly. Unexpected corpus findings and uncertainties about the contents of corpora are indeed difficult to reconcile with formal language teaching regulated by syllabus and textbook content. Closely related to this were the comments made in regard to the need for guidelines on the assessment of corpus tasks. This was mentioned both by teacher educators during the expert interviews and by the trainees in the case study. Again, this shows that pedagogical concerns play a dominant role.

Another aspect that illustrates the need to adjust tools and resources based on the needs of classroom users is the case of corpus analysis software. As has been shown throughout this study, the concordancer plays a central role in the analysis of corpora. It is the functionality of this text retrieval software that provides access to the language data in corpora, counts the occurrences of language items, and makes language patterns visible. As a consequence, it is highly important that this software is user-friendly and that this concept is defined by the requirements of classroom users. The results of the survey of teacher educators reported in Chapter 5 confirmed the need for such software. More than a third of those respondents who were either very or at least somewhat familiar with corpus linguistics but chose not to use corpora in their teaching, reported lack of suitable tools and resources as a reason for this. The software reviews presented by the teacher trainees in the case study (Chapter 6) showed that practical considerations dictated by the realities of the classroom were at the forefront of their minds. To them it was important that the software was easy to use, simple to install, and that it produced quick results, and provided functions for materials design. In response to these findings, a proposal for a tailor-made software for language teachers and learners was made in Chapter 7. Based on the profiles of classroom users drawn up in Section 4.3.2, the software was designed to have a maximally intuitive interface, short navigational pathways, and a customisable toolbar to ensure a user-friendly approach. Furthermore, drawing on the results from the analysis of learners as corpus users in Section 4.3.4, prompts were integrated as scaffolding devices in order to help improve search strategies. In addition, on-screen editing facilities (e.g. highlighting, underlining in multiple colours) were designed to help make patterns more visible and serve as a form of input enhancements.

Throughout the case study it became apparent that computer-related difficulties were an unnecessary source of worry and distraction to the trainees. This was also noted in several studies analysed in Section 4.2. Providing a targeted and user-friendly software solution for classroom concordancing is thus seen as a significant step towards advancing the use of corpora, and it is a prime example of adjusting such a research tool for the classroom context.

(iii) Teachers play a pivotal role in the popularisation of corpus use in language education but their perspectives on teaching with corpora have remained largely unexplored.

The use of corpora for language learning is not generally a part of standard curricula. Thus, teachers are in no way obliged to use corpora as part of their teaching. As a consequence, teachers are not likely to make use of corpora in their classrooms, unless they can see the benefits of the approach (in other words, if they have the necessary motivation), and unless they have the skills that enable them to use corpora to create successful learning scenarios. Teachers are thus the main conduit between research and classroom: if teachers do not use corpora, then this valuable resource will continue to be limited to the confines of specialised research environments, most likely in tertiary contexts. Mauranen (2004a: 208) has rightly observed that in order "[t]o make a serious contribution to language teaching, corpora must be adopted by ordinary teachers and learners in ordinary classrooms.". However, the role of teachers in the process of teaching with corpora, the challenges to that role, and how to train teachers accordingly, are areas that have yet to be fully explored. The discussion of studies on learner and teacher responses in Section 4.2 has highlighted the lack of studies on teachers teaching with corpora. As a consequence, little is known about difficulties that teachers, not corpus experts, may experience when using corpora in their classrooms. The analysis in Section 4.3.3 on learners and teachers as users of corpora has demonstrated the considerable challenges for learners using corpora. This led to the conclusion that the teacher's task in using corpora with learners and guiding them in their training is a complex task that is frustrated by a persisting lack of classroom-ready teaching materials, by fundamental changes to the traditional role of teachers, and by the need to integrate corpora into existing curricula.

As was mentioned in the previous section, it is of great importance to inform the process of using corpora in the classroom by educational requirements. Given that teachers play such a pivotal role in introducing corpora into mainstream teaching, it is of utmost importance to gain more knowledge about the challenges of using corpora from their perspective. The case study with teacher trainees on learning *and* teaching with corpora (Chapter 6) has provided valuable insight into these challenges. Most significantly, the evaluation of the reflective essays, the DDL task created by the trainees, and their feedback, showed that to them teaching with language corpora is mostly about teaching and to a much lesser extent about corpora. In other words, issues in regard to classroom management, learning processes, and their role as teachers dictated their uses and views of corpus resources. Difficulties in locating and selecting appropriate corpora, uncertainty about the content of corpora as well as the unknown outcome of learning tasks paired with technical problems in relation to concordancers were some of the main concerns the teacher trainees had listed in their feedback on creating a DDL task.

Seidlhofer (2000b: 24) has argued that it should be applied linguists who "should make these developments [newly emerging facts uncovered through corpus linguistic research] accessible and relevant, and this, as we have seen, is by no means straightforward. It is in this sense that the buck stops with us". This study has shown that it is just as important to include teachers' opinions and concerns into the process of integrating corpora into language education in order to advance the use of corpora in language classrooms.

(iv) Only adequate training enables teachers to use corpora for teaching purposes. This training is ideally placed in pre-service language teacher education.

The level of language proficiency (particularly for non-native teachers of a language), the knowledge of corpus linguistics and computer technology has to be quite high in order for teachers to confidently use corpora in the classroom. As Mauranen (2004a: 199-200) emphasises, using corpora in the language classroom is challenging on several levels:

> Since corpora do not only provide new resource material and new exercises, but actually a new way of looking at language, thereby demanding wholly new *types* of exercises, the time and effort required

> for teacher initiation is probably more than for many other pedagogical innovations. (Mauranen 2004a: 199-200)

The in-depth analysis of learners and teachers as corpus users in Sections 4.3.3 revealed that learning and teaching with corpora indeed presents both groups with a number of potential challenges. Appropriate training for learners that ensures a gradual introduction to corpora is of great importance because corpus tasks were shown to be demanding for learners on three levels: firstly, corpora are a new learning resource; secondly, concordancers are an unfamiliar technology; and thirdly, inductive, research-like learning tasks differ from guided, traditional learning activities. The task of training learners is by default the responsibility of the teacher, and the complexity of this task is considerable. This shows that teachers themselves need to develop a substantial understanding of the subject and familiarity with the tools and resources if they are expected to train learners in this approach.

Thus, in order to advance the use of corpora in language education, teachers require training to acquire corpus literacy on the one hand, and training on how to teach with corpora on the other. This training is best situated in pre-service LTE where teacher trainees can experience the use of corpora for language learning from two perspectives: as learners *and* as teachers. If teacher trainees can discover the potential of corpora for their own learning, then this may foster intrinsic motivation to make use of corpora in their profession as teachers. It also allows teacher trainees to explore and address the challenges that such an approach entails. The context of pre-service LTE offers time and opportunity for such a learning experience. As a consequence, the case study presented in this book involved a course for teacher trainees on learning *and* teaching with corpora. Furthermore, the teacher educators who participated in the expert interviews stressed the importance of integrating corpora into LTE in order to make prospective teachers aware of corpus-based language descriptions and in order to foster lifelong learning strategies. Furthermore, the teacher educators emphasised the significance of introducing corpora in the pre-service LTE in order to guarantee successful delivery of a sound theoretical background and to provide sufficient learning opportunities with corpora to enable teachers to create rich learning environments with these tools and resources in their future classrooms.

Future research

As was identified by participants of the survey and the expert interviews, as well as by the teacher trainees in the case study, providing accessible, versatile, and 'classroom-ready' corpus teaching materials is another key factor in enabling teachers to integrate corpora into their teaching more readily. Specifically, it is of great importance to identify and promote those areas in which corpora appear to have the most potential. Future research should also focus on identifying suitable corpus activities for individual learner scenarios (e.g. learning context, language proficiency, etc.). Based on the outcomes from this present study, it further seems desirable for future materials to include a stronger focus on pedagogical aspects in order to demonstrate the undeniable relevance this approach has for language learning. This includes an investigation into which corpus tasks are most compatible with the parameters of language classrooms. Another concern voiced by teachers trainees and teacher educators is the difficulty of grading corpus tasks. This should feature in relevant teaching materials as well.

More research studies on teacher perceptions are needed in order to gain better insight into their views of teaching with corpora. In particular, longitudinal studies are necessary in order to determine what the effects of introducing teachers to corpora in pre-service LTE are on their future classroom practices. More research also needs to be done to determine the extent of corpus literacy that teachers need to possess to successfully teach with corpora.

Limitations of this study

There are some limitations to this study that need to be acknowledged. Due to the small number of participants and its exploratory nature, evidence from the case study presented in Chapter 6 can only serve to draw tentative conclusions and generalisations. In particular, it is important to notice that the research presented here is situated within the context of pre-service LTE in Germany. Therefore, the results are shaped and influenced by the characteristics of this environment. Furthermore, the participants were training to teach a language that was not their native language. While this is an important consideration when regarding the results of this study, it should also be noted that this is a very common situation in language education. Therefore, the main insights gained from this study should be transferable and applicable in other LTE contexts. A further limitation of this study is that it cannot show whether the course that was at the centre of the case study had any effect on the future teaching practices of the participants.

Conclusion

The use of computer technology lies at the heart of the corpus approach in language research as well as language education. As a result, corpus applications in the classroom fall into the field of CALL. Levy (2007: 180) has recently pointed out that long-term research projects in CALL can be problematic because "the technology itself is constantly evolving and changing; it does not wait for the researcher, and, as a rule, it evolves rapidly and independently, in its own commercial timeframe". In this sense, corpora and concordances have proven to be more resilient to the fast-paced technological changes which have caused CALL to become "increasingly multifaceted, especially because of its increasingly diverse material means and modes of delivery [...], and its channels for communication and interaction" (2007: 182). While improvements to corpora and corpus software packages based on educational requirements are highly desirable, the basic technology and the underlying principals of using corpus data remain the same as thirty years ago when researchers first suggested the use of concordancers with language learners. Even though the impact of corpora in mainstream language teaching does not yet reflect the enthusiasm of the research community, the corpus approach continues to generate great interest, as is attested by the steadily growing number of studies undertaken internationally with groups of learners from a diverse range of contexts. As this study has shown, the potential of the corpus approach for raising language awareness, improving language proficiency, and increasing learner autonomy is considerable. The fact that central areas of language learning (for example, vocabulary and grammar as well as writing skills) can be so successfully targeted with this approach, makes it all the more likely that concordancing is not "simply a passing trend [in CALL] with little or no lasting value for teaching and learning" (Levy 2007: 188).

However, the persisting gap between research and practice begs the question whether or not promoting the use of corpora in language teaching and learning is an effort worthwhile to be continued. The main hypotheses underlying this present study were that teachers are the key to advance the use of corpora in language education, that they need adequate training, and that this training ideally takes place in pre-service LTE. One important question that is left to be addressed is whether or not the integration of corpus training for teachers in LTE is feasible. Chambers (2007: 13) has previously pointed out that LTE is a "key area for introducing new developments in language learning" but she also concedes the difficulty of finding time and space within LTE programmes for the integration of teaching units on corpus linguistics. This was echoed by the participants of the survey of teacher educators (Chapter 5). While only a minority of the respondents argued that corpus linguistics had no immediate relevance to the training of EFL teachers, almost half of the respondents based their decision to not use corpora for teaching on the fact that the curriculum was full already and that corpus linguistics is not relevant enough to include it. This was in fact the most frequent reason given for not using corpora for teaching.

I believe that the outcomes from the case study, presented in Chapter 6, have demonstrated convincingly that this approach has indeed significant potential in pre-service LTE and well beyond the limits of specific corpus research. The evaluation of the case study has shown that participants viewed the corpus activities as a meaningful use of computers, and a simple training unit on concordancing created a natural focus on the trainees' future teaching subject (English) and fostered critical perspectives to evaluate future teaching materials. The focus on aspects of how to teach with corpora proved in fact to have great potential for raising both language and teaching awareness of the participants.

Furthermore, as the examples of direct corpus applications in Chapter 3 have shown, corpora and concordancers could theoretically be used in a great range of courses that are part of LTE programmes: for example, corpus stylistics in literary studies, corpora as a reference tool for academic writing, and of course corpora to improve language proficiency. However, this development is only possible if teacher educators can see the value of using corpora in this context. As Farr (2010a: 629) has recently pointed out, "teacher educators also need to take an active and responsible role in affording corpus integration the required space in initial and in-service programmes, not as a segregated specialisation, but as a thread woven through many components of the course content and delivery". It is hoped that this present study has contributed a number of convincing arguments to this discussion in favour of integrating corpora into pre-service LTE. More studies are needed to investigate possible uses of corpora in teacher training and evaluate responses to the approach by trainees.

Stubbs (2004: 106) has observed that "[m]uch 'corpus linguistics' is driven purely by curiosity". The use of corpora in language education has the potential to create a similar curiosity and fascination with language that shines through almost every publication reporting on corpus-based language studies. This approach invites the language learner or teacher to question known facts of language, to inquire further into the use of language, and to discover more details about language. Tribble and Granger (1998: 208-209) concluded that the use of corpora in language learning and teaching is a "methodology which raises as many questions as it might appear to answer" but that "the major advantage of DDL is that it presents language as 'an intriguing mystery to be explored' [...]". If corpora can contribute in this way, the effort of advancing their popularisation for classroom use is well worth continuing.

List of References*

Aarts, B. (2000): "Corpus linguistics, Chomsky and fuzzy tree fragments", *Corpus Linguistics and Linguistic Theory. Papers from the Twentieth International Conference on English Language Research on Computerized Corpora (ICAME 20) Freiburg im Breisgau 1999*, ed. C. Mair & M. Hundt. Amsterdam; Atlanta, GA: Rodopi. 5-13.

Aarts, J. & W. Meijs (eds.) (1984): *Corpus Linguistics: Recent Developments in the Use of Computer Corpora in English Language Research.* Amsterdam: Rodopi.

Abercrombie, D. (1965): "Pseudo-procedures in linguistics", *Studies in Phonetics and Linguistics*, ed. D. Abercrombie. London: Oxford University Press. 114-119.

Ackerley, K. & F. Coccetta (2007): "Enriching language learning through a multimedia corpus", *ReCALL* 19(3), 351-370.

Ahmad, K., G. Corbett & M. Rogers (1985): "Using computers with advanced language learners: an example", *The Language Teacher* 9(3), 4-7.

Aijmer, K. (2002): "Modality in advanced Swedish learners' written interlanguage", *Computer Learner Corpora, Second Language Acquisition and Foreign Language Teaching*, ed. S. Granger, J. Hung & S. Petch-Tyson. Amsterdam; Philadelphia, PA: John Benjamins. 55-76.

Aijmer, K. (ed.) (2009): *Corpora and Language Teaching.* Amsterdam; Philadelphia, PA: John Benjamins.

Allan, Q.G. (1999): "Enhancing the language awareness of Hong Kong teachers through corpus data: the *TeleNex* experience", *Journal of Technology and Teacher Education* 7(1), 57-74.

Allan, Q.G. (2002): "The TELEC secondary learner corpus", *Computer Learner Corpora, Second Language Acquisition and Foreign Language Teaching*, ed. S. Granger, J. Hung & S. Petch-Tyson. Amsterdam; Philadelphia, PA: John Benjamins. 195-211.

Allan, R. (2006): *Data-driven Learning and Vocabulary: Investigating the Use of Concordances with Advanced Learners of English.* (CLCS, Occasional Paper 66). Dublin: Trinity College Dublin.

Allan, R. (2009): "Can a graded reader corpus provide 'authentic' input?", *ELT Journal* 63(1), 23-32.

Allwright, D. (1988): "Autonomy and individualization in whole-class instruction", *Individualization and Autonomy in Language Learning*, ed. A.

* All WWW references in this bibliography were last verified on 3 July 2011.

Brookes & P. Grundy. London: Modern English Publications and the British Council. 35-44.

Altenberg, B. (2002): "Using bilingual corpus evidence in learner corpus research", *Computer Learner Corpora, Second Language Acquisition and Foreign Language Teaching*, ed. S. Granger, J. Hung & S. Petch-Tyson. Amsterdam; Philadelphia, PA: John Benjamins. 37-54.

Amador Moreno, C.P., A. Chambers & S. O'Riordan (2006): "Integrating a corpus of classroom discourse in language teacher education: the case of discourse markers", *ReCALL* 18(1), 83-104.

Anthony, L. (2004): *AntConc 4.* Retrieved from http://www.antlab.sci.waseda.ac.jp/antconc_index.html.

Ashford, S., P. Aston & R. Hellyer-Jones (1995): *Learning English – Green Line New 1*. Stuttgart: Klett.

Ashford, S., P. Aston & R. Hellyer-Jones (1996): *Learning English – Green Line New 2*. Stuttgart: Klett.

Aston, G. (1995): "Corpora in language pedagogy: matching theory and practice", *Principle and Practice in Applied Linguistics*, ed. G. Cook & B. Seidlhofer. Oxford: Oxford University Press. 257-270.

Aston, G. (1997a): "Enriching the learning environment: corpora in ELT", *Teaching and Language Corpora*, ed. A. Wichmann, S. Fligelstone, T. McEnery & G. Knowles. London; New York, NY: Longman. 51-64.

Aston, G. (1997b): "Involving learners in developing learning methods: exploiting text corpora in self-access", *Autonomy and Independence in Language Learning*, ed. P. Benson & P. Voller. London; New York, NY: Longman. 204-214.

Aston, G. (1997c): "Small and large corpora in language learning", *PALC 97: Practical Applications in Language Corpora*, ed. B. Lewandowska-Tomaszczyk & P. J. Melia. Łódź: Łódź University Press. 51-62.

Aston, G. (2000): "Corpora and language teaching", *Rethinking Language Pedagogy from a Corpus Perspective*, ed. L. Burnard & T. McEnery. Frankfurt am Main; New York, NY: Peter Lang. 7-17.

Aston, G. (ed.) (2001a): *Learning with Corpora*. Bologna: CLUEB.

Aston, G. (2001b): "Learning with corpora: an overview", *Learning with Corpora*, ed. G. Aston. Bologna: CLUEB. 7-45.

Aston, G., S. Bernardini & D. Stewart (eds.) (2004): *Corpora and Language Learners*. Amsterdam; Philadelphia, PA: John Benjamins.

Atkins, S., J. Clear & N. Ostler (1992): "Corpus design criteria", *Literary and Linguistic Computing* 7(1), 1-16.

Baker, P. (2009): "The BE06 Corpus of British English and recent language change", *International Journal of Corpus Linguistics* 14(3), 312-337.

Barlow, M. (2000): "Parallel texts in language teaching", *Multilingual Corpora in Teaching and Research*, ed. S. Botley, T. McEnery & A. Wilson. Amsterdam; Atlanta, GA: Rodopi. 106-115.

Barlow, M. (2002): *MonoConc Pro 2.2*. Houston, TX: Athelstan. Retrieved from http://www.athel.com/ mono.html.

Barlow, M. (2004): "Software for corpus access and analysis", *How to Use Corpora in Language Teaching*, ed. J. M. Sinclair. Amsterdam; Philadelphia, PA: John Benjamins. 205-221.

Barlow, M. & S. Burdine (2006): *Phrasal Verbs and Collocations – American English*. (CorpusLAB Series). Houston, TX: Athelstan.

Bednarek, M. (2008): "Teaching English literature and linguistics using corpus stylistic methods.", *Bridging Discourses: Proceedings ASFLA Congress 2007 – Online*. Available at <http://www.asfla.org.au/wp-content/uploads/ 2008/07/teaching-english-literature-and-linguistics.pdf>.

Beeby, A., P. Rodriguez Inés & P. Sánchez-Gijón (eds.) (2009): *Corpus Use and Translating: Corpus Use for Learning to Translate and Learning Corpus Use to Translate*. Amsterdam; Philadelphia, PA: John Benjamins.

Belz, J.A. (2004): "Learner corpus analysis and the development of foreign language proficiency", *System* 32(4), 577-591.

Belz, J.A. (2006): "At the intersection of telecollaboration, learner corpus analysis, and L2 pragmatics: considerations for language program directions", *Internet-mediated Intercultural Foreign Language Education*, ed. J.A. Belz & S.L. Thorne. Boston, MA: Thomson Heinle. 207-246.

Belz, J.A. & N. Vyatkina (2005): "Learner corpus analysis and the development of L2 pragmatic competence in networked intercultural language study: the case of German modal particles", *Canadian Modern Language Review* 62(1), 17-48.

Belz, J.A. & N. Vyatkina (2008): "The pedagogical mediation of a developmental learner corpus for classroom-based language instruction", *Language Learning & Technology* 12(3), 33-52.

Benson, P. (2001): *Teaching and Researching Autonomy in Language Learning*. Harlow; New York, NY: Longman.

Benson, P. (2006): "Autonomy in language teaching and learning", *Language Teaching* 40(1), 21-40.

Benson, P. (2008): "Teachers' and learners' perspectives on autonomy", *Learner and Teacher Autonomy: Concepts, Realities, and Responses*, ed. T. Lamb & H. Reinders. Amsterdam; Philadelphia, PA: John Benjamins. 15-32.

Berber Sardinha, A.P. (1999): "Beginning Portuguese corpus linguistics: exploring a corpus to teach Portuguese as a foreign language", *D.E.L.T.A.* 15(2), 289-299. Available at <http://www.scielo.br/pdf/delta/v15n2/a03v15n 2.pdf>.

Bernardini, S. (2000): "Systematizing serendipity: proposals for concordancing large corpora with learners", *Rethinking Language Pedagogy from a Corpus Perspective*, ed. L. Burnard & T. McEnery. Frankfurt am Main; New York, NY: Peter Lang. 225-234.

Bernardini, S. (2001): "'Spoilt for choice': a learner explores general language corpora", *Learning with Corpora*, ed. G. Aston. Bologna: CLUEB. 220-249.

Bernardini, S. (2002): "Exploring new directions for discovery learning", *Teaching and Learning by Doing Corpus Analysis*, ed. B. Kettemann & G. Marko. Amsterdam; New York, NY: Rodopi. 165-182.

Bernardini, S. (2004): "Corpora in the classroom: an overview and some reflections on future developments", *How to Use Corpora in Language Teaching*, ed. J.M. Sinclair. Amsterdam; Philadelphia, PA: John Benjamins. 15-36.

Berry, R. (1994): "Using concordance printouts for language awareness training", *Exploring Second Language Teacher Development*, ed. C.S. Li, D. Mahoney & J. Richards. Hong Kong: City University Press. 195-208.

Bialystok, E. (1978): "A theoretical model of second language learning", *Language Learning* 28(1), 69-83.

Bialystok, E. (1981): "The role of linguistic knowledge in second language use", *Studies in Second Language Acquisition* 4(1), 31-45.

Biber, D. (1993): "Representativeness in corpus design", *Literary and Linguistic Computing* 8(4), 243-257.

Biber, D. (2006): *University Language: A Corpus-based Study of Spoken and Written Registers*. Amsterdam; Philadelphia, PA: John Benjamins.

Biber, D., S. Conrad & V. Cortes (2004): "*If you look at ...*: lexical bundles in university teaching and textbooks", *Applied Linguistics* 25(3), 371-405.

Biber, D., S. Conrad & R. Reppen (1994): "Corpus-based approaches to issues in applied linguistics", *Applied Linguistics* 15(2), 169-189.

Biber, D., S. Conrad & R. Reppen (1998): *Corpus Linguistics: Investigating Language Structure and Use*. Cambridge: Cambridge University Press.

Biber, D., S. Johansson, G. Leech, S. Conrad & E. Finegan (1999): *Longman Grammar of Spoken and Written English*. Harlow: Pearson Education Ltd.

Biber, D. & R. Reppen (2002): "What does frequency have to do with grammar teaching?", *Studies in Second Language Acquisition* 24(2), 199-208.

Bloch, J. (2009): "The design of an online concordancing program for teaching about reporting verbs", *Language Learning & Technology* 13(1), 59-78.

Bogner, A., B. Littig & W. Menz (eds.) (2009): *Interviewing Experts*. Basingstoke; New York, NY: Palgrave Macmillan.

Bogner, A., & W. Menz (2009): "The theory-generating expert interview: epistemological interest, forms of knowledge, interaction", *Interviewing Experts*, ed. A. Bogner, B. Littig & W. Menz. Basingstoke; New York, NY: Palgrave Macmillan. 43-80.

Borg, S. (1994): "Language awareness as a methodology: implications for teachers and teacher training", *Language Awareness* 3(2), 61-71.

Boulton, A. (2007a): "But where's the proof? The need for empirical evidence for data-driven learning", *Proceedings of the BAAL Annual Conference 2007*, ed. M. Edwardes. London: Scitsiugnil Press. 13-16. Available at <http://hal.archives-ouvertes.fr/docs/00/32/67/04/PDF/2007_boulton_BAAL _proof.pdf>.

Boulton, A. (2007b): "DDL is in the details ... and in the big themes", *Cproceedings of the Corpus Linguistics Conference: CL2007*, ed. M. Davies, P. Rayson, S. Hunston & P. Danielsson. University of Birmingham. Available at <http://ucrel.lancs.ac.uk/publications/CL2007/paper/126_Paper. pdf>.

Boulton, A. (2008a): "DDL: reaching the parts other teaching can't reach?", *Proceedings of the 8th Teaching and Language Corpora Conference*, ed. A. Frankenberg-Garcia. Lisbon: Associação de Estudos e de Investigação Cien-tifíca do ISLA-Lisboa. [Author's Manuscript]. 38-44. Available at <http://hal.archives-ouvertes.fr/docs/00/32/67/06/PDF/2008_boulton_TaLC_ reaching.pdf>.

Boulton, A. (2008b): "Looking for empirical evidence of data-driven learning at lower levels", *Corpus Linguistics, Computer Tools, and Applications: State of the Art*, ed. B. Lewandowska-Tomaszczyk. Frankfurt am Main: Peter Lang. [Author's manuscript]. Available at <http://hal.archives-ouvertes.fr/ docs/00/38/49/08/PDF/2008_boulton_PALC_looking.pdf>.

Boulton, A. (2009a): "Corpora for all? Learning styles and data-driven learning [Article #150]", *Online Proceedings of the Corpus Linguistics Conference, CL2009, University of Liverpool, UK, 20-23 July 2009*, ed. M. Mahlberg, V. González-Díaz & C. Smith. Available at <http://ucrel.lancs.ac.uk/publica tions/cl2009/150_FullPaper.doc>.

Boulton, A. (2009b): "Data-driven learning: reasonable fears and rational reas-surance", *Indian Journal of Applied Linguistics* 35(1), 81-106. Available at <http://hal.archives-ouvertes.fr/docs/00/39/68/29/PDF/2009_boulton_IJO AL_rational.pdf>.

Boulton, A. (2009c): "Testing the limits of data-driven learning: language profi-ciency and training", *ReCALL* 21(1), 37-54.

Boulton, A. (2010): "Data-driven learning: taking the computer out of the equa-tion", *Language Learning* 60(3), 534-572.

Boulton, A. (forthcoming a): "Data-driven learning: on paper, in practice", *Corpora in Language Teaching*, ed. T. Harris & M. Moreno Jaén. Bern: Peter Lang. [Author's manuscript]. 1-37. Available at <http://hal.archives-ouvertes.fr/docs/00/39/38/09/PDF/2009_boulton_LANG _paper.pdf>.

Boulton, A. (forthcoming b): "Learning outcomes from corpus consultation", *Exploring New Paths in Language Pedagogy: Lexis and Corpus-based*

Language Teaching, ed. M. Moreno Jaén, F. Serrano Valverde & M. Calzada. London: Equinox. [Pre-publication version]. Available at <http://hal.archives-ouvertes.fr/docs/00/50/26/29/PDF/2010_Boulton_NEW_PATHS_outcomes.pdf>.

Brants, T. (2006): "Part-of-speech tagging", *Encyclopedia of Language & Linguistics*, ed. B. Keith. Oxford: Elsevier. 221-230.

Braun, S. (2005): "From pedagogically relevant corpora to authentic language learning contents", *ReCALL* 17(1), 47-64.

Braun, S. (2006): "ELISA: a pedagogically enriched corpus for language learning purposes", *Corpus Technology and Language Pedagogy. New Resources, New Tools, New Methods*, ed. S. Braun, K. Kohn & J. Mukherjee. Frankfurt am Main: Peter Lang. 25-47.

Braun, S. (2007): "Integrating corpus work into secondary education: from data-driven learning to needs-driven corpora", *ReCALL* 19(3), 307-328.

Braun, S., K. Kohn & J. Mukherjee (eds.) (2006): *Corpus Technology and Language Pedagogy. New Resources, New Tools, New Methods*. Frankfurt am Main: Peter Lang.

Breen, M.P. (1985): "Authenticity in the classroom", *Applied Linguistics* 6(1), 60-70.

Breyer, Y. (2006a): "Love's labour's lost: The troublesome relationship between Corpus Linguistics Research and its application in EFL Teacher training in Germany". Paper presented at the *Corpus Linguistics Conference: CL 2005*, July 14-17 2005, University of Birmingham, England.

Breyer, Y. (2006b): "*My Concordancer*: tailor-made software for language learners and teachers", *Corpus Technology and Language Pedagogy. New Resources, New Tools, New Methods*, ed. S. Braun, K. Kohn & J. Mukherjee. Frankfurt am Main; New York, NY: Peter Lang. 157-176.

Breyer, Y. (2009): "Learning and teaching with corpora: reflections by student teachers", *Computer Assisted Language Learning* 22(2), 153-172.

Brodine, R. (2001): "Integrating corpus work into an academic reading course", *Learning with Corpora*, ed. G. Aston. Bologna: CLUEB. 138-176.

Bullock, A. (1975): *A Language for Life: Report of the Committee of Enquiry appointed by the Secretary of State for Education and Science under the Chairmanship of Sir Alan Bullock F.B.A.* London: Her Majesty's Stationery Office. Available at <http://www.educationengland.org.uk/documents/bullock/>.

Burdine, S. & M. Barlow (2007): *Business Phrasal Verbs and Collocations – American English.* (CorpusLAB Series). Houston, TX: Athelstan.

Burnard, L. & T. McEnery (eds.) (2000): *Rethinking Language Pedagogy from a Corpus Perspective: Papers from the Third International Conference on Teaching and Language Corpora*. Frankfurt am Main; New York, NY: Peter Lang.

Carter, R. (ed.) (1990): *Knowledge about Language and the Curriculum: The LINC Reader*. London: Hodder & Stoughton, Ltd.

Carter, R. & M. McCarthy (1996): "Correspondence", *ELT Journal* 50(4), 369-371.

Chalmel, A. (1998): "Konkordanzen: innovative konstruktivistische Lernmedien", *Französisch heute* 1, 45-56.

Chambers, A. (2005): "Integrating corpus consultation in language studies", *Language Learning & Technology* 9(2), 111-125.

Chambers, A. (2007): "Popularising corpus consultation by language learners and teachers", *Corpora in the Foreign Language Classroom*, ed. E. Hidalgo Tenorio, L. Quereda & J. Santana. Amsterdam; New York, NY: Rodopi. 3-16.

Chambers, A. & Í. O'Sullivan (2004): "Corpus consultation and advanced learners' writing skills in French", *ReCALL* 16(1), 158-172.

Chan, T. & H. Liou (2005): "Effects of web-based concordancing instruction on EFL students' learning of verb-noun collocations", *Computer Assisted Language Learning* 18(3), 231-250.

Chandler, B. (1989): *Longman Mini Concordancer*. London: Longman.

Chang, W.-L. & Y.-C. Sun (2009): "Scaffolding and web concordancers as support for language learning", *Computer Assisted Language Learning* 22(4), 283-302.

Charles, M. (2007): "Reconciling top-down and bottom-up approaches to graduate writing: using a corpus to teach rhetorical functions", *Journal of English for Academic Purposes* 6(4), 289-302.

Chi, A. M.-L., K. P.-Y. Wong & M. C.-P. Wong (1994): "Collocational problems amongst ESL learners: a corpus-based study", *Entering Text*, ed. J. Flowerdew & A.K.K. Tong. Hong Kong: Language Centre, Hong Kong University of Science and Technology. 157-165.

Chomsky, N. (1957): *Syntactic Structures*. The Hague: Mouton de Gruyter.

Chomsky, N. (1962): "Transformational approach to syntax", *Studies in American English: Third Texas Conference on Problems of Linguistic Analysis in English (May 9-12, 1958)*, ed. A.A. Hill. Austin: University of Texas. 124-158.

Chomsky, N. (1965): *Aspects of the Theory of Syntax*. Cambridge, MA: MIT Press.

Chujo, K. (2004): "Measuring vocabulary levels of English textbooks and tests using a BNC lemmatised high frequency word list", *English Corpora Under Japanese Eyes*, ed. J. Nakamura, N. Inoue & T. Tabata. Amsterdam; New York, NY: Rodopi. 231-249.

Ciesielska-Ciupek, M. (2001): "Teaching with the internet and corpus materials: preparation of the ELT materials using the internet and corpus resources",

PALC 2001: Practical Applications in Language Corpora, ed. B. Lewandowska-Tomaszczyk. Frankfurt am Main: Peter Lang. 521-531.

Cobb, T. (1997): "Is there any measurable learning from hands-on concordancing?", *System* 25(3), 301-315.

Cobb, T. (1999): "Breadth and depth of lexical acquisition with hands-on concordancing", *Computer Assisted Language Learning* 12(4), 345-360.

Cobb, T., C. Greaves & M. Horst (2001): "Can the rate of lexical acquisition from reading be increased? An experiment in reading French with a suite of on-line resources", *Regards sur la didactique des langues Secondes.* ed. P. Raymond & C. Cornaire. Montréal: Éditions logique. 133-153. [WWW Prepublication; translation from French.] Available at <http://www.lextutor.ca/cv/BouleE.htm>.

Collins, H. (2000): "Materials design and language corpora: a report in the context of distance education", *Rethinking Language Pedagogy from a Corpus Perspective*, ed. L. Burnard & T. McEnery. Frankfurt am Main; New York, NY: Peter Lang. 51-63.

Coniam, D. (1997): "A practical introduction to corpora in a teacher training language awareness programme", *Language Awareness* 6(4), 199-207.

Conrad, S. (2000): "Will corpus linguistics revolutionize grammar teaching in the 21st century?", *TESOL Quarterly* 34(3), 548-560.

Conrad, S. (2004): "Corpus linguistics, language variation, and language teaching", *How to Use Corpora in Language Teaching*, ed. J.M. Sinclair. Amsterdam; Philadelphia, PA: John Benjamins. 67-85.

Cook, G. (1997): "Language play, language learning", *ELT Journal* 51(3), 224-231.

Cook, G. (1998): "The uses of reality: a reply to Ronald Carter", *ELT Journal* 52(1), 57-64.

Cresswell, A. (2007): "Getting to 'know' connectors? Evaluating data-driven learning in a writing skills course", *Corpora in the Foreign Language Classroom*, ed. E. Hidalgo Tenorio, L. Quereda & J. Santana. Amsterdam; New York, NY: Rodopi. 267-287.

Curtin, R., S. Presser & E. Singer (2005): "Changes in telephone survey nonresponse over the past quarter century", *Public Opinion Quarterly* 69(1), 87-98.

Daud, N.M. & N.A.K. Abusa' (1999): "Teaching prepositions using a concordancer", *The English Teacher* 28, 49-57.

Daud, N.M. & Z. Husin (2004): "Developing critical thinking skills in computer-aided extended reading classes", *British Journal of Educational Technology* 35(4), 477-487.

Davidson, T. (1990): "Teaching with the Oxford Concordance Program", *Literary and Linguistic Computing* 5(1), 81-85.

Davie, R., N. Butler & H. Goldstein (1972): *From Birth to Seven: National Child Development Study*. London: Longman.

Davies, M. (2004): "Student use of large, annotated corpora to analyze syntactic variation", *Corpora and Language Learners*, ed. G. Aston, S. Bernardini & D. Stewart. Amsterdam; Philadelphia, PA: John Benjamins. 257-269.

Davis, B. & L. Russell-Pinson (2004): "Concordancing and corpora for K-12 teachers: project MORE", *Applied Corpus Linguistics: A Multidimensional Perspective*, ed. U. Connor & T. Upton. Amsterdam; New York, NY: Rodopi. 147-169.

Davison, N.J. (1983): "An interactive concordance program for the small computer", *CALICO Journal* 1(1), 24-26.

Deeth, M. (1993): "Concordancing using a Word Perfect macro", *ON-CALL* 7(3), 21-30.

Dodd, B. (1997): "Exploiting a corpus of written German for advanced language learning", *Teaching and Language Corpora*, ed. A. Wichmann, S. Fligelstone, T. McEnery & G. Knowles. London; New York, NY: Longman. 131-145.

Donley, K.M. & R. Reppen (2001): "Using corpus tools to highlight academic vocabulary in SCLT", *TESOL Journal* 10(2/3), 7-12.

Donmall, B.G. (ed.) (1985): *Language Awareness*. London: Centre for Information on Language Teaching.

Doughty, C. (1991): "Second language instruction does make a difference", *Studies in Second Language Acquisition* 13(4), 431-469.

Doughty, C. (2003): "Instructed SLA: constraints, compensation and enhancement", *Handbook of Second Language Acquisition*, ed. C. Doughty & M. H. Long. New York, NY: Blackwell. 256-310.

Doughty, C. & J. Williams (eds.) (1998): *Focus on Form in Classroom Second Language Acquisition*. Cambridge: Cambridge University Press.

Doughty, P., J. Pearce & G. Thornton (eds.) (1971): *Language in Use*. London: Edward Arnold.

Edelhoff, C. (1996): "Kommunikative Grundlagen des Englischunterrichts", *Fremde Texte verstehen: Festschrift für Lothar Bredella*, ed. H. Christ & M. Legutke. Tübingen: Gunter Narr. 40-49.

Ellis, R. (2005): "Principles of instructed language learning", *System* 33(2), 209-224.

Ellis, R. (2008): "Explicit knowledge and second language learning and pedagogy", *Encyclopedia of Language and Education. Vol. 6: Knowledge about Language*, ed. J. Cenoz & N.H. Hornberger. New York, NY: Springer. 143-153.

Estling Vannestål, M. & H. Lindquist (2007): "Learning English grammar with a corpus: experimenting with concordancing in a university grammar course", *ReCALL* 19(3), 329-350.

Fairclough, N. (ed.) (1992): *Critical Language Awareness*. London: Routledge.
Fan, M., C. Greaves & M. Warren (1999): "Identifying characteristic patterns in students' writing using a corpus of learner data", *Language Analysis, Description and Pedagogy*, ed. R. Berry, B. Asker, K. Hyland & M. Lam. Hong Kong: Language Centre HKUST. 147-161.
Farr, F. (2008): "Evaluating the use of corpus-based instruction in a language teacher education context: perspectives from the users", *Language Awareness* 17(1), 25-43.
Farr, F. (2010a): "How can corpora be used in teacher education?", *The Routledge Handbook of Corpus Linguistics*, ed. M. McCarthy & A. O'Keeffe. Milton Park; New York, NY: Routledge. 620-632.
Farr, F. (2010b): *The Discourse of Teaching Practice Feedback: A Corpus-based Investigation of Spoken and Written Modes*. New York, NY: Routledge.
Fillmore, C.J. (1992): "'Corpus linguistics' or 'computer-aided armchair linguistics'", *Directions in Corpus Linguistics: Proceedings of Nobel Symposium 82*, ed. J. Svartvik. Berlin; New York, NY: Mouton de Gruyter. 35-60.
Firth, J.R. (1957a): "A synopsis of linguistic theory, 1930-1955", *Studies in Linguistic Analysis*, (Special Volume, Philological Society). Oxford: Blackwell. 1-32.
Firth, J.R. (1957b): "Modes of meaning", *Papers in Linguistics 1934-1951*, London: Oxford University Press. 190-215.
Fligelstone, S. (1993): "Some reflections on the question of teaching, from a corpus linguistics perspective", *ICAME* 17, 97-109.
Flowerdew, J. (1993): "Concordancing as a tool in course design", *System* 21(2), 231-244.
Flowerdew, J. (1996): "Concordancing in language learning", *The power of CALL*, ed. M. Pennington. Houston, TX: Athelstan. 97-113.
Flowerdew, L. (1998): "Integrating 'expert' and 'interlanguage' computer corpora findings on causality: discoveries for teachers and students", *English for Specific Purposes* 17(4), 329-345.
Fox, G. (1998): "Using corpus data in the classroom", *Materials Development in Language Teaching*, ed. B. Tomlinson. Cambridge: Cambridge University Press. 25-43.
Fox, L. (1979): "On acquiring an adequate second language vocabulary", *Journal of Basic Writing* 2(3), 68-75.
Francis, G. (1994): "Grammar teaching in schools: what should teachers be aware of?", *Language Awareness* 3(3-4), 221-236.
Francis, W.N. (1982): "Problems of assembling and computerizing large corpora", *Computer Corpora in English Language Research*, ed. S. Johansson. Bergen: Norwegian Computing Centre for the Humanities. 7-24.

Francis, W.N. (1992): "Language corpora B.C.", *Directions in Corpus Linguistics: Proceedings of Nobel Symposium 82*, ed. J. Svartvik. Berlin; New York, NY: Mouton de Gruyter. 17-32.

Francis, W.N. & H. Kučera (1979): *Brown Corpus Manual: Manual of Information to Accompany A Standard Corpus of Present-day Edited American English, for Use with Digital Computers*. Available at <http://icame.uib.no/brown/bcm.html>.

Frankenberg-Garcia, A. (2004): "Lost in parallel concordances", *Corpora and Language Learners*, ed. G. Aston, S. Bernardini & D. Stewart. Amsterdam; Philadelphia, PA: John Benjamins. 213-229.

Frankenberg-Garcia, A. (2005): "Pedagogical uses of monolingual and parallel concordances", *ELT Journal* 59(3), 189-198.

Frazier, S. (2003): "A corpus analysis of *would*-clauses without adjacent *if*-clauses", *TESOL Quarterly* 37, 443-466.

Gabel, S. (2001): "Over-indulgence and under-representation in interlanguage: reflections on the utilization of concordancers in self-directed foreign language learning", *Computer Assisted Language Learning* 14(3-4), 269-288.

Gabrielatos, C. (2005): "Corpora and language teaching: just a fling or wedding bells?", *TESL-EJ* 8(4). Available at <http://www-writing.berkeley.edu/TESL-EJ/ej32/a1.html>.

Gan, S.-L., F. Low & N.F. Yaakub (1996): "Modeling teaching with a computer-based concordancer in a TESL preservice teacher education program", *Journal of Computing in Teacher Education* 12(4), 28-32.

Garton, J. (1996): "Interactive concordancing with a specialist corpus", *ON-CALL* 10(1), 8-14. Available at <http://www.cltr.uq.edu.au/oncall/garton101.html>.

Gaskell, D. & T. Cobb (2004): "Can learners use concordance feedback for writing errors?", *System* 32(3), 301-319.

Gavioli, L. (1997): "Exploring texts through the concordancer: guiding the learner", *Teaching and Language Corpora*, ed. A. Wichmann, S. Fligelstone, T. McEnery & G. Knowles. London; New York, NY: Longman. 83-99.

Gavioli, L. (2001): "The learner as researcher: introducing corpus concordancing in the classroom", *Learning with Corpora*, ed. G. Aston. Bologna: CLUEB. 108-137.

Gavioli, L. (2005): *Exploring Corpora for ESP Learning*. Amsterdam; Philadelphia, PA: John Benjamins.

Gavioli, L. & G. Aston (2001): "Enriching reality: language corpora in language pedagogy", *ELT Journal* 55(3), 238-246.

Gilmore, A. (2007): "Authentic materials and authenticity in foreign language learning", *Language Teaching* 40(2), 97-118.

Gilmore, A. (2009): "Using online corpora to develop students' writing skills", *ELT Journal* 63(4), 363-372.

Gilquin, G. (2007): "To err is not all: what corpus and elicitation can reveal about the use of collocations by learners", *Zeitschrift für Anglistik und Amerikanistik* 55(3), 273-291.

Goodale, M. (1993): *Concordance Samplers 1: Prepositions*. London: Collins COBUILD.

Goodale, M. (1995): *Concordance Samplers 2: Phrasal Verbs*. London: Collins COBUILD.

Götz, S. & J. Mukherjee (2006): "Evaluation of data-driven learning in university teaching: a project report", *Corpus Technology and Language Pedagogy. New Resources, New Tools, New Methods*, ed. S. Braun, K. Kohn & J. Mukherjee. Frankfurt am Main: Peter Lang. 49-67.

Gove, P.B. (ed.) (1961): *Webster's Third New International Dictionary of the English Language. Unabridged* (3rd ed.). Springfield, MA: G. & C. Merriam Co.

Granath, S. (2009): "Who benefits from learning how to use corpora?", *Corpora and Language Teaching*, ed. K. Aijmer. Amsterdam; Philadelphia, PA: John Benjamins. 47-66.

Granger, S. (1993): "The International Corpus of Learner English", *English Language Corpora: Design, Analysis and Exploitation*, ed. J. Aarts, P. De Haan & N. Oostdijk. Amsterdam; Atlanta, GA: Rodopi. 57-69.

Granger, S. (1994): "The learner corpus: a revolution in applied linguistics", *English Today* 39(10/3), 25-29.

Granger, S. (1998): "The computerized learner corpus: a versatile new source of data for SLA research", *Learner English on Computer*, ed. S. Granger. London; New York, NY: Longman. 3-18.

Granger, S. (1999): "Use of tenses by advanced EFL learners: evidence from an error-tagged computer corpus", *Out of Corpora: Studies in Honour of Stig Johansson*, ed. H. Hasselgård & S. Oksefjell. Amsterdam; Atlanta, GA: Rodopi. 191-202.

Granger, S. (2002): "A bird's-eye view of learner corpus research", *Computer Learner Corpora, Second Language Acquisition and Foreign Language Teaching*, ed. S. Granger, J. Hung & S. Petch-Tyson. Amsterdam; Philadelphia, PA: John Benjamins. 3-33.

Granger, S. (2008): "Learner corpora in foreign language education", *Encyclopedia of Language and Education. Vol. 4: Second and Foreign Language Education*, ed. N. Van Deusen-Scholl & N. H. Hornberger. New York, NY: Springer. 337-351.

Granger, S. (2009): "The contribution of learner corpora to second language acquisition and foreign language teaching: a critical evaluation", *Corpora and Language Teaching*, ed. K. Aijmer. Amsterdam; Philadelphia, PA: John Benjamins. 13-32.

Granger, S. & C. Tribble (1998): "Learner corpus data in the foreign language classroom: form-focused instruction and data-driven learning", *Learner English on Computer*, ed. S. Granger. Harlow: Longman. 199-209.

Granger, S. & S. Tyson (1996): "Connector usage in the English essay writing of native and non-native EFL speakers of English", *World Englishes* 15(1), 17-27.

Greaves, C. (2003): *ConcApp 4*. Retrieved from http://www.edict.com.hk/pub/concapp.

Greene, K. & D. Rubin (1971): *Automated Grammatical Tagging of English.* Providence, RI: Department of Linguistics, Brown University.

Groß, A. (1998): "MultiConcord - Ein paralleles Konkordanzprogramm für den Fremdsprachenunterricht", *TELL & CALL* 4/98, 36-42. Available at <http://www.eduhi.at/dl/gross.pdf>.

Gurney, P.J. (1994): "Diary", *Literary and Linguistic Computing* 9(1), 102-106.

Gut, U. (2006): "Learner speech corpora in language learning", *Corpus Technology and Language Pedagogy. New Resources, New Tools, New Methods*, ed. S. Braun, K. Kohn & J. Mukherjee. Frankfurt am Main: Peter Lang. 69-86.

Hadley, G. (2002): "An introduction to data-driven learning", *RELC Journal* 33(2), 99-124.

Halliday, M.A.K. (1966): "Lexis as a linguistic level", *In Memory of J.R. Firth*, ed. C.E. Bazell, J.C. Catford, M.A.K. Halliday & R.H. Robins. London: Longman. 148-162.

Halliday, M.A.K. (1982): "Linguistics in teacher education", *Linguistics and the Teacher*, ed. R. Carter. London; New York, NY: Routledge. 10-30.

Harris, Z.S. (1951): *Methods in Structural Linguistics*. Chicago, IL: University of Chicago Press.

Hawkins, E.W. (1984): *Awareness of Language: An Introduction.* Cambridge: Cambridge University Press.

Hawkins, E.W. (1992): "Awareness of language/knowledge about language in the curriculum in England and in Wales: an historical note on twenty years of curricular debate", *Language Awareness* 1(1), 5-17.

Hawkins, E.W. (1999): "Foreign language study and language awareness", *Language Awareness* 8(3/4), 124-142.

Hémard, D. & S. Cushion (2000): "Authoring a web-enhanced interface for a new language-learning environment", *ALT-J* 8(1), 41-49.

Hidalgo, E., L. Quereda & J. Santana (eds.) (2007): *Corpora in the Foreign Language Classroom: Selected Papers from the Sixth International Conference on Teaching and Language Corpora (TALC 6)*. Amsterdam; New York, NY: Rodopi.

Higgins, J. (1986): "Introduction: smart learners and dumb machines", *System* 14(2), 147-150.

Hockey, S. & J. Martin (1987): "The Oxford Concordance Program 2.0", *Literary and Linguistic Computing* 2(2), 126-131.

Holbrook, A.L., J.A. Krosnick & A. Pfent (2007): "The causes and consequences of response rates in surveys by the news media and government contractor survey research firms", *Advances in Telephone Survey Methodology*, ed. J.M. Lepkowski, C. Tucker, J.M. Brick, E. de Leeuw, L. Japec, P.J. Lavrakas, M.W. Link & R.L. Sangster. Hoboken, NJ: John Wiley & Sons. 499-528.

Holec, H. (1981): *Autonomy and Foreign Language Learning*. Oxford; New York, NY: Published for and on behalf of the Council of Europe by Pergamon Press.

Holliday, L. (1993): "Solutions to KWIC concordancing using word processors in CALL classes", *ON-CALL* 8(1), 28-31.

Holmes, J. (1988): "Doubt and certainty in ESL textbooks", *Applied Linguistics* 9, 21-44.

Honeyfield, J. (1989): "A typology of exercises based on computer-generated concordance material", *Guidelines* 11(1), 42-50.

Housen, A. (2002): "A corpus-based study of the L2 acquisition of the English verb system", *Computer Learner Corpora, Second Language Acquisition and Foreign Language Teaching*, ed. S. Granger, J. Hung & S. Petch-Tyson. Amsterdam; Philadelphia, PA: John Benjamins. 77-116.

Hulstijn, J. (1989): "Implicit and incidental second language learning: experiments in the processing of natural and artificial input", *Interlingual Processes*, ed. H.-W. Dechert & M. Raupach. Tübingen: Narr. 49-73.

Hundt, M., A. Sand & R. Siemund (1999): *Manual of Information to Accompany the Freiburg-LOB Corpus of British English ('FLOB')*. Available at <http://icame.uib.no/flob/index.htm>.

Hunston, S. (1995a): "A corpus study of some English verbs of attribution", *Functions of Language* 2(2), 133-158.

Hunston, S. (1995b): "Grammar in teacher education: the role of a corpus", *Language Awareness* 4(1), 15-31.

Hunston, S. (2002a): *Corpora in Applied Linguistics*. Cambridge: Cambridge University Press.

Hunston, S. (2002b): "Pattern grammar, language teaching, and linguistic variation", *Using Corpora to Explore Linguistics Variation*, ed. R. Reppen, S.M. Fitzmaurice & D. Biber. Amsterdam; Philadelphia, PA: John Benjamins. 167-183.

Hunston, S. (2007): "Semantic prosody revisited", *International Journal of Corpus Linguistics* 12(2), 249-268.

Hunston, S. (2009): "Semantic prosody revisited", *Words, Grammar, Text: Revisiting the Work of John Sinclair*, ed. R. Moon. Amsterdam; Philadelphia, PA: John Benjamins. 85–103.

Hunston, S. & G. Francis (1998): "Verbs observed: a corpus-driven pedagogic grammar", *Applied Linguistics* 19(1), 45-72.

Hunston, S. & G. Francis (2000): *Pattern Grammar: A Corpus-driven Approach to the Lexical Grammar of English* Amsterdam; Philadelphia, PA: John Benjamins.

ILEA (1980): *Inner London Education Authority: Literacy Survey*. London: ILEA Research and Statistics Group.

James, C. & P. Garrett (1991): *Language Awareness in the Language Classroom*. London, New York, NY: Longman.

Johansson, S. (2007): "Using corpora: from learning to research", *Corpora in the Foreign Language Classroom*, ed. E. Hidalgo Tenorio, L. Quereda & J. Santana. Amsterdam; New York, NY: Rodopi. 17-28.

Johansson, S. (2009): "Some thoughts on corpora and second-language acquisition", *Corpora and Language Teaching*, ed. K. Aijmer. Amsterdam; Philadelphia, PA: John Benjamins. 33–44.

Johns, T. (1983): "Generating alternatives", *Exploring English with Microcomputers*, ed. D. Chandler. Leicester: Council for Educational Technology. 89-97.

Johns, T. (1986): "Micro-Concord: a language learner's research tool", *System* 14(2), 151-162.

Johns, T. (1988): "Whence and whither classroom concordancing?", *Computer Applications in Language Learning*, ed. T. Bongaerts, P. d. Haan, S. Lobbe & H. Wekker. Dordrecht: Foris. 9-27.

Johns, T. (1991a): "Should you be persuaded – two samples of data-driven learning materials", *Classroom Concordancing*, ed. T. Johns & P. King. Birmingham: University of Birmingham. 1-16.

Johns, T. (1991b): "From printout to handout: grammar and vocabulary teaching in the context of data-driven learning", *Classroom Concordancing*, ed. T. Johns & P. King. Birmingham: University of Birmingham. 27-45.

Johns, T. (1993): "Data-driven learning: an update", *TELL & CALL* April(2), 4-10.

Johns, T. (1997): "Contexts: the background, development and trialling of a concordance-based CALL program", *Teaching and Language Corpora*, ed. A. Wichmann, S. Fligelstone, T. McEnery & G. Knowles. London; New York, NY: Longman. 100-115.

Johns, T. (2002): "Data-driven learning: the perpetual challenge", *Teaching and Learning by Doing Corpus Analysis*, ed. B. Kettemann & G. Marko. Amsterdam; New York, NY: Rodopi. 107-117.

Johns, T. & P. King (eds.) (1991): *Classroom Concordancing*. Birmingham: University of Birmingham.

Johns, T., L. Hsingchin & W. Lixun (2008): "Integrating corpus-based CALL programs in teaching English through children's literature", *Computer Assisted Language Learning* 21(5), 483-506.

Kaltenböck, G. & B. Mehlmauer-Larcher (2005): "Computer corpora and the language classroom: on the potential and limitations of computer corpora in language teaching", *ReCALL* 17(1), 65-84.

Keeter, S., C. Kennedy, M. Dimock, J. Best & P. Craighill (2006): "Gauging the impact of growing nonresponse on estimates from a national RDD telephone survey", *Public Opinion Quarterly* 70(5), 759-779.

Kennedy, C. & T. Miceli (2001): "An evaluation of intermediate students' approaches to corpus investigation", *Language Learning & Technology* 5(3), 77-90.

Kennedy, C. & T. Miceli (2002): "The CWIC project: developing and using a corpus for intermediate Italian students", *Teaching and Learning by Doing Corpus Analysis*, ed. B. Kettemann & G. Marko. Amsterdam; New York, NY: Rodopi. 183-192.

Kennedy, C. & T. Miceli (2010): "Corpus-assisted creative writing: introducing intermediate Italian learners to a corpus as a reference resource", *Language Learning & Technology* 14(1), 28-44.

Kennedy, G.D. (1998): *An Introduction to Corpus Linguistics*. London; New York, NY: Longman.

Kettemann, B. (1995): "On the use of concordancing in ELT", *AAA – Arbeiten aus Anglistik und Amerikanistik* 20(1), 29-41.

Kettemann, B. & G. Marko (eds.) (2002): *Teaching and Learning by Doing Corpus Analysis. Proceedings of the Fourth International Conference on Teaching and Language Corpora, Graz 19-24 July, 2000.* Amsterdam; New York, NY: Rodopi.

Kolb, D.A. (1984): *Experiential Learning: Experience as the Source of Learning and Development*. Englewood Cliffs, NJ: Prentice-Hall.

Kowitz, J. (1991): "Using computer concordancers for literary analysis in the classroom", *Classroom Concordancing*, ed. T. Johns & P. King. Birmingham: University of Birmingham. 135-149.

Kramsch, C. (1993): *Context and Culture in Language Teaching*. Oxford: Oxford University Press.

Krashen, S.D. (1982): *Principles and Practice in Second Language Acquisition.* Oxford: Pergamon.

Last, R. (1984): *Language Teaching and the Microcomputer*. Oxford: Blackwell.

Laviosa, S. (2002): *Corpus-based Translation Studies: Theory, Findings, Applications*. Amsterdam; New York, NY: Rodopi.

Lee, C.-Y. & H.-C. Liou (2003): "A study of using web concordancing for English vocabulary learning in a Taiwanese high school context", *English Teaching and Learning* 27(3), 35-56. (ERIC Document Reproduction Service, No ED 480563). Available at <http://www.eric.ed.gov/ ERICWeb Portal/contentdelivery/servlet/ERICServlet?accno=ED480563>.

Lee, D.Y.W. (2010): "What corpora are available?", *The Routledge Handbook of Corpus Linguistics*, ed. M. McCarthy & A. O'Keeffe. Milton Park; New York, NY: Routledge. 107-121.

Leech, G. (1992): "Corpora and theories of linguistic performance", *Directions in Corpus Linguistics: Proceedings of Nobel Symposium 82*, ed. J. Svartvik. Berlin; New York, NY: Mouton de Gruyter. 105-122.

Leech, G. (1993): "Corpus annotation schemes", *Literary and Linguistic Computing* 8(4), 275-281.

Leech, G. (1997): "Teaching and language corpora: a convergence", *Teaching and Language Corpora*, ed. A. Wichmann, S. Fligelstone, T. McEnery & G. Knowles. London; New York, NY: Longman. 1-23.

Levy, M. (1990): "Concordances and their integration into a word-processing environment for language learners", *System* 18(2), 177-188.

Levy, M. (1997): *Computer-assisted Language Learning: Context and Conceptualization*. Oxford: Oxford University Press.

Levy, M. (2007): "Research and technological innovation in CALL", *Innovation in Language Learning and Teaching* 1(1), 180-190.

Levy, M. & G. Stockwell (2006): *CALL Dimensions. Options and Issues in Computer-assisted Language Learning*. Mahwah, NJ; London: Lawrence Erlbaum.

Lewis, M. (2002): *Implementing the Lexical Approach: Putting Theory into Practice*. Boston, MA: Heinle ELT.

Lightbown, P.M. & N. Spada (1990): "Focus-on-form and corrective feedback in communicative language teaching", *Studies in Second Language Acquisition* 12(4), 429-448.

Liou, H.-C., J.S. Chang, H.-J. Chen, C.-C. Lin, M.-L. Liaw, Z.-M. Gao, *et al.* (2006): "Corpora processing and computational scaffolding for a web-based English learning environment: the CANDLE project", *CALICO Journal* 24(1), 77-95.

Little, D. (1995): "Learning as dialogue: the dependence of learner autonomy on teacher autonomy", *System* 23(2), 175-181.

Lixun, W. (2001): "Exploring parallel concordancing in English and Chinese", *Language Learning & Technology* 5(3), 174-184.

Ljung, M. (1990): *A Study of TEFL Vocabulary*. Stockholm: Almqvist & Wiksell.

Long, M.H. (1991): "Focus on form: a design feature in language teaching methodology", *Foreign Language Research in Cross-cultural Perspective*, ed. K. de Bot, R. B. Ginsberg & C. Kramsch. Amsterdam; Philadelphia, PA: John Benjamins. 39-52.

Louw, B. (1993): "Irony in the text or insincerity in the writer? The diagnostic potential of semantic prosodies", *Text and Technology: In Honour of John Sinclair*, ed. M. Baker, G. Francis & E. Tognini-Bonelli. Amsterdam; Philadelphia, PA: John Benjamins. 152-176.

Louw, B. (2000): "Contextual prosodic theory: bringing semantic prosodies to life", *Words in Context: A Tribute to John Sinclair on his Retirement*, ed. C. Heffer, H. Sauntson & G. Fox. [On CD-Rom] ELR Discourse Monograph No. 18, Birmingham.

Low, G. (1992): "Developing a concordancing macro for WordPerfect 5.1", *MUESLI News* October, 9-11. Available at <http://ltsig.org.uk/archives/MN-92-10.pdf>.

Maddalena, S.R. (2001): "An investigation into how corpus analysis may be used in the second language classroom to solve some of the problems surrounding non-native speakers' understanding to seemingly synonymous words", (ERIC Document Reproduction Service, No ED458795). Available at <http://eric.ed.gov/ERICWebPortal/contentdelivery/servlet/ERICServlet?accno=ED458795>.

Mauranen, A. (2004a): "Speech corpora in the classroom", *Corpora and Language Learners*, ed. G. Aston, S. Bernardini & D. Stewart. Amsterdam; Philadelphia, PA: John Benjamins. 195-211.

Mauranen, A. (2004b): "Spoken corpus for an ordinary learner", *How to Use Corpora in Language Teaching*, ed. J.M. Sinclair. Amsterdam; Philadelphia, PA: John Benjamins. 89-105.

McCarthy, M. (2004): *Touchstone. From Corpus to Course Book.* Cambridge; New York, NY: Cambridge University Press. Available at <http://www.cambridge.org/us/esl/touchstone/teacher/images/pdf/CorpusBookletfinal.pdf.

McCarthy, M. (2008): "Accessing and interpreting corpus information in the teacher education context", *Language Teaching* 41(4), 563-574.

McCarthy, M. & R. Carter (1995): "Spoken grammar: what is it and how can we teach it?", *ELT Journal* 49(3), 207-218.

McCarthy, M. & A. O'Keeffe (2010): "Historical perspective: what are corpora and how have they evolved?", *The Routledge Handbook of Corpus Linguistics*, ed. M. McCarthy & A. O'Keeffe. Milton Park; New York, NY: Routledge. 3-13.

McEnery, T. & A. Wilson (1993): "The role of corpora in computer-assisted language learning", *Computer Assisted Language Learning* 6(3), 233-248.

McEnery, T. & A. Wilson (1996): *Corpus Linguistics*. Edinburgh: Edinburgh University Press.

McEnery, T. & A. Wilson (1997): "Teaching and language corpora (TALC)", *ReCALL* 9(1), 5-14.

McEnery, T., R. Xiao & Y. Tono (2006): *Corpus-based Language Studies: An Advanced Resource Book*. London; New York, NY: Routledge.

McIntosh, C., B. Francis & R. Poole (eds.) (2009): *Oxford Collocations Dictionary: For Students of English* (2nd ed.). Oxford: Oxford University Press.

Meunier, F. (2002): "The pedagogical value of native and learner corpora in EFL grammar teaching", *Computer Learner Corpora, Second Language Acquisition and Foreign Language Teaching*, ed. S. Granger, J. Hung & S. Petch-Tyson. Amsterdam; Philadelphia, PA: John Benjamins. 119-141.

Meunier, F. & C. Gouverneur (2009): "New types of corpora for new educational challenges: collecting, annotating and exploiting a corpus of textbook material", *Corpora and Language Teaching*, ed. K. Aijmer. Amsterdam; Philadelphia, PA: John Benjamins. 179–201.

Meyer, C. F. (2002): *English Corpus Linguistics: An Introduction*. Cambridge: Cambridge University Press.

Miceli, T. & C. Kennedy (2002): "An apprenticeship with the CWIC Corpus: a tool for learner writers in Italian". Proceedings of *Innovations in Italian Teaching* (workshop), Griffith University, Australia. 83-94.

Milton, J.C.P. & E.S.-C. Tsang (1993): "A corpus-based study of logical connectors in EFL students' writing: directions for future research", *Studies in Lexis*, ed. R. Pemberton & E.S.-C. Tsang. Hong Kong: Hong Kong University of Science and Technology. 215-246.

Mindt, D. (1986): "Corpus, grammar, and teaching English as a foreign language", *The English Reference Grammar: Language and Linguistics, Writers and Readers*, ed. G. Leitner. Tübingen: Niemeyer. 125-139.

Mindt, D. (1987): *Sprache – Grammatik – Unterrichtsgrammatik. Futuristischer Zeitbezug im Englischen I*. Frankfurt am Main: Diesterweg.

Mindt, D. (1996): "English corpus linguistics and the foreign language teaching syllabus", *Using Corpora for Language Research. Studies in Honour of Geoffrey Leech*, ed. J. Thomas & M. Short. London; New York, NY: Longman. 232-247.

Mindt, D. (1997): "Corpora and the teaching of English in Germany", *Teaching and Language Corpora*, ed. A. Wichmann, S. Fligelstone, T. McEnery & G. Knowles. London; New York, NY: Longman. 40-50.

Mishan, F. (2004): "Authenticating corpora for language learning: a problem and its resolution", *ELT Journal* 58(3), 219-227.

Mishan, F. (2005): *Designing Authenticity into Language Learning Materials*. Bristol: Intellect Books.

Mittens, B. (1991): *Language Awareness for Teachers*. Milton Keynes: Open University Press.

Möllering, M. (2001): "Teaching German modal particles: a corpus-based approach", *Language Learning & Technology* 5(3), 130-151.

Möllering, M. (2004): *The Acquisition of German Modal Particles: A Corpus-based Approach*. Frankfurt am Main: Peter Lang.
Moreno Jaén, M., F. Serrano Valverde & M. Calzada (eds.) (forthcoming): *Exploring New Paths in Language Pedagogy: Lexis and Corpus-based Language Teaching*. London: Equinox.
Morrow, K. (1977): "Authentic texts and ESP", *English for Specific Purposes*, ed. S. Holden. Mansfield: Modern English Publications Ltd. 13-15.
Müller, K. (2001): "Der pragmatische Konstruktivismus. Ein Modell zur Überwindung des Antagonismus von Instruktion und Konstruktion", *Konstruktivistische Schulpraxis: Beispiele für den Unterricht*, ed. J. Meixner & K. Müller. Neuwied: Luchterhand. 3-48.
Müller-Hartmann, A. & M. Schocker-von Ditfurth (2004): *Introduction to English Language Teaching*. Stuttgart: Ernst Klett Sprachen.
Mukherjee, J. (2002): *Korpuslinguistik und Englischunterricht: Eine Einführung*. Frankfurt am Main; New York, NY: Peter Lang.
Mukherjee, J. (2003): "Korpusbasierte Aktivitäten im Englischunterricht: Konzepte and Vorschläge für die Unterrichtspraxis", *Schüleraktivierung im Fremdsprachenunterricht*, ed. G. Fehrmann & E. Klein. Bonn: Romanistischer Verlag. 41-53.
Mukherjee, J. (2004): "Bridging the gap between applied corpus linguistics and the reality of English language teaching in Germany", *Applied Corpus Linguistics: A Multidimensional Perspective*, ed. U. Connor & T. Upton. Amsterdam; New York, NY: Rodopi. 239-250.
Mukherjee, J. (2006a): "Corpus linguistics and English reference grammars", *The Changing Face of Corpus Linguistics: Papers from the 24th International Conference on English Language Research on Computerized Corpora (ICAME 24)*, ed. A. Renouf. Amsterdam; New York, NY: Rodopi. 337-354.
Mukherjee, J. (2006b): "Corpus technology and language pedagogy: the state of the art – and beyond", *Corpus Technology and Language Pedagogy. New Resources, New Tools, New Methods*, ed. S. Braun, K. Kohn & J. Mukherjee. Frankfurt am Main: Peter Lang. 5-24.
Mukherjee, J. (2009): *Anglistische Korpuslinguistik: Eine Einführung*. Berlin: Erich Schmidt.
Murison-Bowie, S. (1993): *MicroConcord: Manual*. Oxford: Oxford University Press.
Murison-Bowie, S. (1996): "Linguistic corpora and language teaching", *Annual Review of Applied Linguistics* 16, 182-199.
Nesselhauf, N. (2003): "The use of collocations by advanced learners of English and some implications for teaching", *Applied Linguistics* 24(2), 223-242.
Nesselhauf, N. (2004a): "How learner corpus analysis can contribute to language teaching: a study of support verb constructions", *Corpora and*

Language Learners, ed. G. Aston, S. Bernardini & D. Stewart. Amsterdam; Philadelphia, PA: John Benjamins. 109-124.

Nesselhauf, N. (2004b): "Learner corpora and their potential for language teaching", *How to Use Corpora in Language Teaching*, ed. J.M. Sinclair. Amsterdam; Philadelphia, PA: John Benjamins. 125-152.

Nesselhauf, N. (2005): *Collocations in a Learner Corpus*. Amsterdam: Johns Benjamins.

Nunan, D. (1989): *Designing Tasks for the Communicative Classroom*. Cambridge: Cambridge University Press.

Nunan, D. (1991): *Language Teaching Methodology: A Textbook for Teachers*. New York, NY: Prentice Hall.

O'Donnell, M.B. (2008): "KWICgrouper – designing a tool for corpus-driven concordance analysis", *International Journal of English Studies* 8(1), 107-121.

O'Keeffe, A. & F. Farr (2003): "Using language corpora in initial teacher education: pedagogic issues and practical applications", *TESOL Quarterly* 37(3), 389-418.

O'Keeffe, A. & M. McCarthy (eds.) (2010): *The Routledge Handbook of Corpus Linguistics*. Milton Park; New York, NY: Routledge.

Olohan, M. (2004): *Introducing Corpora in Translation Studies*. London; New York, NY: Routledge.

O'Sullivan, Í. & A. Chambers (2006): "Learners' writing skills in French: corpus consultation and learner evaluation", *Journal of Second Language Writing* 15(1), 49-68.

O'Sullivan, Í. (2007): "Enhancing a process-oriented approach to literacy and language learning: the role of corpus consultation literacy", *ReCALL* 19(3), 269-286.

Papp, S. (2007): "Inductive learning and self-correction with the use of learner and reference corpora", *Corpora in the Foreign Language Classroom*, ed. E. Hidalgo Tenorio, L. Quereda & J. Santana. Amsterdam; New York, NY: Rodopi. 207-220.

Pearson, J. (2003): "Using parallel texts in the translator training environment", *Corpora in Translator Education*, ed. F. Zanettin, S. Bernardini & D. Stewart. Manchester: St Jerome. 15-24.

Philip, G. (2009): "Arriving at equivalence. Making a case for comparable general reference corpora in translation studies", *Corpus Use and Translating: Corpus Use for Learning to Translate and Learning Corpus Use to Translate*, ed. A. Beeby, P. Rodriguez Inés & P. Sánchez-Gijón. Amsterdam; Philadelphia, PA: John Benjamins. 50-73.

Polezzi, L. (1994): "Concordancers in the design and implementation of foreign language courses", *Computers & Education* 23(1-2), 89-96.

Prabhu, N.S. (1987): *Second Language Pedagogy*. Oxford: Oxford University Press.
Pravec, N.A. (2002): "Survey of learner corpora", *ICAME* 26, 81-114.
Prodromou, L. (1996a): "Correspondence", *ELT Journal* 50(1), 88-89.
Prodromou, L. (1996b): "Correspondence", *ELT Journal* 50(4), 371-373.
Quaglio, P. (2009): *Television Dialogue: The Sitcom Friends vs. Natural Conversation*. Amsterdam; Philadelphia, PA: Johns Benjamins.
Quirk, R. (1968): "The survey of English usage", *Essays on the English Language, Medieval and Modern*, ed. R. Quirk. London: Longman. 70-87.
Quirk, R., S. Greenbaum, G. Leech & J. Svartvik (1985): *A Comprehensive Grammar of the English Language*. London: Longman.
Rampton, A. (1981): *The Rampton Report: West Indian Children in our Schools. Interim Report of the Committee of Inquiry into the Education of Children from Ethnic Minority Groups, Chairman: Anthony Rampton OBE*. London: Her Majesty's Stationery Office. Available at <http://www.dg.dial.pipex.com/documents/docs1/rampton00.shtml>
Rautenhaus, H. (1997): "Authentische Texte und Konkordanzprogramme im Englischunterricht", *Rostocker Beiträge zur Sprachwissenschaft* 3, 141-166.
Reed, A. (1977): "CLOC: a collocation package", *ALLC Bulletin* 5(2), 168-173.
Renouf, A. (2007): "Corpus development 25 years on: from super-corpus to cyber-corpus", *Corpus Linguistics 25 Years On*, ed. R. Facchinetti. Amsterdam; New York, NY: Rodopi. 27-49.
Renouf, A. & J. Banerjee (2007): "Lexical repulsion between sense-related pairs", *International Journal of Corpus Linguistics* 12(3), 415-444.
Reppen, R. (2010): *Using Corpora in the Language Classroom*. Cambridge: Cambridge University Press.
Rilling, S., A. Dahlmann, S. Dodson, C. Boyles & O. Pazvant (2005): "Connecting call theory and practice in preservice teacher education and beyond: processes and products", *CALICO Journal* 22(2), 213-235.
Rilling, S. & O. Pazvant (2002): "Computer concordancing for ESP materials", *TESOL Journal* 11(3), 43-44.
Rohrbach, J.-M. (2003): "'Don't miss out on Göttingen's nightlife': Genreproduktion im Englischunterricht der Jahrgangsstufe 9", *Praxis des neusprachlichen Unterrichts* 50(4), 381-389.
Rojas, R. & U. Hashagen (eds.) (2000): *The First Computers: History and Architectures*. Cambridge, MA: MIT Press.
Römer, U. (2004a): "A corpus-driven approach to modal auxiliaries and their didactics", *How to Use Corpora in Language Teaching*, ed. J.M. Sinclair. Amsterdam; Philadelphia, PA: John Benjamins. 185-199.
Römer, U. (2004b): "Comparing real and ideal language learner input: the use of an EFL textbook corpus in corpus linguistics and language teaching",

Corpora and Language Learners, ed. G. Aston, S. Bernardini & D. Stewart. Amsterdam; Philadelphia, PA: John Benjamins. 151-168.

Römer, U. (2005): *Progressives, Patterns, Pedagogy: A Corpus-driven Approach to English Progressive Forms, Functions, Contexts and Didactics*. Amsterdam; Philadelphia, PA: John Benjamins.

Römer, U. (2008): "Corpora and language teaching", *Corpus Linguistics. An International Handbook (Vol. 1)*, ed. A. Lüdeling & M. Kytö. Berlin: Mouton de Gruyter. 112-130.

Roussel, F. (1991): "Parallel concordances and tonic auxiliaries", *Classroom Concordancing*, ed. T. Johns & P. King. Birmingham: University of Birmingham. 71-101.

Rüschoff, B. & M. Ritter (2001): "Technology-enhanced language learning: construction of knowledge and template-based learning in the foreign language classroom", *Computer Assisted Language Learning* 14(3-4), 219-232.

Rundell, M. (2008): "The corpus revolution revisited", *English Today* 24(1), 23-27.

Rundell, M. & P. Stock (1992): "The corpus revolution", *English Today* 8(2), 9-14.

Russell, D.B. (1965): "COCOA: A word-count and concordance generator", *Atlas Computer Laboratory, Chilton: 1961-1975*. Available at <http://www.chilton-computing.org.uk/acl/applications/cocoa/p001.htm>.

Rutherford, W.E. (1987): *Second Language Grammar: Learning and Teaching*. London: Longman.

Rutherford, W.E. & M. Sharwood Smith (1985): "Consciousness-raising and universal grammar", *Applied Linguistics* 6, 274-282.

Santos Pereira, L.A. (2004): "The use of concordancing in the teaching of Portuguese", *How to Use Corpora in Language Teaching*, ed. J.M. Sinclair. Amsterdam; Philadelphia, PA: John Benjamins. 109-122.

Saussure, F. d. (1983 [1916]): *Cours de linguistique générale*. London: Duckworth.

Schlüter, N. (2002): *Eine korpuslinguistische Analyse des englischen Perfekts mit Vermittlungsvorschlägen für den Sprachunterricht*. Tübingen: Narr.

Schmidt, R.W. (1990): "The role of consciousness in second language learning", *Applied Linguistics* 11(2), 129-158.

Scott, M. (2004): *Wordsmith Tools 4. Oxford*: Oxford University Press.

Scott, M. (2008): *Wordsmith Tools 5*. Liverpool: Lexical Analysis Software Ltd.

Scott, M. & Johns, T. (1993): *MicroConcord*. Oxford: Oxford University Press.

Sealey, A. & P. Thompson (2004): "'What do you call the dull words?' Primary school children using corpus-based approaches to learn about language", *English in Education* 38(1), 80-91.

Sealey, A. & P. Thompson (2007): "Corpus, concordance, classification: young learners in the L1 classroom", *Language Awareness* 16(3), 208-223.

Seidlhofer, B. (2000a): "Operationalizing intertextuality: using learner corpora for learning", *Rethinking Language Pedagogy from a Corpus Perspective*, ed. L. Burnard & T. McEnery. Frankfurt am Main; New York, NY: Peter Lang. 207-223.

Seidlhofer, B. (2000b): "Where the buck stops: approximations in applied linguistics", *Kognitive Aspekte des Lehrens und Lernens von Fremdsprachen: Festschrift für Willis J. Edmondson*, ed. C. Riemer. Tübingen: Gunter Narr. 12-25.

Seidlhofer, B. (2002): "Pedagogy and local learner corpora: working with learning-driven data", *Computer Learner Corpora, Second Language Acquisition and Foreign Language Teaching*, ed. S. Granger, J. Hung & S. Petch-Tyson. Amsterdam; Philadelphia, PA: John Benjamins. 213–234.

Sharwood Smith, M. (1981): "Consciousness-raising and the second language learner", *Applied Linguistics* 2(2), 159-168.

Sharwood Smith, M. (1991): "Speaking to many minds: on the relevance of different types of language information for the L2 learner", *Second Language Research* 7(2), 118-132.

Shin, D. & P. Nation (2008): "Beyond single words: the most frequent collocations in spoken English", *ELT Journal* 62(4), 339-348.

Sinclair, J.M. (1982b): "Reflections on computer corpora in English language research", *Computer Corpora in English Language Research*, ed. S. Johansson. Bergen, Norway: Norwegian Computing Centre for the Humanities. 1-6.

Sinclair, J.M. (1985): "Selected issues", *Language in the World*, ed. R. Quirk & H.G. Widdowson. Cambridge: Cambridge University Press. 248-254.

Sinclair, J.M. (1987a): *Collins COBUILD English Language Dictionary*. London: Collins.

Sinclair, J.M. (ed.) (1987b): *Looking Up: An Account of the COBUILD Project in Lexical Computing and the Development of the COLLINS COBUILD English Language Dictionary*. London: Collins ELT.

Sinclair, J.M. (1991a): *Corpus, Concordance, Collocation*. Oxford: Oxford University Press.

Sinclair, J.M. (1991b): "Shared knowledge", *Linguistics and Language Pedagogy: The State of the Art*, ed. J. Alatis. Washington, DC: Georgetown University Press. 489-500.

Sinclair, J.M. (1992): "The automatic analysis of corpora", *Directions in Corpus Linguistics: Proceedings of Nobel Symposium 82*, ed. J. Svartvik. Berlin; New York, NY: Mouton de Gruyter. 379-397.

Sinclair, J.M. (1996): "EAGLES. Preliminary recommendations on corpus typology". Available at <http://www.ilc.cnr.it/EAGLES/corpustyp/corpus typ.html>.

Sinclair, J.M. (1999): "A way with common words", *Out of Corpora: Studies in Honour of Stig Johansson*, ed. H. Hasselgård & S. Oksefjell. Amsterdam; Atlanta, GA: Rodopi. 157-179.

Sinclair, J.M. (2003): *Reading Concordances: An Introduction*. London; New York, NY: Longman.

Sinclair, J.M. (ed.) (2004a): *How to Use Corpora in Language Teaching*. Amsterdam; Philadelphia, PA: John Benjamins.

Sinclair, J.M. (ed.) (2006): *Collins COBUILD Advanced Learner's English Dictionary* (5th ed.). Glasgow, Scotland: HarperCollins.

Sinclair, J.M. (2007): "Preface", *International Journal of Corpus Linguistics* 12(2), 155-157.

Sinclair, J.M. & M.R. Coulthard (1975): *Towards an Analysis of Discourse: The English Used by Teachers and Pupils*. Oxford: Oxford University Press.

Sinclair, J.M. & A. Renouf (1988): "A lexical syllabus for language learning", *Vocabulary and Language Teaching*, ed. R. Carter & M. McCarthy. London; New York, NY: Longman. 140-160.

Skehan, P. (1981): "ESP teachers, computers and research", *The ESP Teacher: Role, Development and Prospects* (ELT Document 112, British Council). 106-125.

Smith, R.C. (2003): "Teacher education for teacher-learner autonomy", *Symposium for Language Teacher Educators: Papers from Three IALS Symposia (CD-ROM)*, ed. J. Gollin, G. Ferguson & H. Trappes-Lomax. Edinburgh, Scotland: IALS, University of Edinburgh.

Smith, S., A. Chen & A. Kilgarriff (2008): "A corpus query tool for SLA: learning Mandarin with the help of *Sketch Engine*", *Corpus Linguistics, Computer Tools, and Applications: State of the Art*, ed. B. Lewandowska-Tomaszczyk. Frankfurt am Main: Peter Lang. 673-686.

Spiro, R.J., R.L. Coulson, P.J. Feltovich & D.K. Anderson (1988): "Cognitive flexibility theory: advanced knowledge acquisition in ill-structured domains (Technical Report No. 442)", *The Tenth Annual Conference of the Cognitive Science Society*, Hillsdale, NJ: Erlbaum (Eric Document Reproduction Service No. ED 302821). 375-383.

St John, E. (2001): "A case for using a parallel corpus and concordancer for beginners of a foreign language", *Language Learning & Technology* 5(3), 185-203.

Stenström, A.-B., G. Andersen & I.K. Hasund (2002): *Trends in Teenage Talk: Corpus Compilation, Analysis and Findings*. Amsterdam; Philadelphia, PA: John Benjamins.

Stevens, V. (1991a): "Classroom concordancing: vocabulary materials derived from relevant, authentic text", *English for Specific Purposes* 10, 35-46.

Stevens, V. (1991b): "Concordance-based vocabulary exercises: a viable alternative to gap-fillers", *Classroom concordancing*, ed. T. Johns & P. King. Birmingham: University of Birmingham. 47-61.

Stevens, V. (1991c): "Create your own concordancer with a one-line DOS command", *MS-DOS Newsletter* 5(1), 2-3.

Stubbs, M. (1995a): "Collocations and semantic profile: on the cause of the trouble with quantitative studies", *Functions of Language* 2, 23-55.

Stubbs, M. (2004): "Language corpora", *The Handbook of Applied Linguistics*, ed. A. Davies & C. Elder. Oxford: Blackwell. 106-132.

Stubbs, M. (2009): "Memorial article. John Sinclair (1933-2007). The search for units of meaning: Sinclair on empirical semantics", *Applied Linguistics* 30(1), 115-137.

Sun, Y.-C. (2003): "Learning process, strategies and web-based concordancers: a case study", *British Journal of Educational Technology* 34(5), 601-613.

Sun, Y.-C. & L.-Y. Wang (2003): "Concordancers in the EFL classroom: cognitive approaches and collocation difficulty", *Computer Assisted Language Learning* 16(1), 83-94.

Svalberg, A. (2007): "Language awareness and language learning", *Language Teaching* 40(4), 287-308.

Swain, M. (1998): "Focus on form through conscious reflection", *Focus on Form in Classroom Second Language Acquisition*, ed. C. Doughty & J. Williams. Cambridge: Cambridge University Press. 64-81.

Swain, M. (2000): "The output hypothesis and beyond: mediating acquisition through collaborative dialogue", *Sociocultural Theory and Second Language Learning*, ed. J.P. Lantolf. Oxford: Oxford University Press. 97-114.

Swain, M. (2006): "Languaging, agency and collaboration in second language learning", *Advanced Language Learning: The Contributions of Halliday and Vygotsky*, ed. H. Byrnes. London; New York, NY: Continuum. 95-108.

Szakos, J. (2000): "Producing and using corpora in Chinese language education", *Rethinking Language Pedagogy from a Corpus Perspective*, ed. L. Burnard & T. McEnery. Frankfurt am Main; New York, NY: Peter Lang. 187-192.

Thompson, P. (2006): "Assessing the contribution of corpora to EAP practice", *Motivation in Learning Language for Specific and Academic Purposes*, ed. Z. Kantaridou, I. Papadopoulou & I. Mahili. Macedonia: University of Macedonia [CD ROM].

Thorndike, E.L. (1921): *The Teacher's Word Book*. New York, NY: Teachers College, Columbia University.

Thurstun, J. & C.N. Candlin (1997): *Exploring Academic English: A Workbook for Student Essay Writing*. Sydney, Australia: National Centre for English Language Teaching and Research.

Thurstun, J. & C.N. Candlin (1998): "Concordancing and the teaching of the vocabulary of academic English", *English for Specific Purposes* 17(3), 267-280.

Todd, R.W. (2001): "Induction from self-selected concordances and self-correction", *System* 29(1), 91-102.

Tognini-Bonelli, E. (2001): *Corpus Linguistics at Work*. Amsterdam; Philadelphia, PA: John Benjamins.

Tognini-Bonelli, E. & J.M. Sinclair (2006): "Corpora", *Encyclopedia of Language and Linguistics*, ed. K. Brown. Amsterdam: Elsevier Science. 206-219.

Tribble, C. (1990): "Concordancing and an EAP writing programme", *CAELL Journal* 1(2), 10-15.

Tribble, C. (2000): "Practical uses for language corpora in ELT", *A Special Interest in Computers*, ed. P. Brett & G. Motteram. Whitstable: IATEFL. 31-41.

Tribble, C. (2001): "Corpora and language teaching: adjusting the gaze". Paper presented at the 22nd ICAME: Future Challenge for Corpus Linguistics, Université Catholique de Louvain, Centre for English Corpus Linguistics.

Tribble, C. & G. Jones (1997): *Concordances in the Classroom: A Resource Guide for Teachers*. Houston, TX: Athelstan.

Trinczek, R. (2009): "How to interview managers? Methodical and methodological aspects of expert interviews as a qualitative method in empirical social research", *Interviewing Experts*, ed. A. Bogner, B. Littig & W. Menz. Basingstoke; New York, NY: Palgrave Macmillan. 203-216.

Tsui, A.B.M. (2004): "What teachers have always wanted to know and how corpora can help", *How to Use Corpora in Language Teaching*, ed. J.M. Sinclair. Amsterdam; Philadelphia, PA: John Benjamins. 39-61.

Turnbull, J. & J. Burston (1998): "Towards independent concordance work for students: lessons from a case study", *ON-CALL* 12(2), 10-21. Available at <http://www.cltr.uq.edu.au/oncall/turnbull122.html>.

Van Essen, A. (1996): "Language awareness in a historical, pedagogical, and research perspective", *Zeitschrift für Fremdsprachenforschung* 7(1), 60-69.

Van Essen, A. (2008): "Language awareness and knowledge about language: a historical overview", *Encyclopedia of Language and Education. Vol. 6: Knowledge about Language*, ed. J. Cenoz & N.H. Hornberger. New York, NY: Springer. 3-14.

Van Lier, L. (1991): "Language awareness: the common ground between linguist and language teacher", *Linguistics and Language Pedagogy: The*

State of the Art, ed. J. Alatis. Washington, DC: Georgetown University Press. 528-546.

Van Lier, L. (1996): *Interaction in the Language Curriculum: Awareness, Autonomy and Authenticity*. London; New York, NY: Longman.

Van Lier, L. (1998): "The relationship between consciousness, interaction and language learning", *Language Awareness* 7(2/3), 128-145.

Varley, S. (2009): "I'll just look that up in the concordancer: integrating corpus consultation into the language learning environment", *Computer Assisted Language Learning* 22(2), 133 -152.

Virtanen, T. (1997): "The progressive in NNS and NS student compositions: evidence from the International Corpus of Learner English", *Corpus-based Studies in English: Papers from the Seventeenth International Conference on English Language Research on Computerized Corpora*, ed. M. Ljung. Amsterdam; Atlanta, GA: Rodopi. 299-309.

Watt, R.J.C. (2004): *Concordance 3.2*. Retrieved from http://www.concordance software.co.uk/concordance_software_download.htm.

Watt, R.J.C. (2009): *Concordance 3.3*. Retrieved from http://www.concordance software.co.uk/concordance_software_download.htm.

West, M. (1953): *A General Service List of English Words, with Semantic Frequencies and a Supplementary Word-list for the Writing of Popular Science and Technology*. London; New York, NY: Longman.

Whistle, J. (1999): "Concordancing and learner autonomy: an experiment with first and second year undergraduates", *CALL and the Learning Community*, ed. K. Cameron. Exeter: Elm Bank. 443-453.

Widdowson, D. (1979): *Explorations in Applied Linguistics*. Oxford: Oxford University Press.

Widdowson, H.G. (1980): "Models and fiction", *Applied Linguistics* 1(2), 165-170.

Widdowson, H.G. (1984c): *Teaching Language as Communication*. Oxford: Oxford University Press.

Widdowson, H.G. (1990): *Aspects of Language Teaching*. Oxford: Oxford University Press.

Widdowson, H.G. (1991): "The description and prescription of language", *Linguistics and Language Pedagogy: The State of the Art*, ed. J. Alatis. Washington, DC: Georgetown University Press. 11-24.

Widdowson, H.G. (1996): "Comment: authenticity and autonomy in ELT", *ELT Journal* 50(1), 67-68.

Widdowson, H.G. (1998): "Context, community, and authentic language", *TESOL Quarterly* 32, 705-716.

Widdowson, H.G. (2000): "On the limitations of linguistics applied", *Applied Linguistics* 21(1), 3-25.

Widdowson, H.G. (2003): *Defining Issues in English Language Teaching*. Oxford: Oxford University Press.

Willis, D. (1990): *The Lexical Syllabus: A New Approach to Language Teaching*. London: Collins ELT.

Willis, D. (1993): "Syllabus, corpus and data-driven learning", *IATEFL Annual Conference Report: Plenary Papers*. 25-31.

Willis, D. (2003): *Rules, Patterns and Words: Grammar and Lexis in English Language Teaching*. Cambridge: Cambridge University Press.

Willis, D. & J. Willis (1988): *Collins COBUILD English Course*. London: Collins COBUILD.

Willis, J. (1998): "Concordances in the classroom without a computer: assembling and exploiting concordances of common words", *Materials Development in Language Teaching*, ed. B. Tomlinson. Cambridge: Cambridge University Press. 44-66.

Wolff, D. (2001b): "Zum Stellenwert von Lehrwerken und Unterrichtsmaterialien in einem konstruktivistisch orientierten Fremdsprachenunterricht", *Konstruktivistische Schulpraxis: Beispiele für den Unterricht*, ed. J. Meixner & K. Müller. Neuwied: Luchterhand. 187-207.

Wright, T. & R. Bolitho (1993): "Language awareness: a missing link in language teacher education?", *ELT Journal* 47(4), 292-304.

Wyatt, D.H. (1987): "Applying pedagogical principles to CALL courseware development", *Modern Media in Foreign Language Education: Theory and Implementation*, ed. W.F. Smith. Lincolnwood, IL: National Textbook. 85-98.

Yeh, Y., H.-C. Liou & Y.-H. Li (2007): "Online synonym materials and concordancing for EFL college writing", *Computer Assisted Language Learning* 20(2), 131-152.

Yoon, H. (2008): "More than a linguistic reference: the influence of corpus technology on L2 academic writing ", *Language Learning & Technology* 12(2), 31-48.

Yoon, H. & A. Hirvela (2004): "ESL student attitudes toward corpus use in L2 writing", *Journal of Second Language Writing* 13(4), 257-283.

Zanettin, F., S. Bernardini & D. Stewart (eds.) (2003): *Corpora in Translator Education*. Manchester: St Jerome.

Zorzi, D. (2001): "The pedagogic use of spoken corpora: learning discourse markers in Italian", *Learning with Corpora*, ed. G. Aston. Bologna: CLUEB. 85-107.

Online Concordancers

BNC Simple Search.
Available at <http://www.natcorp.ox.ac.uk/using/index.xml.ID=simple>.
BYU-BNC: The British National Corpus. (Davis, M. 2004-).
Available at <http://corpus.byu.edu/bnc>.
Collins WordbanksOnline English Corpus Sampler
Available at <http://www.collinslanguage.com/wordbanks/default.aspx>.
Compleat Lexical Tutor.
Available at <http://www.lextutor.ca>.
WebCorp.
Available at <http://www.webcorp.org.uk>.

Websites

American National Corpus.
Available at <http://www.americannationalcorpus.org>.
Association for Language Awareness.
Available at <http://www.lexically.net/ala>.
Cambridge University Press.
Available at <http://www.cambridge.org>.
Compleat Lexical Tutor.
Available at <http://www.lextutor.ca>.
Department of Education, NRW, Germany.
Available at <http://www.schulministerium.nrw.de/BP/Schulsystem/Qualitaetssicherung/Standards/Kernlehrplaene/index.html>.
EAGLES.
Available at <http://www.ilc.cnr.it/EAGLES96/home.html>.
Longman Dictionary of Contemporary English Online.
Available at <http://www.ldoceonline.com>.
Kultusministerkonferenz.
Available at <http://www.kmk.org/information-in-english.html>.
MICASE: Michigan Corpus of Academic Spoken English.
Available at <http://micase.elicorpora.info>.
myCOBUILD.com.
Available at <http://www.mycobuild.com/about-collins-corpus.aspx>.
Oxford Text Archive.
Available at <http://ota.ahds.ac.uk>.
Project Gutenberg.
Available at <http://www.gutenberg.org>.

Index

English Corpus Linguistics

Edited by Thomas Kohnen and Joybrato Mukherjee

Vol. 1 Roberta Facchinetti / Frank Palmer (eds.): English Modality in Perspective. Genre Analysis and Contrastive Studies. 2004.

Vol. 2 Grace Y. W. Tse: A Corpus-based Study of Proper Names in Present-day English. Aspects of Gradience and Article Usage. 2005.

Vol. 3 Sabine Braun / Kurt Kohn / Joybrato Mukherjee (eds.): Corpus Technology and Language Pedagogy. New Resources, New Tools, New Methods. 2006.

Vol. 4 Clemens W. A. Fritz: From English in Australia to Australian English. 1788–1900. 2007.

Vol. 5 Christiane Brand: Lexical Processes in Scientific Discourse Popularisation. A corpus-linguistic study of the SARS coverage. 2008.

Vol. 6 Sebastian Hoffmann / Stefan Evert / Nicholas Smith / David Lee / Ylva Berglund Prytz: Corpus Linguistics with *BNCweb* – a Practical Guide. 2008.

Vol. 7 Lars M. Blöhdorn: Postmodifying Attributive Adjectives in English. An Integrated Corpus-Based Approach. 2009.

Vol. 8 Uta Katharina Elisabeth Schäpers: Nominal versus Clausal Complexity in Spoken and Written English. Theory and Description. 2009.

Vol. 9 Ulrike Gut: Non-native Speech. A Corpus-based Analysis of Phonological and Phonetic Properties of L2 English and German. 2009.

Vol. 10 Sandra Boggel: Metadiscourse in Middle English and Early Modern English Religious Texts. A corpus-based study. 2009.

Vol. 11 Donald Sims MacQueen: The Integration of MILLION into the English System of Number Words. A Diachronic Study. 2010.

Vol. 12 Tanja Rütten: How to Do Things with Texts. Patterns of Instruction in Religious Discourse 1350–1700. 2011.

Vol. 13 Yvonne Alexandra Breyer: Corpora in Language Teaching and Learning. Potential, Evaluation, Challenges. 2011.

www.peterlang.de

Peter Lang · Internationaler Verlag der Wissenschaften

Aquilino Sánchez / Moisés Almela (eds.)

A Mosaic of Corpus Linguistics

Selected Approaches

Frankfurt am Main, Berlin, Bern, Bruxelles, New York, Oxford, Wien, 2010.
VI, 291 pp., num. tab. and graph.
Studien zur romanischen Sprachwissenschaft und interkulturellen Kommunikation. Edited by Gerd Wotjak. Vol. 66
ISBN 978-3-631-58789-8 · hardback € 58,80*

The growth experienced by Corpus Linguistics over the last two decades has complicated the definition of the discipline. There is at present no consensus as to what corpus linguistics exactly is. Is it a methodology, a theoretical framework, a research paradigm? The goal of this book is multi-purpose. It provides material for a discussion of the notion of "corpus linguistics", an overt discussion of the limits of this discipline and a comparison of some of the main approaches. And at the same time it offers a collection of selected papers representative of a range of approaches and applications associated with corpus research.

Content: Corpus-driven Approach · Corpus-based Approach · Discourse Functions · Discourse Organization · Text Type · Genre · Early Modern English · Clinical Linguistics · Lexical Bundles · Specialized Corpora · Distributional Data · Semantic Roles · Corpus Annotation · Constraint Grammar · Accessibility · Cognitive Focus

Frankfurt am Main · Berlin · Bern · Bruxelles · New York · Oxford · Wien
Distribution: Verlag Peter Lang AG
Moosstr. 1, CH-2542 Pieterlen
Telefax 0041(0)32/3761727

*The €-price includes German tax rate
Prices are subject to change without notice

Homepage http://www.peterlang.de

Kolibri 360 GmbH
Ferdinand-Jühlke-Straße 7
99095 Erfurt, Deutschland
produktsicherheit@kolibri360.de